The Irish Triangle

The Irish Triangle

CONFLICT IN NORTHERN IRELAND

Roger H. Hull

PRINCETON UNIVERSITY PRESS
PRINCETON, N.J.

To Peace

1945824

Every nation-state is an island, entire of itself; yet, every nation-state is also a piece of the continent, a part of the main; if war therefore ravages a nation-state, the world is the less, as well as if the entire world were so ravaged; any wars and the death and destruction resulting from those wars diminish us, because we are all involved in mankind; and therefore never send to know for whom the bell tolls; it tolls for us all.

ACKNOWLEDGMENTS

A BOOK is rarely the product of one person. In this instance, it certainly was not. The idea for the analysis, for instance, was that of British historian Sir John Wheeler-Bennett; the helpful critique was supplied by Professors Neill H. Alford, Jr., Richard B. Lillich, and John Norton Moore of the University of Virginia School of Law; the time to finish the work was the result of the flexible schedule that former Governor Linwood Holton of Virginia permitted me to follow; and the much-needed moral support was provided by my family and Ms. Lillie Siegel. Without their collective help and the funds provided by the University of Virginia School of Law to cover some of my typing and xerox costs, this work would have been far more difficult and unpleasant to complete.

The views, however, expressed in the book—which was written prior to my appointment to the Department of State—are mine and do not necessarily represent the views of any state institution or the United States Government or any agency thereof.

March 13, 1975

CONTENTS

The Irish Triangle

CHAPTER I

Introduction

CONFLICT, all conflict, is tragic. What compounds that tragedy is the lack of fresh ideas with which to put an end to seemingly unending death and destruction. For that reason, the growing belief among both Catholics and Protestants in Northern Ireland that the British Government has run out of ideas to curb the violence in Ulster is, to say the least, disturbing. For that reason, too, an analysis of the struggle in Northern Ireland might not only serve as an interesting scholastic and theoretical exercise but also shed some light on what could be done to bring peace to that troubled land.

In analyzing conflict situations, it is both fashionable and tempting to try to fit the struggle at hand into what may be an existing, albeit unsuitable, framework. Such frameworks and the accompanying comparisons and generalizations are, for the most part, appropriate and helpful, since a conflict may be more clearly understood if it can be viewed as part of a whole. Sometimes, however—as in the case of Northern Ireland—any such attempt is likely to be a strained and futile exercise that confuses rather than clarifies.

The conflict raging in Ulster does not easily or naturally fit into an analytical framework. It is not, as some writers would have us believe,[1] merely another instance of ethnic nationalism; it is not just a further example of religious strife. While there are, to be sure, elements of the struggle which have counterparts in other conflicts, the roots of the

[1] For the view that the Ulster conflict is not very distinct in its primary cause from other struggles, see Connor, *Nation-Building or Nation Destroying?* 24 WORLD POLITICS 319, 339 (1972).

triangular Catholic-British-Protestant strife in Northern Ireland are unique.

To say that these roots are unique, to say that the Ulster conflict is distinct, for example, from the Flemish-Walloon, Hindu-Moslem, Arab-Jew, or black-white schisms in other parts of the world, is not to say that the struggle in Northern Ireland is or should be treated in a vacuum. If that were the case, a study of the turmoil would, of necessity, be of limited value. If, however, the study recognizes that the struggle, though unique, must be viewed not in isolation but from the larger perspective of the world community and in terms of the legal norms established by that community, it can prove instructive for two reasons. First of all, and of cardinal significance, the study might provide new ideas for solving the bitter, never-ending strife in Ulster. Secondly, it might reveal that the legal norms are ineffective or unrealistic and that they should be reformulated.

That the conflict in Northern Ireland has been a never-ending one is beyond dispute. What is subject to question, however, is when it began. To some the starting point is 1968, when the civil rights demonstrations erupted; to others that point is 1922, when Ulster and the Irish Free State, as the Republic of Ireland was then called, decided to go their separate ways; and to still others—perhaps most— the origin of the troubles can be traced back to 1690, the date of the Battle of the Boyne, or even to 1607, the year of the "flight of the Earls" and the start of the Ulster plantation.

Although each of these dates is important, it would appear that if a full understanding of the struggle is to be obtained, an analysis, however brief, of Irish history from 1171—the year that the armies of Henry II first set foot in Ireland—to the present must be made. To fail to do so is to sever hundreds of years of history from the struggle and to paint an incomplete picture of the strife.

Of course, to state that the Ulster conflict is never-ending is not to say that it will never end. Even though a walk through the Bogside in Derry (Londonderry)[2] or down Falls or Shankill roads in Belfast will certainly challenge one's optimism and make him question just how far mankind has advanced, it will not erode that optimism, for the walk will reveal that few of the participants want the struggle to continue. It will also reveal that while the politicians politic, the preachers preach, and the writers write, the people—Catholics and Protestants alike—suffer.

If the conflict is to end, these politicians, preachers, and writers must combine efforts to bring the people of Northern Ireland together. It may have been understandable, if not acceptable, to have neighbor fighting neighbor fifty years ago, when the partition of Ulster was effected; it is neither understandable nor acceptable today.

Yesterday and today in Northern Ireland often blend together in such a way as ostensibly to erase the history of the area. Since the troubles of former times are relived as contemporary events, the past and the present are almost one. The resulting effect of this "merger" is at once confusing and harmful, since "discussions of massacres and battles, political pogroms that took place two or three hundred years ago, are a part of the everyday language of the Ulsterman."[3] As such, they have a chilling, negative effect on improved relations among the people of Northern Ireland.

Language has also been more subtly perverted. Ever since the eighteenth century, the conflict has been "so steeped in party and sectarian animosity, that a writer who has done his utmost to clear his mind from prejudice, and bring together with impartiality the conflicting statements of partisans, will still, if he is a wise man, always doubt whether he has succeeded in painting with perfect fidelity the delicate gradations of provocation, palliation, and guilt."[4] With

---

[2] Catholics refer to the city as Derry; Protestants refer to it as Londonderry.

[3] Eliot & Hickie, ULSTER: A CASE STUDY IN CONFLICT THEORY 29 (1971).

[4] Lecky, A HISTORY OF IRELAND IN THE EIGHTEENTH CENTURY 421 (1913).

the passage of time the conflict has become increasingly complex and objectivity more elusive. If that objectivity is to be attained, unprejudiced individuals must sift through the "conflicting statements of partisans"—and writers without any connection with the conflict are less likely to be prejudiced.

Objectivity, of course, means different things to different people. To some people, it is clearly distinguishable from neutrality; to them, objectivity is nothing more, nothing less than a precise documentation of the course of a particular investigation. Such a definition, however, is defective. Although a perfect balance can rarely be struck since the competing positions are infrequently of equal worth, that balance (which has inappropriately been labeled "a meaningless neutrality the only purpose of which is to protect"[5] the writer) should be sought. Without it, it is all too easy for the writer, under the veil of objectivity, to impress his views—either consciously or unconsciously—on unsuspecting readers.

Objectivity in the sense of neutrality is therefore important. Were a writer to inform his readers that he is simply presenting *his* interpretation of the facts, there would be little danger, for the reader would then be on notice that what he was perusing might or might not be objective. Since, however, writers generally do not so inform their readers and since they array their views as the product of unbiased scholarship, readers are oftentimes dangerously misled. As a result, readers piously mouth the subjective and often inaccurate words of those authors for whom they have respect, but who, as evidenced by advocacy scholar-

[5] For support of the first definition of objectivity and a simultaneous attack on this writer's position, see *The Irish Inheritance*, 48 NEW YORKER 135 (October 21, 1972). But see Durant & Durant, THE LESSONS OF HISTORY 12 (1968) for the view that "even the historian who thinks to rise above partiality for his country, race, creed, or class betrays his secret predilection in his choice of materials, and in the nuances of his adjectives."

ship which subordinates scholarly research to the questionable demands of partisanship, have little respect for them.

Paradoxically, however, neutral objectivity is not enough. After presenting the facts qua facts, a writer must set forth his personal views and policy recommendations. Without those views and recommendations, his analysis will lack the clearly labeled value choices which he has undoubtedly, and unavoidably, made; with them, his analysis is more likely to be both complete and helpful, assuming that the writer has separated his personal views and policy recommendations from the ostensibly objective delineation of the facts.

In the case of the Ulster conflict, this mode of analysis is especially crucial. With passions aflame on the three sides of the struggle, only a dispassionate presentation that balances the arguments and evidence of the contending factions and that is anchored by personal views and policy recommendations can expose the conflict in all its horror and help lead to the peace desired by the vast majority of all the people in Northern Ireland.

In an effort to present dispassionately the Ulster tragedy, each chapter of the book has been divided into five parts: a noncontroversial introductory statement of the pertinent facts or law; the facts or law as seen from Dublin, London, and Belfast; and personal conclusions. This approach, when combined with the selective use of terminology having certain connotations (such as the terms North of Ireland, Northern Ireland, and Ulster), most accurately and fairly captures the triangular division in Northern Ireland. To be sure, there are a great many more viewpoints than would appear to be represented by the Dublin-London-Belfast labels. These labels, however, should be viewed as "umbrellas" under which the beliefs and demands of diverse participants to the struggle can be separated into three easily differentiated categories. By way of illustration, the Dublin label reflects the belief—shared, among others, by the Irish Republican Army, the Civil Rights Association, and the Dublin Government—that changes, large-scale

7

changes, must be introduced on the Northern scene; the London label represents the view that some change is both morally right and politically expedient in Northern Ireland; and the Belfast label joins divergent groups—including Unionists and Paisleyites—who commonly believe both that the status quo in Ulster must be maintained and that far too many concessions have already been made to illegal forces.

Within the Dublin-London-Belfast sections of each chapter, arguments will be marshaled in such a way as to present the particular viewpoint most forcefully. Two factors, though, should be borne in mind: first, abusive and irresponsible rhetoric will be used in an effort to capture the sense of separateness that has settled over Northern Ireland; and second, the arguments raised may well include claims that have not been made by the particular participant but which should be set forth if that participant's position is to be understood in the most favorable light.

After juxtaposing the Dublin, London, and Belfast claims, personal conclusions will be drawn. While these conclusions will be set forth in a frank manner and without predilections, they will still represent the subjective viewpoint of only one person. As such, they may well fall into the age-old trap of absolutism, since it is all too easy to simplify complex issues by announcing dogmatic (and unhelpful, if not harmful) findings.[6] Nevertheless, these conclusions, de-

---

[6] Nowhere is the "problem of certainty" treated better than in Bertrand Russell's classic statement: "But if philosophy is to serve a positive purpose, it must not teach mere skepticism, for, while the dogmatist is harmful, the skeptic is useless. Dogmatism and skepticism are both, in a sense, absolute philosophies; one is certain of knowing, the other of not knowing. What philosophy should dissipate is certainty, whether of knowledge or of ignorance. Knowledge is not so precise a concept as is commonly thought. Instead of saying 'I know this,' we ought to say 'I more or less know something more or less like this.' It is true that this proviso is hardly necessary as regards the multiplication table, but knowledge in practical affairs has not the certainty or the precision of arithmetic." B. Russell, *Philosophy for Laymen*, in UNPOPULAR ESSAYS 21, 27 (1969).

spite misgivings about the difficulty of and potential harm in their certainty, will attempt to allocate both praise and blame and to propose, where appropriate, new actions that might be taken, decisions that might be made, or "yesable propositions"[7] that might be propounded. In each instance, however, the conclusions will be advanced with the realization that the delineations of opposing positions are of cardinal significance, for they—and they alone—will enable the reader to assess intelligently the "is" and "ought to be" of Northern Ireland.

The "is–ought to be" controversy in Ulster is not limited to the historical and political issues. Of major import, too, are the legal questions raised by the conflict—questions that, by their nature, internationalize the strife—and the fact that participants to the conflict (and not only scholars) are asking them. While the Northern Ireland tragedy is historically unique in many ways, its legal impact is not. For that reason, the focus on specific international legal issues, such as civil strife, the laws of war, human rights, domestic jurisdiction, and humanitarian intervention, may well have a bearing on future struggles. An examination of what the law is in each of these areas and how it is applied in Ulster not only will show which participants are adhering to the prescriptions of the law but also may reveal the strength of that law. Conversely, it may just as readily demonstrate that what is labeled as international law is unjust, unsound, or unworkable, and that that law must be improved before it is generally accepted by members of the world community. In a world where future safety depends on the rule of law, such an examination would appear worthwhile.

As might be expected, there are writers who simply do not believe in international law. To some of them, international law is nothing more than a solidification of the status

---

[7] Fisher has advanced the theory of the "yesable proposition." Pursuant to this theory, each side to the conflict attempts to give its opponents a proposition to which they can assent. See R. Fisher, INTERNATIONAL CONFLICT FOR BEGINNERS (1969); see also review by Stanley Hoffmann, 65 AM. J. INT'L L. 845 (1971).

quo and a protection for the inequitable; to others, it does not exist, except as a figment of the world community's imagination.[8] The fact remains, though, that international law, despite definite weaknesses and occasional ineffectiveness, is significant. The proof of that assertion rests in the recognition by all states of both the existence of international law and the obligation to observe it. For instance, even "entrenched dictators spend no end of effort to persuade their own people that they are not law breakers and to rationalize their own politics for a law-conscious public opinion."[9] Admittedly, there are times when the law is violated and other times when "it is manipulated in a self-serving and post-facto fashion or becomes assimilated into the tradition of formulating pious self-avowals in legal rhetoric";[10] admittedly, too, it must be recognized that international law has long played a subordinate role to politics. To make these admissions, however, is not to deny the existence of international law but to realize that it is at this time a rather loose guide for governmental action within an agreed framework, not an inviolable body of law with the power to restrain all governments from doing that which they want to do whenever they want to do it.

If an effective and comprehensive international law is to become an accepted fact in the not too distant future, both cynical disenchantment with that law and overoptimistic

[8] For support of the former view, see Higgins, *The Place of International Law in the Settlement of Disputes by the Security Council*, 64 AM. J. INT'L L. 1, 10 (1970). For support of the latter view, see Kennan, AMERICAN DIPLOMACY 1900–1950 83 (1962); see generally Kennan at 82–89 for a more complete critique of what he calls the legalistic-moralistic approach, and Morgenthau, POLITICS AMONG NATIONS 275–311 (3rd ed., 1961).

[9] R. Jackson, *The Challenge of International Lawlessness*, INT. CONCILIATION 683, 684 (1941).

[10] Falk, *Law, Lawyers, and the Conduct of American Foreign Relations*, 78 YALE L. J. 919, 929 (1969). See also Hoffmann, *Introduction* to Scheinman & Wilkinson, eds., INTERNATIONAL LAW AND POLITICAL CRISES xiv (1969); J. N. Moore, LAW AND THE INDO-CHINA WAR 8–46 (1972).

10

faith in its efficacy must be discarded. In their place international law, with its existing defects, must be bared to the world, for only by stripping the law of its gloss of perfection and exposing it to healthy criticism will it be possible to create a more perfect system of law—a system under which all disputes are resolved by "peaceable persuasion rather than bellicose coercion."[11]

To facilitate the development of such a system of law, efforts must be made to clarify and distinguish permissible and impermissible actions in conflicts such as the Ulster struggle. Through this process of clarification and distinction, the elusive goal of effective international law may become a reality, and, concomitantly, a minimum world public order may be built. To be sure, the process will not directly provide the restraints sought. Indirectly, however, it will aid both goals by increasing consent and reducing the need for coercion, thereby establishing a minimum world public order from which the transition to a more complete international law and world public order can be effected.

Despite the present low capability of the world community to enforce certain aspects of that which is called international law, there is no reason to deprecate those areas of the law that are presently unenforced or unenforceable, for, trite as it may sound, law at its worst is still far preferable to violence at its best. Moreover, by continuing to distinguish the permissible from the impermissible, the weaknesses of the existing system of law will be exposed and new pillars developed on which to lay improved international legal structures.

The relevance of studies of conflicts such as the Ulster struggle to the evolution of an improved system of inter-

11 McDougal & Lasswell, *The Identification and Appraisal of Diverse Systems of Public Order*, 53 AM. J. INT'L. L. 1, 3 (1959). See also McDougal, *Some Basic Theoretical Concepts about International Law: A Policy-Oriented Framework of Inquiry*, 4 J. CON. RES., 337, 343 (1960). See generally McDougal & Feliciano, LAW AND MINIMUM WORLD PUBLIC ORDER 59 (1961).

national law and a minimum world public order is subject to debate. It has been argued, for example, that law is irrelevant in a crisis situation in which there is violence. This point of view should be rejected. Crises are important to study because the permissibility-impermissibility factor can best be assessed when viewed in a practical light and because a vast segment of law is applicable only after a conflict has commenced. Even more importantly, though, the role of law in crises must constantly be reaffirmed, since any other position comes perilously close both to embracing Hermann Goering's view that "in a life and death struggle there is no legality"[12] and to relegating the peoples of the world to anarchy.

If, therefore, international legal development is to be expedited, the experiences of particular crises must be examined. The conflict in the North of Ireland is no exception, for the legal questions presented—civil strife, the laws of war, human rights, domestic jurisdiction, and humanitarian intervention—are among the most volatile issues of the day in the international field. Indeed, no delineations of the limits of permissibility or impermissibility are more vital in a search for an effective and just body of international law. For that reason, following an analysis of the history of the problem in Northern Ireland and of the relationship of Northern Ireland to Great Britain, these issues will be treated in detail in separate chapters. Rather than simply stating the law, though, and applying that law to the struggle, the procedure will be, once again, to view the problem from the Dublin-London-Belfast focal points and then to advance conclusions as to who is violating what and as to the efficacy of the law. In addition, suggestions will be made, where appropriate, to improve the law in each area.

Writing nearly three hundred and fifty years ago, Grotius, in discussing the reasons for his study of international law,

---

[12] Quoted in Leman, *The Prisoners of Vietnam*, VIET REPORT 5 (1966).

stated that "there is no lack of men who view this branch of law with contempt as having no reality outside of an empty name. On the lips of men quite generally is the saying . . . that in the case of a king or imperial city nothing is unjust which is expedient. Of like implication is the statement that for those whom fortune favors might makes right, and that administration of a state cannot be carried on without injustice."[13]

Much the same can be said for a study of the legal considerations of the Ulster conflict. Men are contemptuously saying that international law in general is meaningless and, in particular, has no applicability to Northern Ireland; men are saying that the Irish Republican Army, the British Army, and the Protestant extremists are justified in using any means to attain their ends; men are saying that since the Protestants are in the majority in Ulster or since the Catholics are dominant in certain areas of the Six Counties, they each have the right, within their spheres of control, to impose their will on the minorities whom fortune does not favor; and men are saying that whatever the Dublin, London, or Belfast Governments decide to do must be administratively just. But men can be wrong—and in this instance they are. The problem is to show how and when and where and why they are wrong. Therein lies the objective of the following pages. And if that objective is attained, perhaps some new ideas for bringing peace to Northern Ireland will be found and the viability of the applicable legal norms established.

13 Grotius, PROLEGOMENA TO THE LAW OF WAR AND PEACE 3–4 (1957). The work was first published in 1625.

CHAPTER II

Myth and Reality: The Conflict in Northern Ireland from Three Perspectives

IT has been said that "history never makes up its mind, but like a man climbing a ladder, reaches up to grasp the Left that it may pull itself up to the Right, and with each seizure, it imagines that it has ascended to the stars."[1] Just how high the Northern Ireland climb has reached is a matter of some debate, although no one, not even the staunchest defender of Ulster, would claim that it has yet "ascended to the stars." In assessing that climb, it is obvious, moreover, that the measurement of the climb depends upon one's frame of reference, for the history of Northern Ireland, as already noted, is viewed differently in Dublin, London, and Belfast.

Despite these disparate viewpoints, however, there are certain facts which are accepted by all, certain facts about which there is no dispute. Although to some people these facts may appear irrelevant to the present-day struggle, they are cited here in order to provide a full understanding of the Ulster conflict. And such an understanding, in turn, is a prerequisite to an analysis of the international legal questions raised by the conflict.[2]

The modern history of Ireland begins with the Celtic invasions, the first of which was in the sixth century B.C. and the last of which was that of the Gaels or Goidels during

---

[1] Thompson, THE IMAGINATION OF AN INSURRECTION: DUBLIN, EASTER 1916 243 (1967).

[2] The texts of many of the documents and statutes referred to in this chapter may be found in Curtiss & McDowell, IRISH HISTORICAL DOCUMENTS: 1172–1922 (1943).

14

the first century B.C.[3] Nearly four hundred years later, in 432
A.D., Saint Patrick—the man whose teachings were to have
a profound effect on the course of Irish history—landed in
Ireland. For more than thirty years Saint Patrick preached,
established churches, and appointed priests, and, by the
time he died in 465, Christianity was established and pagan-
ism was on the decline. In the three centuries thereafter,
Ireland remained free from invasion and Christianity flour-
ished. With the coming of the Norse invasions in the ninth
century, however, both Ireland and Christianity came under attack. Although the Norse were defeated in 1014 at
Clontarf, Ireland and Christianity were left greatly weakened.

In an attempt to ameliorate the situation and to restrain
vice, improve morals, implant virtue, and propagate Christianity, Pope Adrian IV granted Ireland to Henry II of England in 1172.[4] Even though the English were briefly over-
powered by the Scots who invaded Ireland in 1315 and
dominated the island for three years, English influence and
control may be said to stem from 1172.

But it was an unusual control. Although the island was
militarily conquered and the land apportioned among the
English and those Irish who were willing to become English
in allegiance, dress, and speech, the native Irish "Gaelicized"
their conquerors. To arrest this process, the Statutes of Kil-

[3] For accounts of the modern history of Ireland, see generally Beckett,
A SHORT HISTORY OF IRELAND (1961); Kee, THE GREEN FLAG (1972);
T. Jackson, IRELAND HER OWN: AN OUTLINE HISTORY OF THE IRISH STRUG-
GLE (1970); and MacManus, THE STORY OF THE IRISH RACE (1972).

[4] The Bull Laudabiliter, the Papal decree pursuant to which the
grant was made, came in response to a request from Henry II. It has
been argued that, in fact, the intentions of Henry II were based on
geopolitical, not religious, considerations; it has even been argued that
the Papal Bull was a forgery. What is in any case ironic, however, is
that Henry II, who had almost been excommunicated for ostensibly
instigating the murder of Thomas à Becket, was an ally of the Pope
in 1172. See MacManus, IRISH RACE 319–30. The actual invasion, which
preceded the grant, occurred in 1171.

15

kenny were passed in 1366 to preserve English influence by setting up a barrier between the two races—a barrier that prohibited English-Irish marriages, the use of Gaelic among the English, the living of Irish among the English, and Irish dress, names, and laws.

The Statutes of Kilkenny, however, proved to be ineffective. Slowly, the authority of the English was reduced to the Pale, an area consisting of Dublin and the surrounding countryside. In an effort to broaden the strip held by the English, Richard II came to Ireland in 1394, but he retired when he realized that he lacked the necessary manpower to accomplish his goal.

As the "Gaelicizing" process continued and the English were absorbed into the Irish populace, Henry VII became fearful that his representatives in Ireland might usurp his powers. Consequently, Poynings' Law was passed in 1494. It provided that the Irish Parliament could not meet unless the King and Council in England had been informed of the reasons for the meeting and of the bills proposed to be passed and unless both the King and Council had indicated their consent to proceed.

In 1534 Henry VIII started to extend his authority over Ireland. By 1541 he had become the King of Ireland. More importantly, he introduced the policy of "conciliation and fusion"—the "conciliation of the great by confirming them in their lands, granting them new titles, and sharing with them the spoil of the religious houses; the fusion of the colonial and the native populations by a complete abandonment of the policy of segregation and by the extension of English law to the whole country."[5]

Shortly thereafter, in 1558, Elizabeth came to the throne

[5] Beckett, A SHORT HISTORY 48. Royal supremacy over the church was formally established by the 1534 Act of Supremacy, pursuant to which subjects were required, if asked, to take an oath acknowledging the supremacy of King over Pope. England thus broke with Rome prior to the adoption of Protestantism. See also MacManus, IRISH RACE 362–67.

—and England became Protestant. The same metamorphosis was prescribed for Ireland, where a replica of the Church of England was established in the form of the Church of Ireland. But the native Irish remained Catholic. Indeed, it might not be unfair to say that "the fact that the ruling English were Protestant only confirmed the Irish in their attachment to the Roman Church."[6]

By 1607 the Tudor conquest—or reconquest—of Ireland was complete. Following years of fighting between the English and an Irish-Spanish alliance, the English were victorious. After the departure of the Earls of Tyrone and Tyrconnell in 1607, a departure which was occasioned by successive military defeats at the hands of the English and which came to be known as the "flight of the Earls," the Ulster lands of the Earls were handed over to English and Scottish settlers, and the most important plantation in Ulster history was begun.

Although the English were once again in military control, the Irish retained control of lands other than those in Ulster and the Dublin area. When, therefore, the Irish revolted in 1640, Cromwell, after ending the insurrections at Drogheda and Wexford, ordered every Irishman who was unable to establish his "constant good affection" for England to forfeit a portion of his estate. The result was that whereas the majority of landlords had been Catholic in 1640, the majority of landlords in 1652 were Protestants.

In 1689 James II came to Ireland from France as a first step in his attempt to recapture the English throne. After being warmly welcomed by Irish Catholics, he called the Irish Parliament into session and had the Parliament revoke the Cromwellian settlement (thereby reinvesting Irish Catholic landowners with their old lands) and declare that the English Parliament was incompetent to pass laws for

---

[6] Palmer, A HISTORY OF THE MODERN WORLD 79 (1960). Thereafter, the "Catholic priests, deprived of status, income, and church buildings, and often in hiding, became national leaders of a discontented people" (*ibid.*).

17

Ireland, that the Irish House of Lords was the court of final appeal, that there would be complete religious freedom, and that all landowners who did not reaffirm their allegiance to James II would have their lands confiscated. One year later at the Battle of the Boyne—a battle in which Catholics were allied with France and led by an English king, and Protestants were allied with England and led by a Dutch prince —James II was defeated by William of Orange, the Irish Parliament was declared illegal since the provisions of Poynings' Law had not been followed, and the work of the Parliament was undone.

The Treaty of Limerick ended the two-year struggle. Signed in 1691 and approved by William III, the Treaty was not accepted by the Irish Parliament until 1697. It provided that Irish soldiers had the option of serving with the King of France or returning home unmolested, an option that was exercised by 10,000 Irishmen and immediately labeled "the flight of the wild geese." It also provided that Catholics, in return for an oath of allegiance to William III, would not have "less toleration" than they had enjoyed prior to James II's accession.

Prior to the adoption of the Treaty of Limerick, the Irish Parliament passed a series of laws, which, together with other laws passed between 1696 and 1746, came to be known as the Penal Laws. In brief, the Penal Laws denied to Catholics the right to open or teach in a school (thus leading to the development of education by "hedge schoolmasters," teachers who held their classes surreptitiously under hedges in the fields), sit in Parliament, vote, hold public office, serve in the army, or intermarry with Protestants. Until the passage of Yelverton's Act in 1782, Catholics were, therefore, second-class citizens. With the passage of Yelverton's Act, however, Poynings' Law was modified to provide that the Irish Parliament's acts were to be transmitted to England without alteration by the Lord Lieutenant and Council in Ireland; and with its passage the Penal Laws were largely repealed.

18

This phase of accommodation, though, was short-lived. With the coming of the French Revolution, the formation of the Society of United Irishmen (whose avowed purpose was to break the ties with England), and the abortive rising of 1798, the English realized that Ireland was "weak" and that the Irish constitutional experiment must end. In 1800 the Union with Ireland Act was passed by Westminster, thereby abolishing the Irish Parliament and uniting England and Ireland.

No sooner had that union been effectuated, however, than new insurrections flared up and new demands arose—the brief "revolt" of Robert Emmet in 1803; the movement of Daniel O'Connell which resulted in the 1829 Catholic Emancipation; the Young Ireland movement of the 1840s and the Rising of 1848; the great famine of the 1840s with its accompanying cry for relief; the birth of the Irish Republican Army in the 1850s and the sharp rise in Fenianism in the 1860s; Charles Parnell's effort to reform the land system, an effort which resulted in the Land Act of 1881; and, finally, the campaign, commencing in the 1880s, for Home Rule. Although the Home Rule Bills of 1886 and 1893 were not enacted, the Government of Ireland Act 1914 did grant Ireland home rule—but its effective date was postponed by the Suspensory Act 1914 until the termination of World War I. Before that date arrived, the Easter Rising of 1916 had occurred, a republic had been declared, and war had ravaged the whole of Ireland.

Even after the Government of Ireland Act 1920 had been enacted and quasi home rule had been granted, the fighting and bitterness continued. Although the 1920 Act provided for home rule for twenty-six of Ireland's thirty-two counties, it also stated that the remaining six counties (six of the nine counties of the historic kingdom of Ulster) were to remain part of Britain.[7] Both the twenty-six county govern-

[7] The original nine counties of Ulster were Armagh, Antrim, Cavan, Donegal, Down, Fermanagh, Londonderry, Monoghan, and Tyrone; the six counties that formed the "new" Ulster were Armagh, Antrim,

ment in the South and the six county government in the North were to have a parliament, and the Northern and Southern Governments were to join in a Council of Ireland. Since Southerners rejected the concept of dividing the island, though, the fighting continued. Within months of the passage of the 1920 Act, however, the Anglo-Irish Treaty of 1921 was signed, thus ending hostilities between Britain and Ireland, recognizing the provisions of the 1920 Act as they pertained to the North, leaving the border question to a Boundary Commission, and granting dominion status to the South as the Irish Free State.

Even then, the fighting in Ireland did not end. When the Treaty was passed by the Dail Eireann (Southern Parliament), the anti-Treaty faction organized as a separate force, and civil war between the Free State and Republican, anti-Treaty forces followed suit. Although the fighting terminated in 1923, the bitterness over the Treaty and the resulting civil war remains to this day.

The Boundary Commission established under the Treaty to make adjustments in the North-South border failed to make a final report. Instead, in 1925 those provisions of the Treaty pertaining to the Boundary Commission were deleted, and, in lieu thereof and as a concession to the South, the Irish Free State's financial obligations to Britain were cancelled.

During the 1920s and 1930s both the North and South developed politically into separate entities. In 1936 the Irish Free State's powers were broadened to provide that the King of England could act for Ireland only if so advised by Irish ministers; in 1937 the people of Ireland voted for a new—and far-reaching—Constitution; in 1938 the ports of Berehaven, Lough Swilly, and Queenstown, which under the Anglo-Irish Treaty were to be used by Britain, were returned to Ireland; and in 1939 the Free State declared her

Down, Fermanagh, Londonderry, and Tyrone. Historically, Ireland was divided into the kingdoms of Connacht, Leinster, Munster, and Ulster.

neutrality in the hostilities between Britain and Germany—
a position that was maintained throughout World War II—
while at the same time the people of the North flocked to
England's defense.

The South's break with Britain was completed in 1949.
Under the terms of the Ireland Act 1949, the Irish Free
State became the Republic of Ireland. But the Act also
stated that the North-South border could not be changed
without the consent of the people of the North and that
Britain could intervene in the North's internal affairs only
to control a breakdown of law and order.

To reduce the likelihood of sporadic violence—there had
been such violence since the partition of Ireland—acts, such
as the Public Order Act 1951 (which made the wearing of
political uniforms illegal), were passed. Nevertheless, violence did erupt in the mid-1950s. From 1956 until 1962,
when it realized the futility of continued activity, the Irish
Republican Army conducted an ineffective but destructive
bombing and shooting campaign in the North to effectuate
a union of North and South.[8]

After the IRA announced that it would terminate hostilities, a brief period of peace came to Northern Ireland. That
the period was brief is evidenced by the fact that in September 1964 riots followed the removal of the Irish tricolor—
the green, white, and orange flag of the Republic of Ireland—from the Republican Party headquarters in Belfast.
Thereafter, a new "lull of peace," highlighted by the historic but inconclusive talks in December 1965 between Prime
Ministers Lemass and O'Neill, settled over Ulster. But the
lull proved to be the proverbial lull before the storm.
Beginning in June 1966, supporters of existing Northern
policies attacked the O'Neill efforts at reconciliation. By

8 See Bell, THE SECRET ARMY: THE IRA, 1916–1970 310–34 (1971);
Coogan, THE I.R.A. 309–44 (1970); Sunday Times Insight Team, ULSTER
17–21 (1972) (hereafter cited as Insight Team, ULSTER). The terms
"Irish Republican Army" and "IRA" will be used interchangeably in
this study.

1967, moreover, the Northern Ireland Civil Rights Association[9] had been founded by middle-class Catholics who felt that Catholics were the object of discrimination in Ulster.

The weapon used by the civil rights activists was "the march." Whereas the IRA sought to achieve its goals by the bomb and the bullet, the CRA tried to demonstrate and march to its ends. On October 5, 1968 the first large-scale civil rights march was held in Derry (Londonderry). Thereafter, in rapid succession, there were marches and countermarches, demonstrations and counterdemonstrations, as the flames of war burst forth across an already troubled land and the foundations of the Northern Government and Parliament (Stormont) began to be consumed.

The pattern that early emerged was that a march (or countermarch) or demonstration (or counterdemonstration) would be followed by riots in the surrounding area. Immediately after the riots, a commission or tribunal would be established to make an official inquiry into the disturbance. Government followed government as the march-riot-commission cycle was repeated endlessly. During that period the only discernible changes were increasing differences among both the pro and anti-Stormont forces and the increasing role of Britain in the struggle.

When the CRA campaign began, the battle lines were quite clearly drawn. By the 1970s, however, those lines had been redrawn so often that parties, positions, and leaders changed almost daily. Although it was still a simple matter to distinguish IRA from Unionist Party policies, it was more difficult to discern noticeable differences between the Official

9 The terms "Northern Ireland Civil Rights Association," "NICRA," "Civil Rights Association," and "CRA" will be used interchangeably hereafter. The Civil Rights movement might really be said to have begun with the effort of Mrs. Patricia McClusky in 1963 to end discriminatory housing methods in Dungannon. See Carroll, *The Search for Justice in Northern Ireland*, 6 N.Y.U. J. INT'L L. & POL. 28, 30–31 (1973). In addition, in August 1966, a secret meeting was held to discuss plans for the formation of NICRA. See Insight Team, ULSTER, 47.

and Provisional IRA, the Nationalist Party and the Social Democratic and Labor Party, the Alliance Party and Unionist Party, and the Democratic Unionist Party, Ulster Defense Association, Ulster Vanguard, and Vanguard Unionist Progressive Party.

A split in the Sinn Fein (the political arm of the Irish Republican Army) resulted in the 1969 Official-Provisional schism. The Officials favored participation in the governmental process and left-wing, Marxist social policies; the Provisionals supported continued abstention from government and unification of the North and South by whatever means necessary. (And more recently, the Irish Republican Socialist Party has broken away from the Official IRA and accused the Officials of being Stalinist, hypocritical, and reformist).

The Nationalist Party, as the name implied, had as its sole objective a united Ireland. Similarly, the Social Democratic and Labor Party (SDLP)—which was formed in August 1970 by Austin Currie, Paddy Devlin, and John Hume and which brought together the Republican Labour Party, the Northern Ireland Labour Party, members of the Nationalist Party, and Independents—sought equality of Catholics and Protestants and, since in its view equality could not be attained in the North, union with the Republic of Ireland.

When Terence O'Neill was forced to resign in 1969, the New Ulster Movement of Catholics and Protestants, which had backed the independent Unionists of O'Neill against the official Unionists, merged with the Northern Ireland Liberal Party to form the Alliance Party. Headed by Bob Cooper and Oliver Napier, it endorsed the link with Britain, the 1969 reform program, complete governmental partnership of Catholics and Protestants, an end to internment, and a referendum on a united Ireland. Conversely, the Unionist Party, under the leadership of Brian Faulkner, advocated the continued tie with Britain and a separate parliament.

Formed by Rev. Ian Paisley and Desmond Boal in 1971, the Democratic Unionist Party became both the successor to the Protestant Unionist Party (created by Paisley in 1969 to provide an alternative to the Unionist Party) and Paisley's political vehicle. The Ulster Defense Association, although not a political party, had as its aim the preservation of a British Ulster and, if that were denied, the continued existence of two Irelands, even if Ulster were forced to make a unilateral declaration of independence. The Ulster Vanguard, formed in February 1972 by William Craig and labor leader Billy Hull, endorsed the existing Constitution, majority rule, the British electoral system, and a policy of opposition to both direct rule and a united Ireland. And the Vanguard Unionist Progressive Party, a March 1973 creation of William Craig, advocated a federal relationship between Great Britain and Ulster and criticized Britain's 1973 White Paper as a sell-out.[10]

Yet if it was difficult to distinguish the participants in the struggle, it was even more difficult, if not impossible, to control them, for a concession to one resulted in an immediate and often violent reaction from another. In an effort ostensibly to facilitate that control, the Public Order (Amendment) Act 1969 and the Criminal Justice (Temporary Provisions) Act 1970 were passed. But these acts, together with the policy of internment that was initiated on August 9, 1971 under the provisions of the Special Powers Act, not only failed to result in additional control but ac-

[10] On the Official-Provisional split, see Rose, GOVERNING WITHOUT CONSENSUS 231 (1971); on the Nationalist Party, see *ibid.*, 228–29; on the SDLP, *ibid.*, 230–33; on the Alliance Party, *ibid.*, 226, and O'Callaghan, *Paisley Waits in the Wings*, 83 NEW STATESMAN 380, 381 (1972); on the Democratic Unionist Party see Kramer, *Letter from Ireland*, 48 NEW YORKER 46, 73 (February 19, 1972) and Rose, GOVERNING WITHOUT CONSENSUS, 226; on the Ulster Defense Association, see T. Buckley, *Double Troubles of Northern Ireland—A Visit with the Protestant Militants*, NEW YORK TIMES MAG. 36, 114 (December 10, 1972); on the Ulster Vanguard, see A. Boyd, BRIAN FAULKNER AND THE CRISIS OF ULSTER UNIONISM 97–98 (1972); and on the Vanguard Unionist Progressive Party, see *The Vanguard Unionist Progressive Party*, UNIONIST REV. 3 (September 1973).

tually aggravated the situation. Accordingly, and as a last resort, Britain suspended the Stormont Parliament and assumed direct control of Northern Ireland on March 24, 1972.

At first, direct rule seemed to have a soothing effect on the struggle. This effect, however, soon was replaced by a renewed campaign of violence from extremists on both sides. With its trump card of direct rule played, Britain searched for another answer. That answer was contained in a 1973 White Paper which, among other things, called for the sharing of power between elected representatives of the Catholic and Protestant communities and a Council of Ireland consisting of Northern and Southern members.

For several months, optimism reigned in Ulster, for—at last—an end to the conflict seemed in sight. With the relentless pressure supplied by striking Protestant workers opposed to the power-sharing experiment and to the possibility of the union of North and South, the optimism waned; with the forced end to the experiment resulting from the May 1974 resignation of the Unionist members, direct rule and pessimism returned to Northern Ireland. And in July 1974 Britain issued another White Paper, a paper which advanced Britain's latest proposed solution to the struggle that had, alternately, been smoldering and raging for over eight hundred years.[11]

The Dublin Viewpoint

Regardless of where a review of Irish history begins, it is not a pleasant process for Irishmen, for "Anglo-Irish history is for Englishmen to remember, for Irishmen to forget."[12] Since it first conquered the island under the pretext of ad-

---

11 Northern Ireland Constitutional Proposals (Cmnd. 5259) cited hereafter as 1973 White Paper) and The Northern Ireland Constitution (Cmnd. 5675) (cited hereafter as 1974 White Paper) are discussed in some detail under "The London Viewpoint," below.

12 Bennett, The Black and Tans 10–11 (1960).

vancing the cause of Christianity, "Britain has enslaved Ireland, doomed the Irish peasants to unparalleled suffering and gradual extinction from starvation, driven them from the land and compelled them to leave their native country in hundreds of thousands and millions and emigrate to America."[13] Indeed, even to an Englishman, Britain's role in Ireland is not only a "frightful document against ourselves" but also a crime unmatched in the history of the modern world.[14]

In an attempt to preserve their authority and influence, the English passed the Statutes of Kilkenny. By these laws the seeds of discord were planted and a permanent barrier was raised between the two races. Thus, although the intent of the statutes was essentially defensive, their effect was far broader than contemplated, for, by limiting interaction between the two peoples, the statutes fostered attitudes that are still felt today.

Another type of planting had an even greater effect on sectarian hostility. While the seeds of discord had germinated in the years following the Statutes of Kilkenny, violent sectarian animosity first grew uncontrollably following the Protestant plantation in 1607. Although race and religion certainly engendered that animosity, "land supplie[d] a much stronger motive for sectarian ill-feeling."[15] In effect, the plantation was purely a land question—the taking of land from the native (Catholic) Irish and the giving of that land to the Protestant invaders.

13 Lenin, LENIN ON IRELAND 12 (1970).

14 The quotation, attributed to novelist William Thackeray, reads in full: "It is a frightful document against ourselves—one of the most melancholy stories in the whole world of insolence, rapine, brutal endless persecution. . . . There is no crime ever invented by the eastern or western barbarians, no torture of Roman persecutors or Spanish inquisitors, no tyranny of Nero or Alva but can be matched in the history of the English in Ireland." Quoted in Bryan, THE IMPROBABLE IRISH 185 (1969).

15 O. Edwards, THE SINS OF OUR FATHERS: ROOTS OF CONFLICT IN NORTHERN IRELAND 6 (1970).

With the coming of the Williamite wars, the situation deteriorated for the native Irish. Even though the Treaty of Limerick provided that Catholics were not to have "less toleration" than they had prior to James II's reign, the Treaty was not ratified until a number of laws penalizing Catholics had been passed and "a legal stipulation had been accepted that the Treaty meant that the least favourable conditions for Catholics prior to 1685 were to become the most favourable conditions for Catholics in the future."[16] Moreover, the Penal Laws that preceded and followed ratification of the Treaty of Limerick not only severely demoralized and enfeebled the Irish but also, by prohibiting Catholics from holding public posts or becoming lawyers, forced large numbers of the best brains among Catholics to emigrate, thereby leaving the priests as the sole and unchallenged teachers of the Irish people and the Irish as the most thoroughly repressed people of Western Europe.

Towards the end of the eighteenth century and through the efforts of Irishmen like Henry Grattan and Englishmen like Edmund Burke, the Penal Laws were largely repealed, and the gap between Catholics and Protestants was narrowed. Thereafter, as a result of the demand of the Catholic Convention of 1792 that Catholics be restored to a position of equality with Protestants, the Catholic Relief Act (1793) was passed, and the last vestiges of the Penal Code were swept away. But Catholic-Protestant equality still had not been attained.

Even if that equality had been secured, it would undoubtedly have been an equality among unequals, since in 1793 there were Protestants and there were Protestants. The ruling Protestants—with whom equality in 1793 was an impossibility—were Episcopalians and, more importantly, landowners. Although their ascendancy was attained with the aid of Presbyterians (Dissenters), the Episcopalians ranked

16 Jackson, IRELAND HER OWN 84. "The cheque which was signed at Limerick was not honored when presented at the bank." Gray, THE IRISH ANSWER: AN ANATOMY OF MODERN IRELAND 76 (1966).

their Presbyterian allies with the "mere Irish," for the Episcopalians viewed the difference between the Dissenters and Catholics as "one of degree and not of kind, inasmuch as [the Dissenters], like the Catholics, held land instead of owning it."[17]

In an effort to improve the economic and social position of all Irishmen and to substitute the common name of Irishman in place of the denominations of Protestant, Catholic, and Dissenter, the Society of United Irishmen was founded in 1791 by Samuel Neilson. Wolfe Tone, the most famous of the United Irishmen and a man who regarded the connection with Britain "as the curse of the Irish nation,"[18] drew up the Society's declaration. The declaration provided that English influence in Ireland was the great grievance of the country, that the most effective way to reform it was by a reform of Parliament, and that no reform could be of any use unless it included the Catholics.

While Neilson, Tone, and other United Irishmen were trying to bring the people of Ireland together, the Protestant Episcopalians were striving to keep them apart. In 1795 they formed the Orange Society to preserve their political, social, and economic ascendancy. Although it later become more broadly based, the Orange Order in 1795 was composed entirely of churchmen and "functioned as a 'union-smashing' force."[19] By employing this "semi-religious, semi-political,

17 Good, ULSTER AND IRELAND 23 (1919).

18 In his speech from the dock in 1798, after being intercepted by British warships on his way to Ireland to participate with French forces in the Rising, Tone stated that "from my earliest youth I have regarded the connection between Great Britain and Ireland as the curse of the Irish nation, and felt convinced that, whilest it lasted, this country could never be free or happy." Sullivan, Sullivan, & Sullivan, SPEECHES FROM THE DOCK 21 (1968). The full text of Tone's speech is at 21–27.

19 Jackson, IRELAND HER OWN 145; Beckett, A SHORT HISTORY 136. The Orange toast is quite instructive in revealing the attitude of the Order: "To the Glorious, Pious, and Immortal Memory of the Great and Good King William who saved us from Rogues and Roguery, Slaves and Slavery, Knaves and Knavery, Popes and Popery, from

totally fascist organization,"[20] the Protestant Ascendancy maintained the laws of the country, divided Catholics and Protestants so that the working classes could never unite to overthrow it, and created a society "which established Episcopalianism, made Presbyterianism a second-class religion and Roman Catholicism an outlaw sect."[21]

This effort was aided by Britain. After the Rising of 1798, Britain, fearful of an Irish-French alliance, moved quickly to eliminate the Irish threat by abolishing the Irish Parliament and uniting the two islands. At first, Catholics looked favorably upon the Union with Ireland Act 1800, since they viewed union as the only way of removing the religious hatred and intolerance that the Orange Order had revived in the period immediately preceding union and as the most promising way by which the Roman Catholics might obtain political power. But, as is often the case, it was not until much later that the Catholics—and others—realized "that the Act of Union really left a small caste in control, and the rest of the people of Ireland in the position of outcastes from which they were never allowed to emerge";[22] for, although the Protestant Ascendancy was forced by the Union to subordinate its interest to the British ruling classes, it managed to retain its dominance over the Irish people.

Nevertheless, despite Orangeism and Union, Catholics

---

brass money and wooden shoes; and whoever denies this Toast may he be slammed, crammed and jammed in the muzzle of the great gun of Athlone, and the gun fired into the Pope's Belly, and the Pope into the Devil's Belly, and the Devil into Hell, and the door locked and the key in an Orangeman's pocket."

20 Devlin, THE PRICE OF MY SOUL 53 (1969).

21 Edwards, SINS OF OUR FATHERS 74. See also Coogan, THE I.R.A. 3. As William Gladstone stated during the Home Rule debates, the Protestant Ascendancy was "like a great tree of noxious growth, lifting its head and poisoning the land as far as its shadow [could] extend." Quoted in Armour, FACING THE IRISH QUESTION 113 (1935); also see generally 112–26.

22 Armour, FACING THE IRISH QUESTION 119. See also Good, ULSTER AND IRELAND 66–67.

and Protestants lived together in relative peace until 1829 when the Catholic Emancipation Act resulted in the admission of Catholics to Parliament. Although the 1829 Act's chief proponent, Daniel O'Connell, is regarded—and rightly so—as one of the giants in Irish history, his less-than-temperate statement that the act would result in a Catholic Ascendancy must also be regarded as a tragic error. Until that time, an element of goodwill existed between Catholics and Protestants, and movements were made up of members of both religions; until that time, too, people like the demonic Henry Cooke, a Protestant minister, had no success in beating the drums of Orangeism and inflaming the passions of Protestants.

As Catholics and Protestants aligned themselves along religious lines, Britain, as became painfully evident during the famine of the 1840s, was interested only in keeping Ireland under sufficient control "to eliminate competition and provide England with an abundance of food."[23] Britain could not, in fact, be said to be anti-Catholic, for those of both Celtic and Saxon blood were repressed. While Protestants were being told that Catholic property and lives were being taken, Catholics were being informed that Britain was the shield between Catholics and the revival of the Protestant Ascendancy that Britain itself had created. In short, Britain was interested in what had to be done for Britain, not what should be done for Ireland. Ireland was, accordingly, consistently oppressed and converted into an impoverished nation that was reduced to supplying Britain with, in addition

[23] Collins, THE PATH TO FREEDOM 58 (1922). Collins also remarked that economic suppression was not the sole means of subjugation, for spiritual subjection was introduced "to forget our former national and economic freedom and acquiesce and grow passive in our servitude." Although he was describing Ireland at a later date, the description is really a timeless one. As early as 1699, the English Parliament had prohibited the export of woolen goods from Ireland to any country except England. And "they were already virtually excluded [from England] by very heavy duties. Under this blow the Irish industry quickly withered away." Beckett, A SHORT HISTORY 112.

30

to food, "prostitutes, casual labourers, pimps, pickpockets, swindlers, beggars and other rabble."[24]

Under these circumstances it was not surprising that on Saint Patrick's Day, 1858, the Irish Republican Brotherhood was founded. Created to resume the work done by the United Irishmen, the Irish Republican Brotherhood, as the name implies, was opposed to any settlement of the "English Question" that compromised its republican aim.

While the Irish Republican Brotherhood was attempting to organize a republican movement, Charles Parnell was successfully arousing support for his attack on landlordism. Through his "three F's" of fixity of tenure, fair rent, and freedom of sale (of a tenant's improvements to the land)— all of which were secured by the Land Act of 1881—Parnell improved the tenant's lot, for before the "three F's" the tenant had no rights.[25] Yet even with these new rights, the tenant's life was a miserable one, because he was still dependent on his crop and he could never challenge the fairness of his rent (which, under the Land Act of 1881, was fixed by a government evaluator).

Parnell was also interested in the larger land question— Home Rule. Indeed, he seemed to realize that everything was, in fact, a struggle for land, be it on an individual or governmental scale. He also seemed to recognize that the Catholic-Protestant schism was not so much a religious problem as it was a land (or economic) issue. Accordingly,

[24] Letter from Frederick Engels to Karl Marx, May 23, 1856, in Marx & Engels, IRELAND AND THE IRISH QUESTION 85 (1972). The work contains various exchanges between Engels and Marx, none of which is favorable to Britain. See also McCaffrey, THE IRISH QUESTION 1800–1922 179 (1968).

[25] To put pressure on opponents of the fair rents campaign, Parnell advocated that tenants show any unscrupulous landlord "your detestation of the crime (unfair rents) he has committed." Jackson, IRELAND HER OWN 325–26. One of the first persons so affected was a Captain Boycott who, as a result of collecting unfair rents, was shunned—"boycotted"—by the surrounding townspeople. *Ibid.*, 326–27; Bryan, THE IMPROBABLE IRISH 85.

31

at the same time that he advanced the cause of tenants' rights, Parnell was one of the chief advocates of Home Rule.

Opposition to Home Rule in 1886 was led by Randolph Churchill. By "playing the Orange Card" and encouraging the Orange Order to threaten to take whatever actions were necessary to defeat Home Rule, Churchill succeeded in perpetuating the Protestant Ascendancy and exacerbating the divisions among the populace. But his machinations were not the sole reason for the defeat of Home Rule. In addition, there was a Protestant fear of Home Rule on religious grounds, a fear based, however, not on whether religious concepts emanated from Geneva or Rome, but on the old maxim that a man hates those people whom he has injured.

Following the defeat of the second Home Rule Bill in 1893, the Irish question seemed to get little attention from Parliament. With the founding of the Sinn Fein ("We Ourselves") by Arthur Griffith in 1905, however, the independence issue was once again a live question. By 1912, despite the bigoted efforts of the Orange lodges to defeat it, a third Home Rule Bill was before Parliament; by 1914, it had passed both Houses, although, with the outbreak of World War I, the bill's effective date was delayed until the cessation of hostilities.

To the Irish the delayed effective date was simply Britain's way of offering Home Rule with one hand to take it away with the other. Rather than wait for the war to end and for Britain to focus her attention and military might on Ireland, a handful of Irishmen decided to take advantage of Britain's indisposition and to force Ireland's independence. While emissaries such as Roger Casement went to Germany for military aid "to get Irish freedom out of the quarrels of the European powers,"[26] a group, headed by James Con-

[26] Hobson, IRELAND YESTERDAY AND TOMORROW 82 (1968). While Casement was in Germany, the Czech leaders, Masaryk and Benes, were in London and Paris, respectively, for the same reasons. "In London, Casement was denounced as a traitor and Masaryk was hailed as a great patriot. Doubtless, in Vienna, the position was reversed. . . . Masaryk ap-

nolly and Padraic Pearse, declared the Irish Republic in
1916. Even though Casement failed and the revolutionary
group was brutally crushed—and both Casement and the
group's leaders were hanged—their failures were turned by
the British into successes which paved the way for Irish
independence. "Ignorant of the Irish and their centuries'
old tradition of reciting the names of the martyrs who had
fallen for Ireland,"[27] the British made martyrs of men whom
no one had followed, much less worshiped.

Those men who had participated in the Rising and were
spared execution became leaders overnight. After his 1917
release from prison for his role in the Rising, Eamon De-
Valera mobilized support for Sinn Fein. In 1918 Sinn Fein
won overwhelming control of the seats allotted to Ireland
in the British Parliament. In lieu of taking their seats at
Westminster, however, the seventy-three elected Sinn Fein
members met in Dublin in January 1919 to organize the
first Dail Eireann. Three months thereafter, on April 1,
1919, DeValera was elected President of the Irish Republic.

No sooner had DeValera and the Dail Eireann put the
wheels of government into motion, than Britain stepped in
to grind them to a halt. To counter British actions, the Irish
Republican Army, descendant of both the 1858 Irish Re-

---

pealed to the victors, Casement to the vanquished. That was the difference between them. Masaryk became the first President of the Czecho-
slovak Republic—Casement was hanged in Pentonville." *Ibid.*, 82–83.

27 Thompson, IMAGINATION OF AN INSURRECTION, 103; see also Forester,
MICHAEL COLLINS—THE LOST LEADER 48 (1971). The executions of the
Easter Rebellion leaders (there were fifteen) provided Ireland with
heroes and martyrs and united the Irish people against Britain. At the
same time, the hanging of Casement, who had attained fame for exposing the Congo and Putumayo atrocities, shocked the world. The
attitude of the men who staged the Rising is captured in Bell's statement that "if the rose tree of Irish freedom had to be watered each
generation with the blood of patriots, then, they were willing, sure
that their sacrifice would in time bring blooms to what seemed in the
Spring of 1916 to be a dry and shattered trunk." Bell, THE SECRET
ARMY 9.

publican Brotherhood and the 1913 Irish Volunteers (a force created to protect the South from both Britain and the North), in 1920 initiated a campaign of guerrilla warfare. Led by Michael Collins, who believed that even though Britain could always replace its soldiers, it could not so easily replace its spies—"another man could step into a spy's place, but he could not step into a dead spy's knowledge"[28]—the IRA struck effectively at British operations.

In response to the IRA attacks, Britain countered with both increased army actions and a repressive irregular force known as the Black and Tans. Although Britain hoped that this two-pronged attack on the fledgling, self-declared Republic would be as effective as Cromwell's murderous campaign nearly three hundred years before, Britain soon realized that the Black and Tans' wanton destruction was having the opposite effect. Instead of subduing the populace, the burning, looting, and torturing by the notorious British force steeled the people of Ireland to further resistance. Moreover, the activities of the Black and Tans and the suicide by starvation of Terence MacSwiney (Mayor of Cork) in a British prison shocked the world into accepting the terrible truth of Britain's rape of Ireland. Reacting to world opinion, Britain shifted its Irish course.

Its shift, however, was back to a plan that Westminster had rejected when Edward Carson, a Northern leader and chief opponent of Home Rule, proposed it eight years earlier. Under the Government of Ireland Act 1920, the six northeastern counties of Ireland were to be carved out and administered by a separate parliament, the remaining twenty-six counties were to be governed by a Southern parliament, and the North and South were to join together in a Council of Ireland. Britain thus attempted to do legislatively and by guile what it had been unable to do militarily, for by separating the "Orange" Northeast from the "Green" South and equating minority and majority, Britain hoped

[28] Thompson, IMAGINATION OF AN INSURRECTION 108. See also Collins, PATH TO FREEDOM 83, and Forester, MICHAEL COLLINS 170.

to defeat the Republican movement. Through the creation of two Irelands, Britain also hoped to force the severed parts of Ireland, which united could have stood alone, to lean separately on Britain, thereby preserving the Irish market for British products. 1945824

At first, the South balked at the proposed settlement. In December 1921 the Anglo-Irish Treaty was concluded, however, and the basic tenets of the 1920 Act were accepted. To the dismay of many persons, but undoubtedly to the delight of the British and the Ulster Protestants, the Treaty created a split in the Southern ranks. Collins and Griffith favored the Treaty because it gave Ireland freedom ("not the ultimate freedom which all nations hope for and struggle for, but freedom to achieve that end")[29] and because they felt that large parts of the North would be shifted to the South by the Boundary Commission, thus making the survival of the North an economic impossibility and forcing the desired union of the North and South; DeValera opposed the Treaty because he wanted more independence than the dominion status granted the South and less of an oath of allegiance to the King of England. After the passage of the Treaty by the Dail by a 64 to 57 vote, the anti-Treaty members walked out and organized as a separate force. The split that no Southerner wanted was complete and civil war followed.

The war was brief but bloody. To the Republicans, the Provisional Government was illegitimate, since the Dail had not been dissolved and the Republic could not be disestablished; to the Provisional Government, the Republicans were leading the country to anarchy. Aside from the tragedy of men fighting each other after years of fighting together, there was the possibility that if the country was reduced to anarchy, the British *"would have been welcomed back, that they would have come not as enemies, but as the only protectors who could bring order and peace."*[30] Fortunately, the

29 Collins, PATH TO FREEDOM 37.

30 *Ibid.*, 25. See also M. Bromage, DEVALERA AND THE MARCH OF A

struggle terminated before this possibility materialized. Equally fortunately, DeValera and the defeated Republicans determined that there would be no "flight of the wild geese" as had occurred in 1691, even though, by refusing to take the prescribed oath of allegiance, they were not permitted to sit in the Dail Eireann.

On December 6, 1922, the first anniversary of the Anglo-Irish Treaty—which was not so much a treaty "as a compromise accepted under threat of arms, and imposed by civil war"[31]—the South proclaimed itself the Irish Free State. Immediately thereafter, the North exercised its option under the Treaty and petitioned the King that the Free State's powers not be extended to Northern Ireland. The question then became what lands were to be included in the excluded area of the North. Pursuant to the terms of Article 12 of the Treaty, a Boundary Commission was set up to settle this question, although since Dublin, London, and Belfast were each to appoint one member and Belfast refused to do so, new legislation was required between Britain and the Free State before the appointment of the Belfast "representative" could be made by London and the commission could meet. After the passage of this legislation, the appointment of the Northern member, and the convening of the commission, it was learned, however, that, contrary to the Free State's expectations, the Boundary Commission was not going to order the transfer of lands to the South but was contemplating transfers of Southern areas to the North. Fearful of this possibility, the Free State entered into the London Agreement of 1925, which confirmed the existing boundary, cancelled Britain's financial claims against the Free State, and abandoned both the nationalists in the North and the hope for all-Ireland unity.

Once the North had obtained its "liberty," it wasted no

NATION 174 (1956); M. Bromage, CHURCHILL AND IRELAND 91 (1964); Churchill, THE AFTERMATH 363–64 (1929).

[31] Greaves, THE IRISH CASE AGAINST PARTITION 13 (1956).

time insuring that the reins of authority would always be in Protestant hands. Boundaries were twisted—gerrymandered—to guarantee the election of Protestant candidates to the Northern Parliament; Catholics were often discriminated against and occasionally victimized by a pogrom; a police force, the Special Constabulary, was created out of a fiercely partisan organization[32] for the sole purpose of protecting Protestant interests; and the Special Powers Act, enacted in 1922 and made permanent in 1933, gave the Minister of Home Affairs or a policeman designated by him a blank check to arrest anyone without a warrant and intern him without the benefit of either a presentation of charges or a trial. In short, the North quickly became a dictatorial "substate" which was ostensibly run for the good of all Protestants but which was actually maintained for the powerful few of the modern Protestant Ascendancy.

At the same time, the Free State moved closer to the harmony it had enjoyed prior to the civil war. Although there were occasional assassinations and although feelings still ran deep, by 1927 the Free State was a working democracy, for in that year the Republicans, who had not participated in the Dail since 1921 because of the required oath of allegiance to the British Crown, made a substantial

---

[32] The Special Constabulary was a Protestant force founded in 1920 as the successor to Carson's Ulster Volunteer Force. There were originally to be three classes: Class A (full-time, small body); Class B (large, part-time, home-based body); and Class C (reserve force for grave emergencies). The A's were disbanded in 1926. Although the B's were to be disbanded, the North balked, and the force was retained in modified form. As such, it was "purely a sectarian organisation from which anybody who [was] not an Orangeman [was] excluded . . . maintained out of public funds through taxation taken equally from those who [could] and those who, because of their religious and political views, [could not] become members." Gallagher, THE INDIVISIBLE ISLAND: THE HISTORY OF THE PARTITION OF IRELAND 192 (1957). See generally ibid., 177–82; Shearman, NORTHERN IRELAND 1921–1971 22–25 (1971); and Wallace, NORTHERN IRELAND: 50 YEARS OF SELF-GOVERNMENT 12 (1971). The terms "B Specials" and "USC" will be used interchangeably in this study.

electoral gain, went through the "form" of taking the requisite oath, and joined the Dail. By 1932 the Republicans had control of the Dail and had formed their first government under the leadership of DeValera; by 1936 DeValera had negotiated the External Relations Act, which, except for formal diplomatic purposes, practically removed the Crown from the Free State Constitution; by 1937 he had provided Ireland with a new constitution, a constitution that substituted "Ireland" for "Irish Free State" and that, pursuant to the provisions of Article 2, claimed to be the constitution for the whole island of Ireland; by 1938 DeValera had regained for Ireland the ports reserved to Britain by the 1921 Treaty; and by 1939 he had announced to a disbelieving Britain that Ireland would maintain a position of neutrality in the onrushing war.

Given the fact that civil war might well have returned to Ireland had DeValera—and DeValera was wholeheartedly supported by the opposition parties—charted a course other than neutrality between the Scylla of the Axis powers and the Charybdis of Britain, there can be no question about the wisdom of his decision. Moreover, in view of Britain's age-old colonial policies toward Ireland, there was no possible justification for DeValera to risk further destruction to Ireland by aiding Britain. Accordingly, despite pleas and threats, DeValera stuck to his "practical declaration of independence" and maintained a rigid neutrality.[33]

After the war, Ireland continued its development, and, in accordance with the terms of the Republic of Ireland Act 1949, Ireland became four-fifths of the republic that

[33] Neutrality was "final, convincing evidence of freedom and in that sense it was a psychological necessity." Mansergh, THE COMMONWEALTH AND THE NATIONS 207 (1948). Nevertheless, foodstuffs and workers were supplied to Britain. Nearly 180,000 Irishmen also served in the British Army, although those members of the Irish Army who left the country to serve in the British Army were, on their return to Ireland, tried on desertion charges, given suspended sentences, denied government jobs, and prohibited from sharing in government relief schemes. See Smyllie, *Unneutral Neutral Eire*, 24 FOR. AFF. 317, 320 (1946).

Connolly and Pearse had declared in 1916. As for the remaining fifth, it continued to develop economically, but it did so only with the assistance of Britain and at the expense of its Catholic community.

By 1964 the first signs of sickness were evident in Ulster; by 1968 the sickness had permeated the entire Ulster body. Although the IRA had conducted an active campaign from 1956 to 1962 to effectuate the long-denied union with the Republic, the campaign had proved unsuccessful because the Catholic populace in the North had not lent its moral or physical support. Yet two years after 1962, when the IRA admitted defeat, the Catholic community began to demonstrate its displeasure with the state of affairs in the North. On Sepember 28, 1964, for instance, riots engulfed West Belfast following the removal of the Irish tricolor from the Republican Party headquarters; on June 6, 1966, as a result of a provocative Protestant march through the Catholic Cromac Square area of Belfast to protest both O'Neill's embryonic policy of reconciliation with the South and the Presbyterian Church's ostensibly "Rome-ward trend," riots again broke out. In each instance, the cause of the riots was an ill-advised and inequitable decision by the Protestant Government, a decision that was no different from the hundreds that preceded it but that the Catholic community, after decades of discrimination, at last refused to accept.

The combination of Stormont's refusal to eliminate discrimination against Catholics and the obvious prejudice of the authorities as reflected in both the Tricolor and Cromac Square riots convinced Catholics and enlightened Protestants alike that the situation in the North could not continue. Within a year, the Northern Ireland Civil Rights Association was founded. Nonsectarian in makeup and desirous of cutting "across the lines of division in the community which Unionist rule had been so careful to emphasize,"[34] NICRA had numerous objectives: to establish the principle of "one man, one vote"; to define the rights of all

34 De Paor, DIVIDED ULSTER 165–66 (1970).

citizens; to allocate jobs and houses fairly; to draw electoral boundaries equitably; to reveal abuses of power (especially the Special Powers Act); to provide guarantees for freedom of speech, assembly, and association; and to inform the members of the public of their rights.

In 1968 a particularly unfair housing decision produced the first civil rights march. Although NICRA was somewhat hesitant to join the August 24, 1968, four-mile march from Coalisland to Dungannon, it finally agreed to lend its support. The march was a total success, if for no other reason than that the Government's rerouting of the march into the Catholic section of Dungannon made people realize that "Northern Ireland was a series of Catholic and Protestant ghettos."[35] In addition, the march demonstrated that the best way to evidence disapproval of government policies was to march peacefully.

A second march was planned immediately—this one for Derry on October 5, 1968. William Craig, Minister of Home Affairs for Northern Ireland, had rerouted the Coalisland-Dungannon march to Catholic areas to make it appear sectarian. That approach having failed, he now tried a new one. On the pretext that the NICRA march would clash with a parade of Orangemen scheduled for the same time, he banned the march. In view of this obvious partisanship on Craig's behalf (obvious because the Orangemen announced their parade after plans for the NICRA march had been made public), Craig's order was defied, and the march held. A clash followed—not, as hypothesized, with the Orangemen but with the police. It was a clash that revealed to the world, through the ever-watchful eyes of television cameras, the rottenness of the Ulster governmental structure. As millions watched, the Royal Ulster Constabulary first blocked the defenseless marchers' escape and then charged them in a savage onslaught. So unjustified was the police action that even the Cameron Commission, a com-

[35] Devlin, PRICE OF MY SOUL 93. The march was the idea of Austin Currie.

40

mission set up by the Government to investigate NICRA's allegations of brutality, had to indict the RUC action.[36]

The Protestants and their Protestant government, though, were just beginning their assault on the Catholic minority. Within four days of the Derry march, two groups—the Derry Citizens' Action Committee and the People's Democracy— had been formed to combat the Protestant threat. Although NICRA agreed in December to give O'Neill time to produce the desired changes and not to hold any further demonstrations or marches in the near future (a march scheduled for Armagh on November 30, 1968 was stopped by a Paisleyite mob and a Protestant crowd broke up a December 4, 1968 CRA meeting in Dungannon), People's Democracy felt that pressure should be maintained on Stormont, that a truce was foolish, and that O'Neill should be shown to have produced no positive changes. Ignoring the fact that O'Neill might well be swept out of office, People's Democracy therefore scheduled a four-day march from Belfast to Derry, a march that was to mark a new low-point in the Ulster tragedy.

On January 1, 1969, the march began. When the marchers reached Burntollet Bridge on January 4, they were attacked by a horde of Paisleyites, hit with planks, bottles, and bars, and, in some cases, thrown into the river. All the while, the police in attendance watched "the gathering of the ambush with staggering complacency";[37] all the while, too, marchers,

[36] See Boyd, HOLY WAR IN BELFAST 195–205 (1969). The force used by the Unionists to disperse the marchers gave the civil rights movement a lift, for "you can slowly crush the Irish, you can take the ground from under their feet and they won't notice they're sinking down; but if you hit them, they will hit back." Devlin, PRICE OF MY SOUL 99.

On the role of the news media, see Bleakley, PEACE IN ULSTER 20 (1972): "Ulster was pitch-forked into the twentieth century by the men and women of broadcasting and the press. They came, they saw, and to the alarm of those in high places they reported what they came across."

The acronym "RUC" will be used interchangeably with Royal Ulster Constabulary in this study.

[37] Insight Team, ULSTER 67 and generally 63–67; Hastings, BARRI-

41

in true civil rights form, made no attempt to defend themselves from the murderous assault. As a follow-up that evening, the RUC roamed the Catholic Bogside of Derry and laid waste to both men and property.

With their truce shattered, the CRA planned to stage a march on April 19, 1969 from Burntollet to Derry. When the Government banned it, CRA officials agreed to observe the ban. Instead, a sit-down was staged by civil rights supporters within the Derry walls, stone-throwing between Paisleyites and the civil rights "sit-downers" began, and a riot developed. As might be expected, the RUC response was to drive the Catholics and their supporters back into the Bogside, thereby reinforcing Catholic opinion that the RUC was anti-Catholic. In the process, the RUC caused the death of an innocent Catholic who, together with his family, was attacked and beaten in his own home.

O'Neill, who in February had been reelected (although he did not receive the show of support that he had hoped for), was forced to resign. Since 1963 O'Neill, in his own words, had tried "to govern an early 17th-century country, in the second half of the 20th century,"[38] but all he had done was alienate both sides. By advocating religious harmony he had, at once, raised Catholic hopes and brought an increasing schizophrenia to the Unionist propaganda machine, which had been "accustomed for all of its life to denying that anything was the matter (which for foreign consumption meant the existence of a harmonious nation and for domestic readers indicated that the Papists would be kept where they belonged) [and which] was now forced to

---

CADES IN BELFAST: THE FIGHT FOR CIVIL RIGHTS IN NORTHERN IRELAND 86–87 (1970).

[38] Quoted in Johnson, *Saving Ulster from Itself*, 77 NEW STATESMAN 608 (1969). Catholics had probably not voted heavily for him because "a strong Catholic vote for O'Neill would [have] insure[d] him against the need for having to make further civil rights concessions." Edwards, SINS OF OUR FATHERS 26.

embark on a separate line that necessary reforms were being taken."[39]

Upon O'Neill's resignation, James Chichester-Clark was
elected Prime Minister by the Stormont members of the
Unionist Party over Brian Faulkner by a margin of 17 to
16 with O'Neill casting the deciding ballot. But Chichester-
Clark was able to do little more than O'Neill—and, in certain instances, far less. One of his first acts, on May 6, 1969,
was to grant amnesty for all political disturbances, an act
that set a dangerous precedent, eliminated any chance for
justice regarding the Burntollet tragedy, and demonstrated
how laws could be violated when Protestant interests demanded that they be violated.

On July 13, it became evident that the Government did
not even have control of its own forces, for on that day a
group of B Specials fired into an unarmed crowd at Dun-
given and revealed to the world "the first terrifying example of the authorities' inability to control the very forces
which Stormont was . . . enlisting to preserve law and order."[40] Although the B Specials had been told *not* to carry
weapons on that day, much less to use them, this "ill-disci-
plined, ill-trained force of patriots and thugs"[41] had taken
it upon themselves to carry and use the weapons that, in-
credibly, they were legally permitted to keep in their homes.

The Battle of the Bogside on August 12, 1969 further
demonstrated the inability of the Unionist Government to
cope with the deteriorating situation. For hundreds of years
the Protestant Ascendancy had maintained its position by
successfully masking its policies of self-aggrandizement under the guise of Protestantism and by manipulating prejudice, genuine fears, and traditions in such a way as to polar-
ize into religious sects set against each other individuals who
were unable to join forces to fight politically for their real

[39] Edwards, SINS OF OUR FATHERS 19.
[40] See Insight Team, ULSTER 100.
[41] *A Future for Ulster*, 232 ECONOMIST 13 (August 23, 1969).

interests; for ten years the Ascendancy had been aided by the power-hungry Ian Paisley and his followers of Protestant poor, wealthy Unionists who wanted the Catholic-Protestant split maintained, and bigots who genuinely hated Catholics. On August 12, 1969, the Ascendancy and Paisleyites once again linked arms in the provocative Apprentice Boys Procession in Derry, a procession commemorating the action of thirteen boys in closing the gates of Derry during the Williamite War and preventing the Governor from delivering the city to the forces of James II.

With memories of the April 19, 1969 RUC assault on the Bogside still fresh, the Bogsiders quickly erected barricades when violence erupted between marchers and residents. The embattled Bogsiders held their own for fifty hours against both the Protestants and RUC, despite the indiscriminate use of CS gas by the RUC against the "Derry families whose only offense was to be obliged—by the unwritten laws of political segregation—to live in Bogside."[42] During this period demonstrations occurred throughout the North as Catholics attempted to keep RUC forces in the Six Counties occupied, thereby preventing the concentration of forces against the beleaguered Bogside. When the battle finally ended, another building stone had been torn from the Ulster foundation, for, as a result of the Unionist Government's inability to restore peace, British troops had entered the fray and replaced the Government forces.

[42] Stetler, THE BATTLE OF BOGSIDE 168 (1970). CS was the military code name for orthochloro-benzylidene matononitrile. It was used by the RUC to compensate for manpower deficiencies in a force that was not only outnumbered and exhausted but also sustaining heavy injuries. *Ibid.*, 81. Although the Himsworth Committee, which examined the effects of CS on Bogside residents, concluded that there was "no evidence that CS gas ha[d] caused any permanent illness to healthy people in the Bogside," it also stated that CS "discriminate[d] observably against those whose age and health [made] them least likely to be involved in the incidents which the army [was] trying to control." *Ibid.*, 137 and 165. See also Devlin, PRICE OF MY SOUL 217-19 for a description of the battle by an active participant.

At first the British troops were cheered by the Catholics as "saviors" and villified by Protestants for their impartial enforcement of the law. Soon, however, Catholics jeered and Protestants cheered. Even though the Downing Street Declaration of August 20, 1969 stated that "every citizen of Northern Ireland [was] entitled to the same equality of treatment and freedom from discrimination as [obtained] in the rest of the United Kingdom,"[43] it was obvious that the law in Northern Ireland "was, in practice, a blunt instrument which, unless used with precise care, would come to seem more a weapon of repression than of justice."[44] With the British armed forces acting as policemen in place of the RUC and the disbanded B Specials and conducting constant searches for arms in Catholic homes, the requisite care was lacking, the law was applied repressively, and the Catholic community was convinced that the Army was, as in the days of old, a force to keep the Protestants in power and the Catholics in place.

As the British welcome wore out among Catholics, a split developed in the IRA ranks. Ever since the civil rights movement began, Protestants had screamed that the movement was just a front for the IRA. The facts, however, refute the charge. Although Cathal Goulding, IRA Chief of Staff, attended a secret meeting in August 1966 to discuss plans for the formation of the CRA and although the IRA deserves some credit for the success of the civil rights movement, the IRA was neither in control of the situation in 1969 nor

[43] Paragraph 6 of the Declaration. The Downing Street Declaration is set forth in Government of Northern Ireland, A RECORD OF CONSTRUCTIVE CHANGE (Cmd. 558) 13–14 (1971) [hereafter cited as 1971 WHITE PAPER].

[44] Insight Team, ULSTER 175. The Criminal Justice (Temporary Provisions) Act 1970 was such a law. Although it provided for minimum six-month jail terms for anyone convicted of certain acts, the act was generally applied against Catholics. Protestants were charged under more flexible and lenient laws, or they had the charges withdrawn by the police before the case went to court. And the Army enforced the act. *Ibid.*, 225–29.

even an organized body. It was, in fact, precisely this inability to lead or to produce the promised aid during the
August riots that made the IRA unpopular in many Catholic areas. It was also this inability that led to the split in the
IRA. Nearly complete by September 1969 when the IRA
leadership seemed willing to negotiate away the barricades
—the Catholics' only real protection—that had been erected
in Belfast and Derry, the split between Official and Provisional factions was finalized at the November IRA Convention, when Goulding and his supporters voted de facto
recognition to the two Irish governments. During the vote,
Sean MacStiofain led a walkout, proclaimed the Provisional
Army Council, and pledged the council's allegiance to a
thirty-two county Republic of Ireland.

To the Official (Red and Green) wing of the IRA, the
ultimate objective is a democratic socialist republic, and the
enemy is British imperialism, Unionism, and Free Statism.
In order to accomplish the objective and defeat this three-
headed enemy, the Officials believe that it is necessary to
subvert the authority of all three parliaments and to establish the authority of the common people in a united socialist
republic in which the brotherhood of man will make religious differences irrelevant. They furthermore feel that if
the timetable can be advanced by contesting elections and
by taking seats in the parliaments concerned, both steps
should be taken. That is not to say that Officials renounce
the use of force, for, so long as Britain upholds its claim to
legislate for Ireland by armed force, they believe that Irishmen must stand ready to resist Britain's claim by any and
all means. It is to say, however, that Officials think that
bombing alone will not bring the Protestants into the Republic or create a socialist republic; it is also to say that
Officials feel that economic, military, and political methods
must be combined if (1) the interim goals of amnesty, cessation of search and arrest operations, free political expression, cancellation of rent debts, a Bill of Rights, British
troop removal, the abolition of emergency powers legisla-

tion, and the end to internment and (2) the final objective of a thirty-two county democratic socialist republic are to be attained.[45] In addition, the Officials are convinced that "the lessons learned by people [in the North] in the course of their struggle for democracy and equality of citizenship, would later be used by them in the further struggle for their economic, social and national rights."[46]

The approach of the Provisional branch of the IRA, though, is "more nationalistic." Aside from its name, which goes back to the 1916 Provisional Government of the Irish Republic, the Provisional (Green) IRA believes that the historic Sinn Fein refusal to participate in or recognize the three parliaments must be maintained, since the failure to do so would undoubtedly weaken the will of the populace to resist. Moreover, the Provos claim that the "national question must take precedence over the social question: not because nationalism is more important than socialism, but because social liberation is impossible without national liberation and must follow rather than precede it."[47] The Provos furthermore think that the border around the Six Counties is an arbitrary one that has no basis either in geography or history and that must, by whatever means necessary, be removed. After the border has been removed, the union with the Republic has been effected, and the eight-hundred-year fight for independence has been successfully terminated, a democratic socialist republic—although not the totalitarian dictatorship of the Left espoused by the Officials—will be developed. Until that time, however, the fight for independence must be unimpeded by grandiose schemes for social advancement.[48]

[45] See THE I.R.A. SPEAKS (1972); MacGiolla, WHERE WE STAND— THE REPUBLICAN POSITION 13–15 (1972).

[46] MacGiolla, WHERE WE STAND 2.

[47] George, *These Are the Provisionals*, 82 NEW STATESMAN 680, 681 (1971). See generally Insight Team, ULSTER 176–97.

[48] IRELAND: THE FACTS 20 (1971). For a detailed description of the Provo social program, see EIRE NUA: THE SOCIAL AND ECONOMIC PROGRAMME OF SINN FEIN 7–49 (1971); WHERE SINN FEIN STANDS 1–2 (1972).

47

Initially, the Provos lacked the strength of the Officials, but the combination of financial support from Dublin militants, the Officials' appeal to communists and militant socialists, the renewed use of CS gas, and massive arms searches and curfews in Catholic areas boosted the stock of the Provos. Even without this boost, however, the Provos were a force with which to be reckoned, since the Provos felt that they could mount effective urban guerrilla warfare with even a handful of people.

The annual Orange parades in 1970, which should have been but were not banned, resulted in further riots—and increased tensions between the Army and the Catholics. Nevertheless, Army-IRA relations remained unaffected by these tensions until February 1971, when, after the failure of a secret attempt by the Army to get the Provos to keep the peace in the Ballymurphy section of Belfast, the first British soldier was killed.[49] In addition to the British soldier there was another, simultaneous, casualty—Chichester-Clark. Although the collapse of his Government was postponed a month, Chichester-Clark's attempt to govern ended with the firing of the bullet, for the escalating troubles were beyond his capabilities to solve.

Although in the opinion of many persons Faulkner was unfit to be Prime Minister, Chichester-Clark's resignation placed him in that position. From the outset, Faulkner demanded that internment be instituted. On August 9, 1971, Britain agreed to Faulkner's demand "so that he might be strengthened against an even more dangerous faction, the Boal-Paisley party, within the Stormont Parliament."[50] For that most flimsy of reasons, 342 people were arrested without

[49] See Insight Team, ULSTER 236–45 for a discussion of this bizarre attempt to maintain peace.

[50] Boyd, BRIAN FAULKNER 69. Faulkner, who had been Minister of Home Affairs from 1959 to 1962, felt that internment was the reason that the IRA campaign of that period had been defeated. He failed to realize that the IRA movement in the 1960s lacked the popular support it had in 1971. See Insight Team, ULSTER 260–61.

charge on the first day of Faulkner's new policy. By December 1971, the number had risen to 1,576.

Internment only succeeded in uniting the Catholic community and showing the world the inhuman depths to which British-Unionist policy had sunk. Despite commissions—Cameron and Hunt and Scarman and Compton—set up to whitewash each perversion of justice and law and despite reports that piously listed the changes that the Unionist Government had implemented, the excesses of that policy were painted in lurid colors for all to see.

Nowhere were these excesses more glaringly evidenced than in the events in Derry on January 30, 1972. In the six months prior to that day, the Army had increasingly brutalized the Catholic populace, but it had done so largely on a case-by-case, individual-by-individual basis; on that day, the Army launched a premeditated campaign of murder against unarmed demonstrators—a campaign whose ostensible purpose was to induce the IRA to stand and fight, force the demonstrators to flee, and enable the Army to kill or capture the bulk of Derry's IRA gunmen.[51] Yet, once again, a government-appointed commission—the Widgery Tribunal—chose to ignore the facts and to exonerate the culpable Army.

Since January 30, 1972, little has changed. True, the imposition of direct rule in March 1972 and the suspension of Stormont "exposed the lie of Ulster's self-proclaimed Englishness by making Ulster truly English ground . . . and proving the Catholic point that for many Ulster Protestants Englishness [has meant] little more than the right to an al-

---

[51] Sayle & Humphrey, *The Verdict They Could Not Print*, 2 CIVIL RIGHTS 3 (June 16, 1973); Messrs. Sayle & Humphrey were members of the *Sunday Times* Insight Team. The idea "was based on the military principle that the way to bring your enemy to battle is to attack something that, for prestige reasons, he will have to defend. . . . Brought to battle, he will then be annihilated by superior strength." In this instance, the belief was that if the demonstrators were attacked, the IRA would have to fight.

most racist domination over Catholics."[52] True, the March 1973 White Paper purported to devise an equitable system of government, even if it failed at least partially by placing primary emphasis on defeating violence with military might, continuing repressive legislation in violation of international law, and advancing an incomplete Charter of Human Rights. True, the December 1973 Sunningdale Agreement calling for a Council of Ireland and the 1974 power-sharing experiment seemed to lay the foundation for an end to Protestant perfidy, until Britain permitted an illegal Protestant strike to demolish those foundations and force a reimposition of direct rule. And true, the 1974 White Paper stated that a consultative convention would be held at the earliest possible time to consider what provisions for a Northern Government would command widespread acceptance.

The fact remains, however, that the abuses that have been carried out by Stormont have been enacted and perpetrated pursuant to powers delegated by Westminster; the fact also remains that the campaign of brutality and discrimination continues; and the fact remains, too, that the promises made in the 1974 White Paper can, unfortunately, be no more believed than those promises breached in the past. Until, therefore, the inhumane Northern laws are suspended, the discrimination in housing and jobs is ended, an impartial police force is introduced, the legal system is reformed, amnesty is granted to all political prisoners, internment is ended, and the Protestant gun clubs are disbanded, civil rights activists can be expected to continue to demonstrate, and the IRA can be expected to maintain its pressure on both the British Army and the Protestant extremists.

THE LONDON VIEWPOINT

To Englishmen the Irish Question has long been one they would be happy to do without. Ever since the grant of

[52] Kramer, *Letter to the Editors*, 48 NEW YORKER 126, 129 (April 15, 1972).

Ireland to Henry II of England in 1172 "to enlarge the boundaries of the Church, to proclaim the truths of the Christian religion to a rude and ignorant people, and to root out the growths of vice from the field of the Lord,"[53] the English have had nothing but difficulties with the Irish. Although various statutes were passed by the English in an attempt to protect their interests, the English generally left the Irish alone and focused their attention on more pressing matters. For that reason, therefore, the Pale—that portion of Ireland under the direct control of the King's representatives—was constantly being diminished by the Irish through the process of assimilation.

The first real attempt to settle Ireland took place during the early seventeenth century. Following the "flight of the Earls" in 1607, the Earls' estates were forfeited and "planted" with English and Scottish settlers. This Anglicizing of the province of Ulster formed the foundation upon which the Northern Ireland of today was built and is the point from which the Catholic-Protestant schism dates.

Still, the power of the Catholic nobility survived both the planting and the subsequent Cromwellian settlement. It was not, in fact, finally overthrown until James II was defeated at the Battle of the Boyne nearly a century later. Thereafter, and until the impact of the French Revolution resulted in a surge of nationalism, the Protestant Ascendancy ruled unchallenged.

Beginning in 1791, with the formation of the Society of United Irishmen, nationalism and renewed civil strife returned to Ireland. After the French-inspired Rebellion of 1798, England, under the leadership of William Pitt, moved to union with Ireland. Simply stated, the objectives were to restore peace, emancipate the Catholics, and consolidate the power and resources of the British Empire for the forthcoming struggle with France. Even without the French threat, however, the Union was not only justifiable but necessary, for, if the Union had not taken place, there would

53 *The Bull Laudabiliter*, in Curtiss & McDowell, IRISH HISTORICAL DOCUMENTS 17.

have been in Ireland two peoples intent on mutual destruction.

In the years following Union, the situation in Ireland improved markedly for both Catholics and Protestants. The sectarian hostility of the pre-Union period was replaced by increased cooperation between the two communities; the Catholic emancipation of 1829 made Catholics and Protestants equal; Pax Britannica kept Ireland secure from the troubles that raged throughout Europe in the nineteenth century; and various acts, such as the Land Act of 1881, secured increased rights for the Irish populace. Despite the peace and tranquillity that Union brought to Ireland, however, Irish politicians, operating under the cover of nationalism but interested only in their own power, began towards the end of the nineteenth century to advocate Home Rule.

As might be expected, there were among the Protestants of Ireland many who feared that the demand for Home Rule was tantamount to a demand for Rome Rule. Although this situation was, to state the obvious, an overreaction on the part of Protestants who were afraid of being subjected to Catholic domination, it was a reaction that was understandable, as subsequent events proved. During the period when Home Rule was being debated, for instance, candidates often found themselves attacked by the Catholic Church. On one occasion, a letter from the Archbishop of Dublin was read from the altars of the city, warning people not to vote for a particular candidate and stating that to do so would be a mortal sin. Approximately four hundred such sins were committed.[54]

When the Home Rule League was formed in 1873 by Isaac Butt and Charles Parnell, it was therefore quite natural for Britain, seeing the ugly head of sectarianism on the horizon, to resist attempts to accede to Home Rule. As the years passed, however, the realism of politics replaced the idealism of good government. By the mid-1880s, Home Rule had become a leading political issue in England, al-

[54] See Bestic, THE IMPORTANCE OF BEING IRISH 83 (1969).

though for a time the brutal Phoenix Park murders of 1882 tended to dam the Home Rule flow.

To the Liberal Party of William Gladstone, Home Rule was the price to be paid for Nationalist (Irish) Party support; to the Conservative Party of Lord Salisbury and Randolph Churchill, Home Rule was the chink in the Liberal armour. Although the issue was one of opportunism for both parties, it would be unfair to say that opportunism was the sole motivating factor. For both Liberals and Conservatives, support or opposition to Home Rule was the result of deep-seated feelings.

Writing to Salisbury in 1885 about Gladstone's proposed Home Rule bill, Churchill stated that he would not "hesitate, if other circumstances were favourable, to agitate Ulster even to resistance beyond constitutional limits."[55] In Churchill's view, there simply was no justification to cut the link with Ireland when doing so meant leaving loyal British citizens unprotected on that island. When, therefore, Gladstone introduced the Home Rule Bill of 1886, Churchill immediately demanded that Ulster be given a separate assembly, which some saw as a ploy to "demand something that cannot be conceded so that nothing at all will be conceded,"[56] but which might more correctly be viewed as a protection for the loyal British subjects in Ireland if Home Rule were granted.

Whatever the reason—ploy, genuine interest in protecting the "Western British," or a combination of ploy and genuine interest—the first Home Rule bill was defeated. Seven years later, the Liberals again introduced a Home Rule bill. Unlike its predecessor, the Home Rule Bill of 1893 was passed by the House of Commons, but it died when it was rejected by the House of Lords.

55 Churchill, 2 LORD RANDOLPH CHURCHILL 28–29 (1906).

56 Gallagher, INDIVISIBLE ISLAND 59. Gallagher's statement continues: "Make the demand so vague that in any case it ceases to be practical. Those who used partition as a weapon in the British party struggle were never agreed on the area to be cut away." See also 65–77.

After seventeen years of Irish appeals, the Liberals tackled Home Rule for the third time. When the Liberals regained power in 1906, they did so with an absolute majority—a majority that precluded the need for Nationalist Party support. Four years later, though, the Liberals' majority had vanished, and that support was again needed. Accordingly, the same deal was struck as in 1886 and 1893, with one very important addition—an addition whose importance far transcended its role in the Irish Question. Rather than face certain defeat in the House of Lords, the Liberals and Nationalists joined forces to pass in 1911 the Parliament Act, and, faced with the threat of the creation of additional peerages, the House of Lords also passed it. Under the terms of the act, three passages of a bill by the House of Commons within a two-year period would make that bill law regardless of how the House of Lords voted on the measure the third time.

With the Parliament Act on the Statute Book, Home Rule became more likely. Led by Bonar Law and F. E. Smith, the Conservatives again rallied around Ulster. Reminiscent of Churchill's actions a quarter of a century earlier, they claimed that Ulster could go to any lengths, however desperate and unconstitutional, and "stopped little short of inciting armed resistance to the King's Government on the part of Ulster in the event of any attempt at coercion."[57] When that effort failed, they tried to compromise by promising support for Home Rule in exchange for the exclusion of a geographical area of Ulster consisting of Antrim, Down, Derry, Tyrone, North Armagh, Mid Armagh, North Fermanagh, and Derry City until such time as this area would consent to the rule of a Home Rule Parliament. They failed again. The Orange Card, which had been a trump card in 1886, was no more effective than a joker twenty-six years later, and, in 1912, the third Home Rule Bill passed the House of Commons. With the hands of the House

[57] Wheeler-Bennett, JOHN ANDERSON: VISCOUNT WAVERLY 49 (1962). See generally Kee, GREEN FLAG 513.

of Lords effectively tied by the Parliament Act, Home Rule seemed, after twenty-six years of parliamentary maneuvering, assured within two years. The shots at Sarajevo, though, made a casualty of Home Rule. With the outbreak of World War I, Britain suspended the effective date of the Home Rule Bill, and Conservatives, Liberals, and Nationalists put politics aside and linked arms against the common enemy.

While all of Britain and the vast majority of Ireland were fighting Germany, however, a few misguided and treacherous Irishmen attempted to take advantage of Britain's preoccupation with the war. Encouraged by Germany to rebel—Germany argued that Ireland would be free of domination if Germany won the war—a small group led a rebellion in 1916. It was, though, a rebellion *in* Ireland, not a rebellion *of* Ireland. After brief fighting, the leaders of the treasonous rebellion were captured, tried, and convicted of their heinous crime, and Ireland returned to normalcy.

Within three years the normalcy had evaporated. Once again, Ireland sought to force its exit from Britain. In 1919 the seventy-three members of the Sinn Fein delegation to the House of Commons refused to go to London, constituted themselves the first Dail Eireann, and declared war upon the King's Government in Ireland. It was not an unbacked declaration of war. For months, Irish gunmen roamed the countryside and conducted a vicious campaign of cold-blooded murder. And on November 21, 1920—Bloody Sunday—an Irish murder squad stealthily descended on a group of unsuspecting and unarmed British officers and, without warning, killed fourteen of them.

In an effort to terminate hostilities, Britain proposed the Government of Ireland Act 1920. The 1920 Act provided for separate parliaments in Belfast and Dublin, thereby granting Home Rule to Ireland but insuring that Northerners, who strenuously opposed Home Rule, would be able to maintain their historic ties with Britain. As Lloyd George stated in presenting the compromise that was designed to placate the objections of both sides, "to place them [the Northerners] under national rule against their will would be as glaring an outrage on the principles of liberty and self-government as the denial of self-government would be for the rest of Ireland."[58]

Reacting arrogantly and unjustifiably, the South at first rejected Lloyd George's reasonable solution. After some thought, however, the South did agree to the basic terms of the Government of Ireland Act 1920. On December 6, 1921, the Anglo-Irish Treaty was signed, pursuant to which the South gave its assent to the 1920 plan. More specifically, the South was to become a self-governing dominion of the British Commonwealth with the same degree of independence as Canada; the North was to be left free to stay out of the dominion and to continue its existing constitutional position within the United Kingdom; and all members of Parliament were to take an oath of allegiance to the Crown. Out of deference to the feelings of Southerners, though, the oath was "qualified." Whereas the oath of all other dominions was one of unqualified allegiance to the Crown, the Irish oath was "primarily to the Constitution and only secondarily to the Crown."[59]

Each provision of the Treaty was the result of strenuous bargaining; each provision was important, as soon became painfully evident. Article 7 of the Treaty provided that the Irish Free State was in time of peace to permit Britain to

[58] Quoted in Mansergh, THE IRISH QUESTION: 1840–1921 207 (1965). For a record of Lloyd George's compromises, see Gwynn, THE HISTORY OF PARTITION (1912–1925) 188–97 (1950).

[59] Mansergh, THE IRISH FREE STATE: ITS GOVERNMENT AND POLITICS 33 (1934). See generally *ibid.*, 26–42; and Beckett, A SHORT HISTORY 180. Article 4 of the Treaty contained the prescribed oath:

> I, . . . , do solemnly swear true faith and allegiance to the Constitution of the Irish Free State as by law established, and that I will be faithful to H.M. King George v, his heirs and successors by law, in virtue of the common citizenship of Ireland with Great Britain, and her adherence to and membership in the group of nations forming the British Commonwealth of nations.

use the harbors of Berehaven, Queenstown (now Cobh), and Lough Swilly and in time of war to permit the use of these ports and of such other facilities as Britain might require. Yet within seventeen years the British, in an apparent attempt to appease the recalcitrant DeValera, seemed to forget the significance of the provisions of Article 7 and returned the three ports to Ireland. Only Winston Churchill, in tones reminiscent of his father, had the foresight to see the gathering storm and to inveigh, but to no avail, against the momentous 1938 decision. Although Churchill realized that events had transformed the British-Irish relationship, he recognized, too, that Ireland was, as it had always been, indispensable to British security.

With the outbreak of World War II, Britain naturally wanted, expected, and tried to get Ireland to "return" the ports, for, without the ports, British ships had only the Ulster bases from which to sail to help keep open Britain's lifeline across the Atlantic. Throughout the course of the war, repeated attempts were made to persuade Ireland to lease the ports. Nevertheless, Ireland, remaining "implacably neutral," kept the ports closed to British ships, thus impeding Britain in its life and death struggle, making Britain all the more dependent on the ports of loyal Ulster, and convincing Britain of the wisdom of the 1920 partition.

In the years following the war, relations with Ireland gradually improved, and, in 1949, Ireland was granted total independence. Ireland, which had been a sovereign state externally associated with the British Commonwealth and which had exercised its sovereignty in such a nearly fatal way, was given the republic it had coveted for nearly forty years.

At the same time that it set the South free, Britain continued to fulfill its obligations to Ulster. When Britain became a welfare state in 1949, Ulster moved in lock step with Britain; when Westminster passed legislation affecting the peoples of England, Stormont passed parallel legislation to provide similar benefits to the people of Ulster.

57

Within a short time, therefore, Ulster—as a result of British support—moved far ahead of the fledgling Southern republic in both social services and benefits. By the mid-1960s, the differences between North and South were not only in the minds but also in the pockets of men.

Despite its activism in matters of economics and even after the 1968 troubles began, Britain remained somewhat aloof from Northern Ireland. While the Government of Ireland Act 1920 reserved certain powers to Britain and gave Britain final and absolute authority over all actions to be taken in Northern Ireland, the purport of the act was to enable the Northerners to govern themselves. Being in full accord with this interpretation, Britain chose to leave the day-to-day operations of Northern Ireland to the Stormont Parliament and the Northern Ireland Government.

This interpretation of Britain's role in Northern Ireland had an important effect. Since Britain adopted, in effect, "a hands-off" approach with respect to Ulster, it had to support the man chosen by the Unionist Party (the party controlling Stormont) to lead Northern Ireland. In addition, the approach meant that, since the successive O'Neill–Chichester-Clark–Faulkner Governments became more punitive as the recent troubles escalated, Britain was seen as the force behind or cause of the increasingly severe government actions.

But the fact that Britain opted, as much as possible, for a "hands-off" approach did not mean that Britain sat idly by. From the very beginning of the civil rights movement in 1968, Britain endeavored to convince Stormont to make the requisite changes to return Northern Ireland to its pre-1968 state of stability. Moreover, through the vehicle of commissions and inquiries, Britain went to great lengths to insure that the facts relative to a particular event or series of events were made known to all, that blame was properly placed, and that justice was done at all times.

In March 1969, the Cameron Commission was appointed to make an examination of the underlying causes of the disturbances in Northern Ireland, commencing with the Dungannon march of August 24, 1968. It found that the 1968 disturbances were part of a worldwide "wave of re-action against constituted authority."[60] It also found that although the CRA was "dedicated to a policy of nonvio-lence," it had members who would not hesitate to use force and it was "an instrument, already constituted and organ-ised, which could without any excessive difficulty be suc-cessfully infiltrated by those whose intentions [were] far other than peaceful and constitutional."[61] More specifically, it concluded that the Coalisland-Dungannon march was car-ried out without any breach of the peace because the march was rerouted and because no provocative banners or sym-bols were displayed; that the Londonderry march of Oc-tober 5, 1968 demonstrated both that left-wingers wanted a conflict with the police and that the march's leaders, such as Gerry Fitt, were "reckless and wholly irresponsible, but that the police had made indiscriminate use of batons and water canon";[62] and that, despite the tragic results, "a se-rious effort was made to protect the marchers at Burntol-let,"[63] for it was "possible that the police, like others, un-derrated the determination of the marchers, and that, as they did not really expect them to get as far as Londonderry, the senior officers omitted to take adequate and timeous measures to provide the necessary protection from physical interference from the opponents of the march."[64] In sum-mary, the Cameron Commission refuted the assertion that "agitation for civil rights [was] a mere pretext for other and more subversive activities,"[65] and it held that although the police had at times acted unjustifiably and indiscrimi-nately, they "were stretched to the utmost limit both in

[60] Cameron, DISTURBANCES IN NORTHERN IRELAND: REPORT OF THE COMMISSION APPOINTED BY THE GOVERNOR OF NORTHERN IRELAND (Cmd. 532) 55 (1969).

[61] *Ibid.*, 79.   [62] *Ibid.*, 24–29.

[63] *Ibid.*, 48; see generally 44–48.

[64] *Ibid.*, 48.   [65] *Ibid.*, 63.

numbers and endurance in endeavouring to carry out their very difficult task."[66]

Prior to the release of the Cameron Commission Report, and as a direct consequence of the disturbances of August 12–19, 1969, the Downing Street Declaration of August 20, 1969 was made. Aside from restating Britain's insistence that Northern Ireland would cease to be part of the United Kingdom *only* when Stormont consented and that "responsibility for affairs in Northern Ireland [was] entirely a matter of domestic jurisdiction," the Downing Street Declaration welcomed the reforms that had been initiated by Stormont to weigh grievances and eliminate inequalities and reaffirmed the pledge of "equality of treatment and freedom from discrimination" for all citizens of Northern Ireland. Finally, the Declaration cited Britain's ultimate responsibility to protect the people of Northern Ireland and stated that Britain had "responded to the requests of the Northern Ireland Government for military assistance in Londonderry and Belfast in order to restore law and order."[67]

Within one week of the Downing Street Declaration, the appointment of the Hunt Commission was announced to report on the Royal Ulster Constabulary and the Ulster Special Constabulary. Whereas the mere announcement of the Cameron Commission had played a role, albeit a minor one, in the resignation of O'Neill, the Hunt Commission wrote the script for the overhaul of the RUC and the demise of the B Specials and set the stage for Chichester-Clark's resignation. In its report, the Hunt Commission decried "the increasing tendency of a minority to flout the law, un-

[66] *Ibid.*, 71; see generally 71–75. Two instances were cited by the Commission where the police had not acted properly: the police charge at, and indiscriminate use of water canon against, demonstrators in Londonderry on October 5, 1968; and the damage inflicted by police on personal property in Londonderry's Bogside on January 4–5, 1969. *Ibid.*, 73.

[67] The full text of the Downing Street Declaration may be found in 1971 WHITE PAPER 13–14.

dermine authority and create anarchy";[68] recommended "that the RUC be relieved of all duties of a military nature"[69] and assume the character and functions of a civil, generally unarmed, police force; and concluded that a "new force, together with [a] police volunteer reserve, should replace the Ulster Special Constabulary."[70] As might be expected, the Hunt Report, although sound and largely adopted, was not well received in the Protestant community. Following rioting on the night of October 11–12, 1969, in which an RUC officer was killed by Protestants protesting against the new disarmament policy of the RUC, the British Army engaged the Protestants for the first time. In an exchange of shots, it killed two of the rioters.

While the Hunt Commission was contemplating the future of Northern Ireland's police forces, the Scarman Tribunal was making an inquiry into the 1969 disturbances. The tribunal concluded that the August riots were unplanned; instead, "they were communal disturbances arising from a complex political, social and economic situation."[71] In addition, it found that the RUC had acted incorrectly on six occasions, and that the USC had been ineffective in restraining Protestant aggression.[72] Furthermore, it stated

[68] Hunt, REPORT OF THE ADVISORY COMMITTEE ON POLICE IN NORTHERN IRELAND (Cmd. 535) 8 (1969).

[69] Ibid., 21; see generally 21–28 for a discussion of proposed changes in the role and organization of the RUC.

[70] Ibid., 42; see 41–42 for the Commission's view of the future of the USC.

[71] Scarman, VIOLENCE AND CIVIL DISTURBANCES IN NORTHERN IRELAND IN 1969: REPORT OF TRIBUNAL OF INQUIRY (Cmd. 566) 11 (1972).

[72] Ibid., 15–19. The six occasions of improper RUC action were the lack of direction in Londonderry on August 12, 1969; the use of USC for riot control in Dungannon on August 13; the similar use of USC in Armagh on August 14; the use of machine guns in Belfast on August 14–15; the failure to prevent the burning of Catholic homes by Protestants in Belfast on August 14–16; and the failure to restrain or disperse mobs or protect lives on August 15 prior to the arrival of the Army. The USC action (or inaction) involved its presence in

61

that although the police descended to the level of the rioters by throwing stones in an attempt to disperse the mobs, the police—reluctant to shoot and forbidden to use CS gas—were subject to severe provocations and lacked the means to defend themselves. Finally, and perhaps most significantly, the tribunal determined that the decision to allow the Apprentice Boys Parade—the event that triggered the riots—was not unreasonable, in light of the fact that a ban would have been viewed in the Protestant community as a sign of weakness in the face of Catholic pressure, would—perhaps—have caused the Government to fall, and would have resulted in the collapse of the reform program.[73]

The reform program referred to by the Scarman Tribunal was a success. Instituted at the urging of Britain, the commitment and steps taken by mid-1971 were, as stated in the 1971 White Paper, far-reaching: a police authority representative of the entire community had been established by the Police Act (Northern Ireland) 1970; a public prosecutor was to be appointed; the USC was replaced by a RUC reserve; a Commissioner of Administration had been appointed; a Commissioner for Complaints had been established to investigate cases of alleged discrimination; universal adult suffrage had been introduced; equality of employment had been adopted by all statutory and local authorities; antidiscrimination clauses were required in all government contracts; a points scheme had been introduced to insure fairness in the allocation of houses; a Ministry of Community Relations had been created; and local government had been reorganized. Indeed, the only unrealized commitment was the undertaking to withdraw those aspects of the Special Powers Act in conflict with international obligations—a commitment that was met with the passage of the Detention of Terrorists (Northern Ireland) Order 1972 and the Northern Ireland (Emergency Provisions) Act 1973.

Belfast on August 14, a presence that evoked Catholic hostility and failed to restrain Protestants.

[73] *Ibid.*, 64–67.

Despite these reforms, however, terrorism and violence escalated rather than declined. Aside from the casualties of bombs and bullets and burnings, Northern Ireland suffered another victim—Chichester-Clark. Unable to stem the rising tide of hostilities, Chichester-Clark resigned and was replaced by Faulkner. When he became Prime Minister on March 23, 1971, the issue of internment immediately arose —and once it arose "the issue was not *whether* internment was to come, but *when* and on what scale."[74] Although Britain was not in favor of internment, it soon found itself supporting Faulkner's demand, since the alternatives available —support of Faulkner, a new, more conservative government, or direct rule—left Britain with no real choice. After several raids by the Army to ascertain IRA membership strength, the British Government decided to institute internment. Accordingly, on August 9, 1971, the Army "lifted" 342 people and distributed them among three holding centers.

In retrospect, internment appears to have been an unwise course of action because it alienated the Catholic community and forced the withdrawal of Catholic leaders from Stormont. However, given the political realities of the situation in Northern Ireland, the increasing problem of violence, and the fact that witnesses could never be found for IRA trials, it was an easily understandable decision. Since Britain wanted above all else to avoid sinking further into the Irish bog, it gambled that a brief policy of internment would bring an end to the senseless Northern Ireland troubles. It lost. Within a year, the situation had deteriorated to the point where still more drastic action was required, for it was obvious that the combination of Stormont control, British support and operational responsibility, and independent commissions was not producing the desired results.

On March 24, 1972, therefore, the British Government suspended Stormont and assumed full and direct responsibility for the administration of Northern Ireland. Having

[74] Insight Team, ULSTER 260 and, generally, 260–68.

realized that new and more radical measures were necessary to end the continuing and escalating campaign of terrorism, Britain proposed that periodic plebiscites be held on the issue of the border with the Republic, that internment be phased out, and that the present division of responsibility between Belfast and London for maintaining law and order be eliminated by transferring full responsibility to Westminster. Although Faulkner accepted the first two proposals, he and his Government rejected the third one, thereby necessitating direct rule by Britain and a return to pre-1920 conditions. In advocating plebiscites and assuming full and direct responsibility for Northern Ireland, however, Britain was in no way suggesting that the consent of Stormont, as required by the Ireland Act 1949 before any change in the border could be made, was being circumvented. Under no circumstances would the provisions of the Ireland Act 1949 be affected by the temporary prorogation of Stormont.

Unfortunately, though, direct rule did not bring a halt to the violence. Catholics and Protestants continued their insane warfare—against each other, against themselves, and against the British Army. Throughout the incessant struggle and despite endless provocations, the British Army maintained its discipline and a "relative peace"; and throughout the struggle, too, Britain—mainly as a result of the efforts of Secretary of State William Whitelaw, in whom the powers formerly exercised by the Northern Ireland Government were vested by the Northern Ireland (Temporary Provisions) Act 1972—continued its search for consensus and peace.

That search led first to the Darlington Conference of September 25–27, 1972. Even though each of the seven parliamentary political parties was invited to attend the conference to discuss suggestions for the future of Northern Ireland, representatives of only three—the Unionist, Alliance, and Northern Ireland Labour parties—attended.[75] Still, the views expressed by the participants at Darlington were of

[75] The views of the three parties are set forth in THE FUTURE OF NORTHERN IRELAND: A PAPER FOR DISCUSSION 45–71 (1972).

great significance. As a result of wide circulation, these views helped form the basis for the next step towards the elusive peace—the 1973 White Paper.

By far the most important "peace initiative" to date, the 1973 White Paper established conditions for a settlement, made constitutional proposals, and provided for a Charter of Human Rights. Citing the fact that there was no more urgent or compelling task than to end the violence and to restore the rule of law, the White Paper reaffirmed Britain's pledge that Northern Ireland would remain a part of the United Kingdom until a majority of its people decided otherwise and stated a threefold pattern of obligations: Britain's obligation to protect all the people of Northern Ireland, to secure their rights and freedoms, and to work towards achieving for them standards of living, employment, and social conditions similar to those in the United Kingdom; Northerners' obligation to respect Parliament's decisions; and the obligation of those Northerners favoring Irish unity both to seek that unity on the basis of consent and to accept the fact that such consent did not at that time (and does not now) exist.[76] In addition, the White Paper elaborately set forth proposals for a Northern Ireland Assembly of about eighty members elected on the basis of proportional representation; committees of the Assembly reflecting the balance of parties in the Assembly; a less powerful Secretary of State for Northern Ireland; an Executive representative of more than one party; a legislative scheme in which powers were "excepted," "reserved," or "transferred"; repeal of the Special Powers Act and the re-enactment into law of the only strictly necessary provisions of that Act; and a Council of Ireland.

[76] 1973 WHITE PAPER 5. On March 8, 1973, a poll was held throughout Northern Ireland regarding the question of Irish unity as opposed to continued membership in the United Kingdom. The results indicated that 6,463 persons voted to have Northern Ireland joined to the Republic outside the United Kingdom; 591,920 persons voted to have Northern Ireland remain part of the United Kingdom. *Ibid.*, 3–4.

Legislation implementing the provisions enumerated in the 1973 White Paper was immediately passed. In June 1973, the first tangible result of that legislation was evidenced when the people of Northern Ireland went to the polls to elect members to the Northern Ireland Assembly and to provide the basis for consensus government; in July 1973, the Special Powers Act was repealed by the Northern Ireland (Emergency Provisions) Act of 1973; in November 1973, an executive body in which Catholics and Protestants shared power was formed; in December 1973, an agreement was reached on a proposed Council of Ireland; and in January 1974, the new system of devolved powers was implemented.

Unfortunately, the delicate balance produced by these actions was not long maintained. In May 1974, following a general work stoppage by the nonelected Ulster Workers' Council and stepped-up Army actions to reopen roads and to distribute gas and oil, the embryonic Government collapsed when the Unionist members of the Executive resigned after their suggestion for negotiations with the Ulster Workers' Council was rejected. Moving swiftly, Britain—in another White Paper—proposed temporary governmental arrangements in July 1974 and announced that a consultative Northern Ireland Constitutional Convention would be convened to consider the future of Ulster. As events unfold, it will be clear whether the 1974 White Paper will attain its desired effect or whether Britain's search for a just and stable society will have to continue.

The Belfast Viewpoint

To most Protestant Ulstermen, the struggle in Northern Ireland today is a continuation of the conflict that began in 1607 with the plantation of Ulster. Then, as today, Protestants were faced with a threatening Papist conspiracy; then, as today, Protestants may have differed among themselves about various issues, but they were united in their opposition to the "forked-tongued pronouncements of the Roman Catholic Church."[77]

The philosophical and spiritual roots of modern Ulster date from the treasonous flight of the Irish Earls. Immediately after the Earls sailed from Lough Swilly to enlist continental support, their lands were forfeited to the Crown. The Crown, in turn, then distributed the lands to English and Scottish planters.

Despite constant harassment and disloyal, sometimes murderous, activities by the Catholic populace, the Protestant community maintained the Ulster Trust until 1689, when James II came to Ireland and was welcomed with open arms by perfidious Catholics. After James II was defeated at the Battle of the Boyne, the Penal Laws were instituted to downgrade the Catholic aristocracy and to put it "out of the power of the Irish again to rebel, gentle means having hitherto always proved ineffectual."[78] While these laws have long been the subject of Catholic calumny, they were—it must be remembered—the result of the 1640 massacre, the Catholic refusal to take an oath of allegiance to the Crown in 1666, the cruel laws of the Jacobite Parliament of 1689, and an army of 30,000 men serving in France and ready, at any time, to invade Ireland.

With the repeal of the last of the Penal Laws in 1793, the tranquillity in Ulster was shattered. No sooner had the Catholics been freed from the restrictions of the Penal Laws than they formed the Defender movement, an organization

[77] Smyth, THE AXIS AGAINST ULSTER 20 (1972). See generally Eliot & Hickie, ULSTER: A CASE STUDY IN CONFLICT THEORY 34 (1971).

[78] Ingram, A CRITICAL EXAMINATION OF IRISH HISTORY 219 (1900); see generally 181–220. At 183 the author states, "we are overwhelmed with rhetorical censures of the Penal laws, but we hear nothing of the prior foreign and domestic events which produced them, namely, the long and terrible struggle with the Popes and their Spanish champions, the introduction by the Jesuits and seminary priests of a new faith which mixed up the truths of religion with treasonable designs, and the perpetual plots and conspiracies of the Papistic faction at home." See also Shearman, NORTHERN IRELAND 1921–1971 11.

whose raison d'être was to commit outrages on the Protestant community in the hope of provoking retaliations which, in turn, would provide the justification for a French invasion. As a direct result of one of these outrages—the Catholic-initiated Battle of the Diamond in 1795—the Orange Order was born.

The Orange Order brought together, from all walks of life, Protestants interested in commemorating and protecting the British-Ulster links established by William of Orange. As such, it tended to be a somewhat novel organization, for by enabling the uninfluential and the unsophisticated to deal with Protestant leaders as equals, the Orange Order transcended the strong denominational antagonisms of Protestant Ulster. Due mainly to this unique organization, the Protestant community in Northern Ireland was able to present a formidable defense against the Catholic menace and to oppose the fatal errors and doctrines of the Church of Rome.

Following Union and the removal of the French threat—a union that Protestants received with mixed emotions, since it both removed the fear of invasion and resulted in a diminution of Protestant authority through the suspension of the Irish Parliament—Protestants again devoted their energies to the fulfillment of their Ulster Trust. Meanwhile, Catholics continued their pernicious ways. Although they were granted the right to sit in Parliament in 1829, Catholics were not satisfied with full equality with their Protestant brethren. Instead, according to Daniel O'Connell, the Catholic Emancipation Act of 1829 was to lead to a Catholic Ascendancy and the persecution that Catholics felt it their duty to initiate.

Given this attitude, it is easy to understand Protestant opposition to the various Home Rule efforts of the nineteenth and early twentieth centuries. Under the Home Rule scheme envisioned by the Liberal-Nationalist conspiracy, Ireland would have been both free of British rule and free to persecute Protestants. For this reason, the Protestant community rose to defeat Home Rule at every opportunity.

Religion was not, however, the sole reason for Protestant opposition to Home Rule. There was, in addition, the compelling argument of economics. Since northern industries formed part of the general British system and depended on Britain for both markets and essential supplies, Home Rule would have had a ruinous effect. Moreover, the business capacity of the average Catholic was the subject of contempt by Ulster leaders such as Carson.

It was, accordingly, with great relief that the Protestants embraced the Conservative Party suggestion that Ulster resist Home Rule. With the support of the Salisburys and Churchills of the Conservative Party, the Ulster Protestants led by Carson felt secure. When, therefore, the third Home Rule Bill became law, Carson and all Ulster felt betrayed, for, while they had been sincere in their actions, they suddenly realized that they had merely been puppets in a Conservative Party political production to attain power.[79]

Yet despite the Conservative Party betrayal, the Protestants of Ulster made an all-out effort to help Britain during the difficult years of World War I. At the same time that the Catholics of the South were stabbing Mother England in the back by rebelling in the streets of Dublin and openly seeking German assistance, the Protestants of the North were fighting side by side with their fellow British citizens.

After the war, the inequities of the third Home Rule Bill were realized by Britain. While the South brazenly declared itself a Republic for the second time in three years, Britain contemplated a more equitable solution; and while the

[79] As Carson bitterly stated: "I was in earnest. I was not playing politics. I believed all this. What a fool I was: I was only a puppet and so was Ulster and so was Ireland in the political game that was to get the Conservative Party into power." Gallagher, INDIVISIBLE ISLAND 84. Ironically, Carson was not an Ulsterman (he was born in Galway), never lived in Ulster, and had no relatives in Ulster. See Ervine, SIR EDWARD CARSON 50–51 (1916).

69

South murdered British soldiers in their beds and conducted a campaign of terror, Britain advanced as a compromise the Government of Ireland Act 1920.

As is wont with compromises, neither Catholic nor Protestant was happy with the proposed solution. The Catholics wanted total independence for all Ireland; the Protestants wanted all Ireland to remain part of the United Kingdom, and, were that objective to prove unacceptable, they wanted the North fully integrated with Britain. Still, both the Catholic and Protestant communities came to accept the 1920 Act and the prescriptions of the Anglo-Irish Treaty of 1921.

At least the Protestant community did. Following ratification of the Treaty by the Dail Eireann, the Catholics of the new "Irish Priest State" turned their guns on themselves. Having grown accustomed to a steady diet of violence, they wasted no time in proving to the world in general and the Ulster Protestants in particular the wisdom of separating the troublesome South from the North.

While burning and shooting enveloped the South, the North turned to the problems of government. Under the able leadership of Sir James Craig, Northern Ireland developed a fine security force to meet the exigencies of the day. To some people the fact that the career of Northern Ireland began with the creation of the Special Constabulary was a matter of condemnation. However, given the disorder in and wild threats emanating from the Free State, it is clear that Craig had no alternative—if the North was to to survive.

At the same time that he was upgrading the military capabilities of Northern Ireland, Craig was laying the economic foundations for Ulster. Of paramount significance in this endeavor was the "contribution." Originally conceived as a yearly contribution to be made by Northern Ireland to Britain for services rendered by Britain and viewed by the Free State as a means of weakening Ulster to the extent that union with the South would be welcomed, the contribution was envisioned differently by Craig. As early as 1925 he thought in terms of a contribution paid by Britain to Northern Ireland to preserve the same standard of living in the North as existed in Britain. And in 1938 that thought became reality when Britain proposed that if a deficit existed as a result of Northern Ireland's inability to finance services at British levels, Britain would assume the deficit.

In 1938, Britain also made the nearly fatal decision to give Ireland the ports reserved to Britain by Article 7 of the Anglo-Irish Treaty of 1921. Fortunately for Britain, Ulster—unlike the South—remained loyal to Britain. While the South declared its neutrality in World War ii and flirted perfidiously with the Axis powers, Ulster remained the bulwark of British security. Since the inclusion of Northern Ireland in the area granted dominion status under the Anglo-Irish Treaty would, in light of the South's subsequent action, have meant its loss to Britain as a strategic base, the decision to permit the British-Northern Ireland tie to continue was of priceless importance. Without the use of the Ulster base during World War ii, the British lifeline across the Atlantic would have been cut; without that lifeline, Britain would have met defeat in the war.

In the years following the war, Northern Ireland continued its economic and social development. With the protection of the Ireland Act 1949, which guaranteed to Northerners that the British connection would be maintained until the people of the North, through their democratically elected representatives in the Stormont Parliament, voted to end the connection, Ulster felt secure. Furthermore, Northern Ireland's feeling of security was enhanced by the memory of the vital role that Ulster played in saving Britain from destruction and the knowledge that Britain would long remember that role.

As opposed to the South, which chose to become a republic, Northern Ireland sought to preserve the parliamentary union with Great Britain, to keep the Ulster window on

71

the world wide open, and to avoid the "risk of falling into the fallacy of 'ourselves alone'."[80] The vehicle for preserving the union was the Unionist Party. Although dissident Catholics were quick to assert that the Unionist Party was able to maintain its domination of Ulster politics only through voting irregularities and gerrymandered districts, an undeniable majority of the Northern populace supported the Unionist Party. In fact, the identification of the Unionist Party with the survival of Northern Ireland has resulted not only in success for the party but also in the longest reign for any single party in the Western world.

The strength of the Unionist Party was demonstrated during the invidious IRA terror campaign of 1956–1962 and in the party's ability to promulgate changes where and when they were justified. Despite being hampered by the Catholic community's refusal to accept the obligation to support the regime, the Unionists tried to promulgate sensible changes. As O'Neill stated, change was an ally, and the finest traditions of Unionism regarded it as such, rather than to "retreat into some fortress mentality of our own, resisting all change, suspicious of every forward-looking idea, hostile and resentful of all who disagree with us."[81]

There were, of course, limits to the acceptability of change. To begin with, the 1965 Lemass-O'Neill talks were perceived as an attempt to change or remove the border with the Republic, and that, to Protestants, was an unacceptable change. Secondly, change was never to be forced, for, while change was welcome, the imposition of change by violence or other forms of coercion was also anathema to the people of Ulster.

With the onset of the so-called civil rights demonstrations, both limits—the question of the border and the imposition of change by force—were raised. For years, Ulster had been traveling the road to progress and prosperity. Now it sud-

[80] O'Neill, ULSTER AT THE CROSSROADS 47 (1969).

[81] Ibid., 56. See also Rose, GOVERNING WITHOUT CONSENSUS 273; Cole, Introduction to O'Neill, ULSTER AT THE CROSSROADS 10–11.

denly found itself at a crossroads, for before it lay not only the road that it had been traveling but also the road to pointless violence and civil strife. Although the vast majority of both the Catholic and Protestant communities wanted Northern Ireland to continue its progressive voyage, a few misguided IRA extremists attempted to force another course on Ulster. Under the cover of the civil rights movement, the IRA hoped to exacerbate religious divisions and to bring down the Unionist Government, thereby leaving the way open for Ulster to travel down a third road— the road to union with the Republic and to Catholic domination.

By claiming that Catholics had long been the subject of discrimination, the IRA managed to arouse a not insignificant portion of the Catholic community. As the number of Catholics misled by this falsehood increased, the number of Protestants who took issue with Catholic demands also rose. Moreover, O'Neill's announcement of reforms in 1968 and his hesitancy to deal firmly with lawbreakers led to a subsequent split within the Unionist Party itself, for there were cabinet members, such as Faulkner, who realized that subversives win if they do not lose and, concomitantly, that governments lose if they do not win.[82]

82 This observation is more fully developed in Gardner, RESURGENCE OF THE MAJORITY 44 (1971). Faulkner resigned as Deputy Prime Minister in January 1969 because he felt that O'Neill was making too many concessions to demonstrators. The exchange between Faulkner and O'Neill that followed was quite sharp. In responding to Faulkner's letter of resignation of January 23, 1969, O'Neill wrote on January 24, 1969: "You also tell me that you remained through what you term 'successive crises.' I am bound to say that if, instead of passively 'remaining' you had on occasions given me that loyalty and support which a Prime Minister has the right to expect from his Deputy, some of these so-called crises might never have arisen." Quoted in Boyd, BRIAN FAULKNER 61.

The reforms announced on November 22, 1968 were that houses would be allocated on a fair basis, citizens' grievances would be investigated by a commissioner and a Community Relations Board, a new Londonderry Area Plan would be implemented, local government

In an attempt to strengthen his hand, O'Neill called for elections in February 1969. Paradoxically, although he won re-election, O'Neill also lost, for the official, anti-O'Neill Unionist candidates did reasonably well, and Paisley, running against O'Neill himself, did remarkably well. Still, O'Neill attempted to accommodate the demands of civil rights activists by appointing a commission to examine the disturbances of 1968 and early 1969. In creating the Cameron Commission, however, O'Neill merely underscored Protestant claims that he was weakening the Ulster foundations and made his position more untenable. Even though some grievances of the demonstrators were genuine, those grievances were exploited by "ill-disposed persons for their own ends, not the least of which [was] a systematic attempt first to discredit and then to undermine all constituted authority . . . in a determination to achieve either the merging of [Ulster] into the Irish Republic or the setting up of a new Irish Workers' Republic."[83] For allowing this exploitation to be perpetrated, O'Neill had to go.

Upon his accession to the captaincy of the Ulster ship of state in the spring of 1969, Chichester-Clark released all political prisoners, including those Protestant Ulstermen whose only crime had been their enthusiastic patriotism. This decision, which was followed shortly afterwards by the start of the "marching season" to celebrate the great victories of Boyne and Londonderry, proved a costly one, since, undoubtedly, many of the IRA prisoners released played large parts in the forthcoming August 12 "Battle of the Bogside."

The "Battle of the Bogside" was quite instructive. When the Protestants marched past the Bogside, the Derry Citi-

---

would be reformed, and the Special Powers Act would be revised when conditions permitted such revision. See generally A COMMENTARY BY THE GOVERNMENT OF NORTHERN IRELAND TO ACCOMPANY THE CAMERON REPORT (Cmd. 534) 3–11 (1969).

[83] *Ibid.*, 2.

zens' Action Committee—the organization whose responsibility included controlling the Catholic community—quickly revealed its inability to restrain the Catholic hooligans
whose object it was to provoke the Protestants to battle. Yet
in a manner which, when juxtaposed with its earlier ama-
teurishness, was highly professional and can only impute
guilt to its actions, the DCAC quickly erected barricades
and made ready for the showdown with the police and
Protestants that it had permitted to develop.

Even after the treacherous Bogside action terminated and
despite the O'Neill experiences, the Chichester-Clark Government continued to make concessions to the Catholic
community. Regardless of the concessions made, they were
never enough for the Catholics. The Catholics, moreover,
escalated rather than reduced their demonstrations against
the Government. Accordingly, the Protestants vowed to
draw the line—and to defend their homeland.

With Britain holding back the forces necessary to dis-
patch the IRA terrorists once and for all, the Protestant
position in general and Chichester-Clark's status in particular became more hazardous. Seemingly bent on following the
incongruous policy of doing as little as possible, Britain allowed the situation to deteriorate. When, finally, the IRA
loosed its murder campaign on the British Army, Britain
got the message. But it was too late—at least for Chichester-
Clark, who, by then, had lost the confidence of the Protestant community.

Following his elevation to Prime Minister in May 1971,
Faulkner quickly convinced Britain of the need to rein-
state internment. By the time it was instituted in August,
it was also a case of the proverbial "too little, too late," for
even with internment the smoke screen of civil rights provided sufficient cover for the Republican conspiracy. Since
Britain had forced Ulster to disband the Special Constabulary and disarm the RUC, security was totally dependent
on the undermanned British Army, an ineffective Ulster
Defense Regiment (the B Specials' successor), and an un-

75

armed police force. Under these circumstances, internment was predictably not as effective as it would have been had not Ulster's best protections been "tossed overboard in an act of national suicide."[84]

Simultanously with his endeavors to install internment, Faulkner attempted to get all responsible elements in the Ulster community to play a constructive role in its institutions. He therefore proposed that three additional parliamentary committees (industrial development, environmental services, and social services) be established, two of which were to be headed by Catholics. While the concept was well received, it floundered when the Catholic opposition left Stormont at the announcement of the reinstatement of internment.

These attempts to broaden the Government were seen as further concessions to the Catholic minority. As had been the case with Faulkner's predecessors, the concessions produced negative reactions among Protestants. It became evident once more that the more equality was granted on paper, the more violent the reactions from both communities became. Not only were the concessions never enough for the Catholic minority, but also they were far too much for the Protestant majority. Since Catholics both rejected the obligation to support the democratically elected regime and aided IRA efforts to overthrow the Government, many Protestants felt that the continuous extension of privileges to Catholics was a naive and even criminal act. Within a short period of time, therefore, a number of Protestant splinter groups had been formed to counter the venomous

---

[84] Paisley, THE DAGGER OF TREACHERY STRIKES AT THE HEART OF ULSTER 7 (1972). The bulwarks of Northern Ireland were the RUC and USC. In order for the IRA to succeed, both had to be destroyed, since the IRA "could never achieve [its] objective and never bring this country into a state of anarchy . . . unless [it] first overthrew these two forces." Paisley, *Action to Defeat Republican Conspiracy*, 84 N. I. PARL. DEBATES (March 14, 1972). The UDR's role was that of a part-time force. Its function was simply to assist the British Army in its security functions. See generally 1971 WHITE PAPER 3.

IRA program of deceit and murder and to pressure the Unionist Government to toe the line.

However much Protestants may have disagreed about concessions and tactics, they were of one mind when it came to the need to restore law and order. To all Protestants the restoration of law and order was the indispensable foundation upon which further progress could be built—and restoration of law and order meant "the cessation not only of riots, shootings, bombing and arson, but also of intimidation, extortion and all forms of civil disobedience."[85] Before further progress could be made, the IRA had to lay down its arms and terminate all such activities.

Even a return to law and order was not viewed by the Paisleyite-Vanguard factions of the Protestant community as implying that all laws were infallible or that the law must never be broken. Since the loyalty of Protestants was to the basic principle of a Protestant government for a Protestant people, a legislative departure from this principle and toward appeasement of Catholics was to be resisted because the resulting laws were, perforce, illegitimate. Hence, those individuals who refused to comply with illegitimate laws were not lawbreakers but ultraloyal.[86]

One law, however, remained sacred to all Protestants— the Government of Ireland Act 1920. With violence mount-

---

[85] See 1971 WHITE PAPER 1.

[86] See generally Rose, GOVERNING WITHOUT CONSENSUS 151–52. This point of view is most clearly expressed in a Stormont speech delivered by Paisley: "It is a process of democracy to change laws that are bad. Are all laws infallible? . . . It is wrong to say that because a law has been made it is a good law. . . . This Parliament came into being and . . . the Unionist Party came to power as a result of resisting the law, defying the police, arming the community and declaring that the Westminster Government's proposal to put us out of the United Kingdom was not acceptable. Let no member of the Government party tell us that the law must never be broken; their whole history rests on an effectual defiance of Westminster's laws." Paisley, *Banning of Parades*, 83 N. I. PARL. DEBATES (January 25, 1972). William Craig, leader of the Ulster Vanguard, took a similar position in an interview with the author in Belfast on August 17, 1972.

ing, Protestants worried that there would be politicians in Britain who would advocate modifying the Britain-Northern Ireland relationship in an attempt to seek a solution to the crisis. They were right. On March 24, 1972, Britain announced to a shocked Ulster and a gleeful Republic the suspension of Stormont and the imposition of direct rule.

Direct rule was imposed after Faulkner refused to consent to the transfer of all responsibilities for law and order from Stormont to Westminster. Although some Protestants felt that Faulkner erred in rejecting Prime Minister Edward Heath's plan, they failed to recognize that not only would such a transfer have been an admission by Stormont of its inability to govern, but it would also have been a mere face-saving sham that would, nonetheless, have left the Northern Ireland Government "bereft of any real influence and authority by removing the most fundamental power of any government."[87] In either case, though, the announcement of direct rule can only be viewed as a victory for terrorists who believe that violence can and does pay and that those persons who shout, lie, or destroy earn for themselves an attention that responsible conduct and honorable behavior do not.

To Protestants, direct rule must be accepted as a setback. The ensuing 1973 White Paper must be similarly viewed. Although it provided for a return to regional government in Ulster, the White Paper also gave the Secretary of State a continuing role in Ulster affairs, referred franchise and election laws to Westminster, envisioned a union with the Republic that—to all Ulstermen—remains anathema, and failed to provide for the automatic return of internal security along with the proposed Assembly. It was accordingly regarded as, at the very least, a quasi setback.

When the provisions of the 1973 White Paper were implemented, they bore out the worst fears of loyal Ulster-

[87] Faulkner, *Statement on Ulster Move*, N. Y. TIMES (March 25, 1972) 9, col. 1. Direct rule is also commented on in Boyd, BRIAN FAULKNER 94-112; NORTHERN IRELAND: THE HIDDEN TRUTH 23 (1972).

men. Despite the Ulster Unionist Council's repudiation, for example, of the proposed Council of Ireland by an overwhelming 80 votes (454–374), plans for this unwanted body continued; despite the obvious opposition by the vast majority of Ulster's citizenry to the new constitutional arrangements of the Assembly and Executive, the unrepresentative Assembly rejected a loyalist coalition motion calling for renegotiation of those arrangements. As a direct consequence of this latter action and in an effort to demonstrate to Britain that both union with the Republic of Ireland (in any form) and power-sharing were unacceptable to the Protestant community, the Ulster Workers' Council initiated a work stoppage that brought Ulster's industry to a standstill and, after the undemocratic Executive refused to negotiate with the Council, forced the Ulster Government to its knees, thereby reinstating direct rule. Whether direct rule will be temporary or permanent depends on whether "the voice of the Ulster majority—which is not a sectarian majority, but a majority of responsible people loyal to the Crown"[88]—continues to make itself heard as it did in the May 1973 local government elections, the June 1973 Assembly elections, and the May 1974 strike.

To insure that it is heard, several points must be realized. First of all, it must be recognized that the Constitution of the Republic of Ireland "validly expresses the beliefs and aspirations of the majority of the Southern Irish people, that as such it is entitled to respect as the expression of a national culture, and that there is something intrinsically absurd and quite possibly fraudulent, in the suggestion that it should be radically altered in order to enable the Southern Irish State to extend its authority over those who do not wish to accept it."[89] Secondly, it must be acknowledged,

[88] Faulkner, STATEMENT ON ULSTER MOVE, 9. See also *The Reflections of Leading Unionist Politicians,* UNIONIST REV. 4 (May 1973); Faulkner, *The White Paper: We Must Be Constructive,* UNIONIST REV. 5 (May 1973).

[89] Utley, ULSTER: A SHORT BACKGROUND ANALYSIS 4–5 (1972). Sug-

as James Craig said long ago, that there are "fewer differences between the Northern Catholic and Protestant than say the Catholic who lives in Tyrone and the Catholic who lives in Cork or Kerry."[90] Finally, it must be stated—loudly and clearly—that union is possible, but only if "the South should return to the Union from which [it was] foolish enough to secede."[91]

CONCLUSIONS

The resolution of competing factual claims is never an easy task. In the case of Northern Ireland, years of turmoil attest to the Gordian dimensions of the problem. By turning back the pages of history, however, the two "ends" of the Ulster cord are revealed, even if the present problem remains firmly knotted.

The first "end" dates back to 1172. With the coming of the English, the Irish became a conquered people. Although they managed to a certain extent to "Gaelicize" their conquerors, the Irish were nevertheless subjected to degrading and harsh treatment, treatment that was perhaps required for England to retain its authority, but which, over the years, resulted in a natural Irish animosity to England. For instance, to the conquering English the Statutes of Kilkenny and the seventeenth-century land and religious programs were necessary, but to the conquered Irish they were necessarily the cause of much bitterness.

In 1607 the second "end" developed. With the planting of English and Scottish Presbyterians in Ulster, the English employed the Machiavellian principle of planting "colonies in one or two of those places which form as it were the

---

gestions have been made to amend the 1937 Constitution of Eire to delete the prohibitions on censorship (Article 40) and divorce (Article 41) and the special position of the Catholic church (Article 44).

[90] Biggs-Davidson, CATHOLICS AND THE UNION 12 (1972).

[91] Ervine, *Ulster and Her People*, 198 SPECTATOR 577, 578 (May 3, 1957).

keys of the land, for it [was] necessary to do this or to maintain a large force of armed men."[92] In the process, they permitted the Protestant Ascendancy to become rooted in the fertile Ulster soil, exacerbated Irish hatred for England, and brought the question of religion to the fore. Even though the Catholics did commit atrocities during the 1640 rising, act unfairly during the 1689 Irish Parliament, and rally around James II, the Protestants, it would appear, were the real "villains." Moreover, but for the treatment Catholics suffered at the hands of Protestants, the Catholic reactions, in all likelihood, would never have occurred. In any case, however, further Protestant action—or reaction—in the form of the Penal Laws was totally unjustified, since the Treaty of Limerick clearly forbade any such laws. Indeed, the only possible explanation for the laws was repression. In this respect, the Penal Laws were successful.

Despite these attempts at dividing the inhabitants of Ireland, Protestants and Catholics remained "partially united" well into the nineteenth century. To those inhabitants who did unite, the goal of an Ireland free of Britain and the Protestant Ascendancy that had been created to guard Britain's interest was, especially after the Union of 1800, far more significant than whether an individual was Catholic or Protestant. As evidence, the names of Tone, Emmet, Butts, and Parnell need simply be cited to substantiate the dual claims that Protestants played leading roles in the early efforts for independence and that religious bigotry evolved not spontaneously but artifically through the actions of those individuals whose economic and political interests were served by dividing the people of Ireland. Simultaneously, though, it must be recognized that British-Protestant Ascendancy interests—the two "ends" of the Ulster cord— did not always coincide. In the Acts of Union, for example,

[92] Machiavelli, THE PRINCE 37 (1960). The English actually had put Machiavelli's principle to use before he developed it. The Pale—Dublin and the surrounding area—was such a plantation beginning in the twelfth century.

the Protestant Ascendancy was forced to relinquish part of its power in order both to satisfy British demands and to protect its remaining power.

Division ultimately became a fait accompli. Mostly through endeavors of the British and Protestant Ascendancy, partly through Catholic wrongs such as the 1795 Battle of the Diamond and O'Connell's intemperate remark about a Catholic Ascendancy, the division was formed by the mid-nineteenth century. Even then, however, the Butts and Parnells continued to advocate the eighteenth-century theme of unite and conquer, although, for the most part, battle lines were increasingly drawn along religious lines.

Originally conceived as a convenient cover for the causes of British expansion and Protestant privilege, the Catholic-Protestant schism was quickly employed by the Conservative Party to manipulate itself into power. With the issue of Home Rule and under the aegis of Randolph Churchill, the Conservatives spoke of the British connection, argued economics, and worked on religious feelings. By "playing the Orange Card," the policy of divide and conquer was successfully used by the Conservatives to defeat the Liberal Party, obtain control of Britain, and maintain the Irish connection until 1914. Even after the third Home Rule Bill became law in 1914, the delay in its effective date occasioned by World War I permitted the Conservatives to develop a more effective strategy to defeat both the Liberal-Nationalist coalition and Home Rule. When the subject re-emerged after the war, the suspended Government of Ireland Act 1914 was jettisoned and replaced by a plan for the partition, and continued manipulation, of Ireland.

Before that plan was formally proposed in the Government of Ireland Act 1920, however, the situation in Ireland changed markedly. With the 1916 Easter Rebellion in Ireland—rightly viewed by Britain as a "stab in the back" but wrongly handled—Ireland became "radicalized." Since Home Rule had been the main plank in the Nationalist Party platform and since Home Rule had proved illusory, the Nationalists in 1918 were replaced by Sinn Fein as the main Irish political voice. In turn, Sinn Fein members met in 1919 in Dublin, abandoned Home Rule, and declared a republic—an act to which Britain responded forcefully by creating the notorious Black and Tans, a group whose repressive actions unified the Catholic populace in hatred against Britain.

With this state of affairs, it was an easy matter for the Conservatives to incite Catholics and Protestants against one another and to prevent a union of North and South. The only real question was the maximum area and population that could effectively be controlled by the privileged minority or modern Protestant Ascendancy. When that detail was finally resolved, the 1920 Act was introduced and passed. Ireland, after initially rejecting the act, consented to it by signing the Anglo-Irish Treaty of 1921. As a result of the Treaty—and let there be no mistake that the Treaty was signed at the point of British guns—the stage was set for civil war in the South, the Conservative Party policy was brought to a successful conclusion, and a line was drawn on the map of Ireland and in the hearts of Irishmen that was to cause only pain and suffering for all but the modern Protestant Ascendancy.

Despite these machinations, however, Catholics and Protestants still joined hands occasionally against the British-Protestant Ascendancy conspiracy. In 1906 and 1932, the workingmen of both communities rebelled in protest against police brutality towards the unemployed of the Catholic Falls Road area of Belfast. Although the union was short-lived in each instance, it was an event that should serve as a reminder and may prove a precursor.

Another reminder of significance in comprehending the present conflict was Ireland's neutrality during World War II. While Ireland's action was understandable given the history of the long struggle for independence from Britain, it was hardly acceptable in view of the fact that Ireland would have been an easy prey for Germany had Britain fallen. In

83

fact, but for the proverbial luck of the Irish—and the concomitant use of Northern bases by Britain—Ireland's refusal to aid Britain would have resulted, at best, in an occupation reminiscent of the Penal Laws period. At the same time, Ireland's neutrality produced two results that had long-range effects, for, it would appear, the declaration of neutrality poignantly demonstrated to Britain the strategic importance of the North and deepened the Catholic-Protestant schism.

The schism was further accentuated by the IRA actions of the 1950s and 1960s. By attempting to coerce a North-South union, the IRA succeeded only in making such a union less likely. Indeed, if there has been one principle that has been true throughout Irish history, it is that the Irish—all Irish—fight hardest when they are hit hardest. With the initiation of the IRA campaign to unite the Six Counties with the South, the antiunion feelings in the North hardened.

The deepened schism and hardened feelings were demonstrated by the Tricolor Riots, the reactions to the Lemass-O'Neill meeting, and the reception given to the civil rights demonstrations. In an open society, a society free of hatred, no such results could have been generated. The modern Protestant Ascendancy had done its work well.

In a sense, it had done its work too well. At first, the divisions established by Britain and maintained by the Protestant Ascendancy had been so controlled that actions or reactions were almost Pavlovian. Over the years, however, these divisions produced elements in each community that were not only full of bitterness and hate but also uncontrollable. By 1970, the situation had deteriorated so completely that reactions to events in Northern Ireland were not so much Pavlovian as Frankensteinian.

When the CRA called its initial march on August 24, 1968, it was a truly nonsectarian organization with laudable objectives. Although extremist elements, such as the IRA, were members of the CRA, the CRA was hardly an extremist group. Despite Protestant claims to the contrary and despite the fact that the IRA, which from 1962 to 1970 was unorganized, tried to benefit from the CRA successes (and deserves some credit for those successes), the CRA remained interested in improving conditions for the people of Northern Ireland within the existing governmental framework. At no time was it interested in destroying the concept of a separate six-county area and in effectuating union with the South, although by 1969 the CRA had become as guilty as its opponents in perceiving the "truth" through its own subjective eyes.[93]

While the Catholic extremists (the IRA) did not emerge as a factor on the Northern Irish scene until 1970, however, the Protestant extremists were causing problems as early as 1964, for, beginning with the 1964 Tricolor Riots and continuing with the 1966 Cromac Square Riots, they made their presence felt. It was, though, at Burntollet, during the Belfast-Derry march of January 1–4, 1969, that the Protestant extremists revealed the insanity and criminality of their actions, actions that were to be repeated on innumerable occasions in succeeding years and that, despite the Cameron Report's acceptance of the event as simply a "disgraceful episode,"[94] were certainly among the most outrageous deeds in Ulster's troubled history.

Protestant extremism had a sometimes overt, sometimes covert ally—the RUC. In the October 5, 1968 Derry march, the RUC action in routing the marchers was reckless and wholly irresponsible, even though the Cameron Commission preferred to apply those adjectives to the actions of the leaders of the march; in permitting the Burntollet affair to occur, the RUC was delinquent, and, in allowing it to degenerate into tragedy, the RUC seemed to be a silent partner of the Protestant extremists; in the sweep through the

---

[93] By the summer of 1969, "truth as such had ceased to exist. Every man had his own unshakable truth, and was guided by it." Hastings, BARRICADES IN BELFAST 201.

[94] Cameron, DISTURBANCES 46.

Bogside on the evening of January 4, 1969, the RUC acted criminally; and in the April 19, 1969 Bogside riot, the RUC once again acted in an, at best, irresponsible fashion.

Britain, meanwhile, seemed content to follow its policy of benign neglect. Although it made attempts to convince the Unionist Government to institute reforms where reforms were justified, Britain protected its interests by supporting that government and adhered to a policy of "partial peace by meeting at any rate the minimum demands of the sect which seemed prepared to make the most trouble, the Protestants."[95] Consequently, as the conflict progressed and more responsible Unionist leaders, such as O'Neill, stumbled and fell, Britain found itself supporting an increasingly "conservative" government, a government that did not seem to realize that reform, without a concomitant change of attitude and additional goodwill, was meaningless in resolving the conflict.

The conflict, accordingly, escalated. As it did and as the RUC and Protestant extremist actions mounted, the Catholic community gave increased support to the civil rights movement. This support was evidenced quite convincingly during the fifty-hour Battle of the Bogside, an incident for which the Derry Citizens' Action Committee has to bear the brunt of the responsibility. Although both the CRA and the Action Committee laid the blame for the ensuing riot on the Government's decision to permit the Apprentice Boys' march on August 12, 1969, the fact remains that there would have been no riot had the Action Committee marshalls exercised the same degree of control over the stone-throwers—the persons throwing paving stones at Protestant marchers—as they did over the barricade-builders. Admittedly, the parade might have been banned given the volatile climate in Northern Ireland, but the decision to permit the march—be it for political reasons or because peaceful demonstrations should be permitted in an ostensibly democratic society—was justified.

[95] Insight Team, ULSTER 310.

What was unjustified was both the Protestant reaction to the Bogside riot and the RUC's complicity in that reaction by failing to control the Protestant hordes, especially in Belfast. As a direct result of that reaction and of Stormont's inability to deal with the situation, Britain introduced on August 14, 1969 the first elements of its Army; as an indirect result of those events, the IRA was reborn.

Even though the IRA had infiltrated the CRA and had benefitted politically from the successes that movement enjoyed, it was not really an organization in 1969. When the Protestants went on the rampage during the week of August 12, therefore, the IRA was unable to back its grandiose promises of support with anything but verbal action and an occasional bullet. Shortly after and because of this action-reaction, the IRA split occurred—and a new armed wing (the Provos) rose phoenix-like from the IRA ashes to provide the Catholic community with its two-edged sword of protection and societal destruction.

Following the 1970 IRA rebirth, the British Army found itself in an increasingly untenable position. Now each side had its extremist element that constantly harassed the other community and urged its own community to reject the status quo. For Catholics, rejection was the result of promised changes that either did not come or came too slowly; for Protestants, rejection was based on the fact that the 1968 reforms and the Hunt Commission proposals to disarm the RUC and disband the USC were concessions to what were regarded as criminal groups; and, for the Army, rejection meant increased tensions and rioting for which it, like any army, was ill-prepared, since "no army, however well it conducts itself, is really adapted for police work."[96] In brief, although the Ulster society improved significantly in terms of equality for all its citizens, the Catholic and Protestant extremists continued to prod themselves and their respective communities to further action.

That action on the part of the IRA produced the first

[96] *Ibid.*, 159. See 1974 WHITE PAPER 14.

British Army death in February 1971, the replacement—
with the aid of Protestant extremists—of Chichester-Clark
with Faulkner in May 1971, and the establishment of internment in August 1971. Obviously, each of these three
events was important; obviously, too, the decision to institute internment was of cardinal significance.

Aside from the fact that internment without charge or
trial would be wrong under any circumstances, internment
as carried out by the British was a disaster. While Protestants—with the notable exception of Paisley, who was ada-
mantly opposed to internment—were quick to laud the
exercise, it was, in fact, an error of great magnitude. Not
only did it fail to reduce violence in any way, but also internment, when combined with the traditional dislikes produced by the tug of history, made Catholics more receptive
to IRA demands for support. Hence, although internment
was to remove the IRA fish from the Catholic water, it
simply enabled those members of the IRA who escaped
capture—and the growing number of bombings and killings
attested to the fact that many members did escape—to swim
in more and deeper water.[97]

As internment failed but continued, the Frankensteinian
reactions of both Catholic and Protestant extremists grew,
for whichever group committed the initial outrage, the
other side quickly retaliated with a like excess. Among the
most condemnable events of the recent conflict, however,
was the atrocity committed not by communal extremists but
by the British Army in Londonderry on January 30, 1972.
Despite the attempts of the Widgery Tribunal to place the
blame equally on both the marchers and the Army, the
facts, as stated by the tribunal itself, indicate that the Army,

[97] This analogy is based on Mao's famous axiom of guerrilla warfare
that the people are the water and the guerrilla army the fish. See
generally Chinh, *Revolutionary War*, in CONTEMPORARY COMMUNISM:
THEORY AND PRACTICE 298–300 (Swearer & Longaker, eds., 1963); Moss,
War in North Ireland, 163 NEW REP. 13, 14 (August 15, 1970).

in an effort to capture members of the IRA, acted in a murderous and wholly unjustified fashion. Even discounting the theory that the Army deliberately fired upon demonstrators in the hope of making the elusive IRA stand and fight and even admitting that elements of the marchers were provocative in throwing stones at the Army, there was no rational way to explain, much less justify, the Army's conduct on that day. In all instances of factual discrepancies, facts must be weighed carefully; in this instance, Widgery to the contrary notwithstanding, the scales were tilted heavily against the Army's version of the events that led to the tragedy.

Out of the horror of Derry's Bloody Sunday—January 30, 1972—came the realization that further action was required. Since Stormont was unable to take that action, Britain suspended Stormont on March 24, 1972 and, for nearly two years, reverted to its pre-1920 policy of direct rule. But it was unable to turn back the clock on the violence in Northern Ireland—not with direct rule, not with the elaborate, well-reasoned and sensible plans proposed in the 1973 White Paper, not with the elections of 1973. And it was unable to do so by implementing the 1973 White Paper plans in 1974 or, after the failure of those plans, by reimposing direct rule in May 1974 and calling in the 1974 White Paper for a consultative constitutional convention.

That clock will never be turned back if the Ulster strings continue to be pulled for the benefit of either Britain or the privileged few of Northern Ireland. Even though conditions have improved tremendously in Ulster, the fact remains that the North today is the result of yesterday's policies in Ulster, that present events are the incontrovertible residue of past expansionist and manipulative policies, and that religion is, as it has always been, a tool to be wielded for economic and political profit. Until these facts are recognized, any number of White Papers will be powerless to end the insane violence; until these facts are admitted, the Christianity of Northern Ireland will continue to be debased by its politics;[98] and until these facts are erased, the question will not be how high the Ulster journey to the stars has reached, but how often the Northern Ireland treadmill must turn before that ascent can be commenced.

[98] In his farewell address, O'Neill stated his views in no uncertain terms: "Ours is called a Christian country. We could have enriched our politics with our Christianity; but far too often we have debased our Christianity with our politics." O'Neill, ULSTER AT THE CROSSROADS 200.

CHAPTER III

Northern Ireland's Status: An Analysis of the Constitutional Position of Ulster

To NON-BRITISH and non-Irish members of the world community, the status of Northern Ireland is a mystery; to the British and Irish that status is not a mystery but a source of continuous, sometimes violent, disagreement. In any attempt to shed light on these opposing viewpoints, the statutory development of Ulster needs to be examined in some detail.

The constitutional position of Northern Ireland rests on nine acts—the Acts of Union of 1800, the Government of Ireland Act 1920, the Irish Free State (Consequential Provisions) Act 1922, the Ireland (Confirmation of Agreement) Act 1925, the Ireland Act 1949, the Northern Ireland (Temporary Provisions) Act 1972, the Northern Ireland Assembly Act 1973, the Northern Ireland Constitution Act 1973, and the Northern Ireland Act 1974. In addition, the Anglo-Irish Treaty of 1921 and the Statute of Westminster 1931 are relevant—although the relevance of the 1931 Statute is tangential—to an understanding of the North's status.

In 1800, in order "to promote and secure the essential interests of Great Britain and Ireland, and to consolidate the strength, power and resources of the British empire,"[1] Great Britain and Ireland were united by the Acts of Union into one kingdom. Although many of their provisions were subsequently repealed, the acts remain the basis for the con-

---

[1] 23 HALSBURY'S STATUTES OF ENGLAND 832 (1970) (cited hereafter as HALSBURY). There were two acts in 1800—the Union with Ireland Act 1800 and the Act of Union (Ireland) 1800. The language quoted is from the Union with Ireland Act 1800. See generally HALSBURY, 832–42. For a full text of the act, see 39 & 40 Geo. 3c.67.

tinued incorporation of Northern Ireland within the United Kingdom.

Under the Government of Ireland Act 1920 (which, somewhat ironically, was entitled "An Act to provide for the better Government of Ireland") separate legislatures and governments were envisioned for the Northern and Southern territories. A Council of Ireland was, moreover, to be established to exercise certain powers over the entire country. Even though the 1920 Act never accomplished its intended objectives, it remains operative in Northern Ireland, "where it forms, in effect, the constitution."[2]

Section 1 of the 1920 Act provided for the establishment of the Parliament of Northern Ireland. Section 4 (1) set forth the legislative power of the Northern Ireland Parliament "to make laws for the peace, order, and good government of . . . Northern Ireland with the following limitations, namely, that [it would] not have power to make laws except in respect of matters exclusively relating to the portion of Ireland within [its] jurisdiction or some part thereof," and that certain matters of imperial concern would be excepted from its jurisdiction. Section 5 prohibited laws interfering with religious equality. Section 9 reserved certain matters to the jurisdiction of Westminster, which, pursuant to Section 4 (1)(14), meant that they were excepted from Stormont's jurisdiction. Section 23 provided for a Northern Ireland contribution of £18 million annually towards the imperial liabilities and expenditures. And Section 75 held that despite the establishment of the Northern Parliament, "the supreme authority of the Parliament of the United Kingdom [would] remain unaffected and undiminished over all persons, matters, and things."

As a result of the South's resistance to the 1920 Act, the hostilities between Dublin and London continued until

[2] Donaldson, *Fundamental Rights in the Constitution of Northern Ireland*, 37 CANADIAN BAR REV. 189, 193 (1959). The text of the 1920 Act may be found at 10 & 11 Geo. 5c.67. The Government of Ireland Act 1920 will hereafter be cited as the 1920 Act.

terminated by the Articles of Agreement for a Treaty between Great Britain and Ireland of December 6, 1921.[3] Under the terms of the Treaty, the South became known as the Irish Free State (Article 1); it was granted the same status as the Dominion of Canada (Article 2); Southern members of Parliament were required to take an oath to the King (Article 4); the South assumed the debt of Great Britain regarding war claims (Article 5); the defense of Ireland by sea was undertaken by Britain (Article 6); the use of certain Irish ports was granted to Great Britain (Article 7); the powers of the Irish Free State were not exercisable with respect to the North, and the 1920 Act was to continue to apply to the North if, within one month of the passage of the legislation ratifying the treaty, the North addressed the King that the Irish Free State's powers not be extended over the North (Article 12); and, if the North so addressed the King, a boundary commission was to be created to determine the border between the North and South (Article 12). The Irish Free State (Agreement) Act 1922 gave the force of law to these articles; the Irish Free State Constitution Act 1922 ratified them.[4]

On the same day that the Irish Free State Constitution Act 1922 was passed, the Irish Free State (Consequential Provisions) Act 1922 was enacted. It provided that the 1920 Act was inapplicable "to any part of Ireland other than Northern Ireland, and, in the event of such an address as is mentioned in Article 12 of the Articles of Agreement," the 1920 Act was to continue in effect for Northern Ireland.[5]

But once the North had petitioned the King, it refused—despite the provisions of Article 12—to name its member to the Boundary Commission. Following some legal maneuvering, that member was finally appointed by London. A

[3] The text of the Anglo-Irish Treaty of 1921 may be found in 30 H.C.T. 775. See also Donaldson, SOME COMPARATIVE ASPECTS OF IRISH LAW 79–82 (1957).

[4] See 4 HALSBURY'S STATUTES OF ENGLAND 636–40 and 641–46 (1968).

[5] HALSBURY 901–909; 13 Geo. 5C.2.

93

short time later, in November 1924, the Boundary Commission held its first meeting. The proceedings, then and thereafter, proved abortive;[6] the Dublin, London, and Belfast representatives accordingly agreed to amend and supplement the 1921 Treaty through the Ireland (Confirmation of Agreement) Act 1925.[7] This act revoked the powers conferred on the Boundary Commission by Article 12, provided the Free State with financial assistance, established the boundaries of Northern Ireland as set forth in Section 1 of the 1920 Act, repealed Section 2 of the 1920 Act (which called for a Council of Ireland) and transferred powers of the proposed Council of Ireland to the Northern Ireland Parliament, and provided that "the Governments of the Irish Free State and of Northern Ireland [were to] meet together as and when necessary for the purpose of considering matters of common interest"[8] (although until the 1965 Lemass-O'Neill talks, there were no such meetings).

By 1925, therefore, *les jeux étaient faits*; by 1925 the grandiose scheme of the 1920 Act had degenerated into an ostensibly firm separation of Belfast from Dublin. In lieu of the proposed temporary demarcation of North and South and a unifying Council of Ireland with powers extending throughout Ireland, a more permanent barrier had been erected between the six and twenty-six county areas of Ireland.

That barrier was made more and more permanent as the South moved towards the republican status espoused by DeValera in 1922. Although the Free State was a far cry from a republic, it gave the South, as Collins had wisely observed in defending the 1921 Treaty, the freedom to at-

[6] See generally HALSBURY at 910. For the documents and unofficial findings of the Boundary Commission—it never made a final report—see Hand, REPORT OF THE IRISH BOUNDARY COMMISSION 1925 (1969). Ironically, the documents and findings were made public for the first time in 1968—the year that the present troubles in the North began.

[7] HALSBURY 910–12; 15 & 16 Geo. 5c.77.

[8] Section 5 of the agreement, set forth in the Schedule to the Ireland (Confirmation of Agreement) Act 1925. See HALSBURY 912.

tain its objective. In fact, it gave the South enough freedom not only to participate in dominion developments but also to lead attempts to enhance the powers of the dominions. The Irish Free State had an important part in both the 1926 and 1930 Imperial Conferences, for instance, where the principle of equality between Britain and the dominions was propounded. And it also maintained a position of leadership in the passage of the Statute of Westminster 1931, which stated that no law made by Westminster was to "extend to any of the . . . Dominions as part of the law of that Dominion otherwise than at the request and with the consent of that Dominion."[9]

Following enactment of the Statute of Westminster 1931, the South moved to still greater freedom. Under the direction of DeValera, the Free State—in rapid succession—removed the oath of allegiance to the King from the Free State Constitution and disputed the 1921 Treaty provision that held that the Treaty should control in the event that the Constitution and Treaty conflicted; passed the Executive Authority (External Relations) Act 1936, pursuant to which the King was to be recognized as the symbol of cooperation if so advised by the Executive Council, thereby giving constitutional form to the policy of "external association" pursued by DeValera since 1922; adopted a new Constitution (which was viewed by some as "a revolution in law" but which Great Britain did not regard as "effecting a fundamental alteration in the position of the Irish Free State");[10]

[9] Preamble to the Statute of Westminster 1931. The statute may be found in Harrison, IRELAND AND THE BRITISH EMPIRE, 1937 344 (1937). Section 4 of the statute provides that "no Act of Parliament of the United Kingdom passed after the commencement of this Act shall extend, or be deemed to extend, to a Dominion as part of the law of that Dominion, unless it is expressly declared in that Act that that Dominion has requested, and consented to, the enactment thereof." *Ibid.*, 345.

[10] Donaldson, ASPECTS OF IRISH LAW 89. The argument advanced by such scholars as Wheare in THE STATUTE OF WESTMINSTER AND DOMINION STATUS (1947) was that the Irish Free State was restricted in its actions by that which could be done by Canada, and, since Canada could not

negotiated an agreement that deleted Articles 6 and 7 from the 1921 Treaty and resulted in the return of three ports to Ireland in exchange for the payment to Britain of £10 million; and declared its neutrality in World War II. Despite Britain's assertions to the contrary, therefore, by 1939 the South's "control of [its] destiny in international affairs was as complete as that of any sovereign state."[11]

In the North, the South's actions were viewed with alarm —and as evidence that the decision to petition the King under the terms of the 1921 Treaty was correct. When the South thereafter formalized its previous acts of independence and declared the Republic of Ireland, the British-Northern forces acknowledged the South's action in the Ireland Act 1949.[12] At the same time, however, they declared, in Section 1 (2), "that Northern Ireland remains part of His Majesty's dominions and of the United Kingdom and . . . affirmed that in no event will Northern Ireland or any part thereof cease to be part of His Majesty's dominions and of the United Kingdom without the consent of the Parliament of Northern Ireland."

Constitutionally, the situation in the North remained unchanged for the next twenty-three years. On March 24, 1972, though, Britain exercised its powers under Section 75 of the 1920 Act and announced that it was assuming full and direct responsibility for the administration of Northern Ireland until a political solution to the conflict could be devised; on March 30, 1972, Parliament passed and the Queen gave the Royal Assent to the Northern Ireland (Temporary Pro-

---

enact such policies, the Irish Free State could not do so. DeValera regarded the 1921 Treaty as a dead letter, however, and felt that the Statute of Westminster provided the Free State with total freedom. See Clokie, *The British Dominions and Neutrality*, 34 AM. POL. SCI. REV. 737, 740 (1940).

[11] Donaldson, ASPECTS OF IRISH LAW 90.

[12] HALSBURY 933–34; 12, 13, & 14 Geo. 6c.41. The Ireland Act 1949 will hereinafter be referred to as the 1949 Act.

visions) Act 1972.[13] By its terms, the act provided both that for a period of one year—which year could be and was extended for a second year—the Secretary of State was to act as chief executive officer for Ulster with the advice and consent of a Northern Ireland Commission to be appointed by him and that the Parliament of Northern Ireland stood prorogued. In brief, the British experiment in parliamentary devolution ground to a halt on March 30, 1972.

The halt was a "quasi-temporary" one, however. Elections were held in June 1973 for an Assembly pursuant to the Northern Ireland Assembly Act 1973; the Assembly met for the first time in July 1973; and the Assembly was given substantial powers by the Northern Ireland Constitution Act 1973.[14] Moreover, a power-sharing Executive of eleven members (six Unionists, four members of the SDLP, and one member of the Alliance Party) was created. Under the system of devolution of limited powers to the Assembly and Executive, Ulster was—from January 1, 1974 to May 29, 1974—once again self-governing.

With the collapse of the Executive in May 1974, though, the Northern Ireland Act 1974 was enacted.[15] Providing for the dissolution of the existing Assembly, temporary arrangements for the governance of Ulster, and elections for and the holding of a consultative constitutional convention to consider what measures for governance of the province would command widespread acceptance, the act ended debate over devolution and turned the Northern clock back to March 1972.

These acts and treaties provide the constitutional foundation for Northern Ireland today. While on their face they

[13] HALSBURY'S STATUTES OF ENGLAND 455–61 (Current Statute Service, 1973). The act was extended by an Order in Council on March 28, 1973.

[14] The Northern Ireland Assembly Act 1973 (1973c.17) may be found in HALSBURY'S STATUTES OF ENGLAND 183–87 (Current Statute Service, 1973); Northern Ireland Constitution Act 1973 (1973c.36).

[15] Northern Ireland Act 1974 (1974c.28).

fit well into the Ulster puzzle, they also might be said to overlap. In this apparent overlap lie three legal questions of some note: What rights does Dublin have with regard to the North? What latitude does London have in dealing with the status of Northern Ireland? And what rights does Belfast have after fifty-five years of stormy existence? It is these questions that will now be examined.

THE DUBLIN VIEWPOINT

With the 1920 Act, Britain mothered Northern Ireland, thereby bringing into being "a quasi-country, subject in most affairs of state to the Westminster government but with its own parliament, at Stormont, its own Prime Minister, its own militia, and its own power to enforce the authority and advantage of its million Protestants over its half-million Catholics."[16] Concomitantly, the British decision to partition Ireland resulted both in a "giant gerrymander—by a major boundary manipulation, a minority of the whole of Ireland was given a veto on the majority's right to decide policy for the nation"[17]—and in the rejection of the principle of self-determination.

For Dublin, partition was viewed as a distasteful but temporary condition. Although the South realized that the North would exercise the option given to it by Article 12 of the 1921 Treaty, it also believed that the Boundary Commission provided for in that article would quickly force the reunion of the two parts of the nation by transferring such large sections of the Six Counties to the South as to make partition economically unfeasible. In addition, Dublin felt that the contribution required by Section 23 of the 1920

[16] Kramer, *Letter to the Editors*, 48 NEW YORKER 126 (April 15, 1972). See also *Stormont and Saigon*, 213 NATION 165 (1971) for the view that Northern Ireland is the "grand-daddy of partitioned monstrosities" and "a vestpocket 'state' which was intended as a timeless sinecure for the Tory-inclined 'landed gentry' and other Protestants."

[17] IRELAND: THE FACTS 12 (1971).

Act would hasten reunification as a result of the strain put on the Northern treasury. For these reasons—and under the threat of renewed military pressure by Britain—the South agreed to the terms of the 1921 Treaty and became the Irish Free State.

But the Free State's faith—if faith there could be after seven hundred and fifty years of British subjugation—was soon shattered. Even though no change was to be made in the contribution for a period of two years commencing May 1921, Britain reduced the Northern Ireland contribution within twelve months—and by 1939 the net contribution "for the whole pre-war period 1922 to 1939 was little more than what the 1920 Act fixed for one year, and there was in fact no true Imperial Contribution at all."[18] Moreover, and more importantly, the Boundary Commission's rumored decision to transfer sections of territory to, not from, the North forced the Free State to sign the 1925 Agreement recognizing the "existing boundary on a de facto basis in exchange for financial assistance from London."[19] However it did not—and it does not today—recognize the de jure separation of North and South.

Having been forced as a not-so-free state into a "free association,"[20] having foresaken its goal of external association, and having pinned its hopes on a treaty that almost seemed to be written in invisible ink, the Free State turned its attention to British Commonwealth affairs—and to breaking the choking tie to Britain. Not satisfied with Article 2 of the Treaty that a change in Canada's status produced a

[18] Gallagher, THE INDIVISIBLE ISLAND: THE HISTORY OF THE PARTITION OF IRELAND 268 (1957); also see generally 266–72.

[19] Rose, GOVERNING WITHOUT CONSENSUS 92 (1971). As is discussed in the text accompanying note 24, the 1937 Irish Constitution lays claim to the six "lost" counties.

[20] Ireland, in truth, was "forced into a free association. That contradiction, that handicap, laid upon dominion status when Lloyd George foreclosed debate on 5 December 1921 with an ultimatum, clung to it like an old man of the sea, shaken off only when dominion status itself was discarded." Mansergh, THE COMMONWEALTH EXPERIENCE 208 (1969).

like change in the Free State, the South helped revolutionize dominion affairs, first through the Imperial Conferences of 1926 and 1930 and then through the Statute of Westminster 1931, "which gave expression to the principle of co-equality of status of the different dominions as well as their autonomous statehood by ending their dependence upon (and the power of) the Imperial Parliament."[21]

The Free State acted even though Britain contended that, despite the changes wrought by the Imperial Conferences and the 1931 Statute, anything repugnant to the 1921 Treaty was inconsistent with the explicit association of the status of the Free State with that of Canada. The Free State could have discarded the British viewpoint as either putting the Canadian status "into cold storage"[22] or implanting "an element of fixity in a settlement designed to guarantee an evolutionary growth in status,"[23] but instead it simply treated the 1921 Treaty as a document which, as a result of British perfidy and the 1931 Statute, no longer had the force of law. The Free State then proceeded to remove the despised oath in 1933, the office of Governor-General in 1936, and the Crown from the Constitution in 1936 (although the Dail unilaterally reinstated it in relation to external affairs in an action subsequently accepted by Britain). In taking these actions, the Free State merely exercised the right granted to it—or to Canada or any of the other dominions—by the Statute of Westminster.

In the 1937 Constitution of Ireland, the Irish Free State

[21] Hogan, THE NEUTRALITY OF IRELAND IN WORLD WAR II 60–61 (1953).

[22] Wheare, asserting that a contrary view would put the Canadian status "into cold storage," stated that any change in Canada's status produced a concomitant change in the Free State's position, since Article 2 of the 1921 Treaty, as claimed above, conferred Canada's status on the Free State. See Wheare, THE STATUTE OF WESTMINSTER AND DOMINION STATUS 260 (1947).

[23] Mansergh, SURVEY OF BRITISH COMMONWEALTH AFFAIRS: PROBLEMS OF EXTERNAL POLICY 1931–1939 27 (1952); also see 288–93. See Hogan, NEUTRALITY OF IRELAND 164–66 for development of this viewpoint.

—or Eire, or Ireland, as its name became pursuant to the terms of Article 4—reaffirmed its independence and sovereignty and restated its claims to the whole of Ireland. Article 2 held that the "national territory consists of the whole island of Ireland, its islands and territorial seas"; Article 3 provided that "pending the re-integration of the national territory, and without prejudice to the right of the Parliament and Government established by this Constitution to exercise jurisdiction over the whole of that territory," the laws of Ireland would extend only to the South of Ireland. In short, the Constitution acknowledged the continued de facto existence of Northern Ireland, as well as the legal claim of Ireland to the Six Counties.

Enacted by the people of Ireland in a plebiscite, the Constitution was said by Britain to conflict with the 1921 Treaty and to be "a revolution in law."[24] It did not and was not. The Constitution was, instead, a further exercise of the powers conferred upon the South by the 1931 Statute of Westminster and of the supreme authority of the people to enact a constitution. Even though Britain may well have regarded the Constitution as "a revolution in law," it concluded that the Constitution was consistent with dominion status and that the 1931 Statute furnished the requisite authority to enact such a Constitution.[25]

[24] "The 'enactment' of the Constitution of Eire by the people is, on the British view, a revolution in law. The result of this revolution was recognized by an executive declaration of the British and Dominion Governments at the close of 1937." Wheare, STATUTE OF WESTMINSTER 276.

[25] See Donaldson, ASPECTS OF IRISH LAW 84; Wheare, STATUTE OF WESTMINSTER 272–73, where the author states that although the 1937 Constitution clearly "confers upon Ireland the status of a sovereign, independent state, it is also clear that it does not necessarily exclude the acceptance by this sovereign, independent state of Dominion Status, at any rate in so far as Dominion Status has been defined in conventional terms. The three conventional requirements of Dominion Status were . . . common allegiance along with Great Britain to the same king . . . equality of status with Great Britain . . . and . . . free association with Great Britain; it is in no way subordinate in any aspect

Similarly, Ireland's declaration of neutrality was further evidence of the South's sovereignty and the breaking of the British connection. Although Ireland and all dominion members of the British Commonwealth were "free as air, each of them to make its own choice—peace or war . . . [and] under no constitutional or contractual obligation to co-operate with Britain in war,"[26] Ireland acted as a sovereign state externally associated with the Commonwealth, not as a dominion, in choosing neutrality.

Yet neutrality did not derive from the concept of external association alone, for external considerations, once again, were the by-product of internal conditions. Memories of the war dead of 1914–1918, the betrayal of the 1921 Treaty, and the people of the Six Counties living in subjugation to a British puppet regime compelled Ireland to neutrality. Indeed, how could Ireland "again wage war to win for others that which [its] principal comrade-in-arms had refused, and [was] still refusing to [it]?"[27] It could not. As final, convincing evidence of its freedom and of its opposition to Britain's "Northern policy," Ireland therefore remained neutral.

Neutrality meant greater independence. It also meant,

---

of its domestic or external affairs. But is it freely associated with Great Britain in the British Commonwealth? And does it owe allegiance to the same King? There seems little doubt that the answer is, Yes." In fact, there *is* little doubt, for Article 29 (4) (ii) of the 1937 Constitution would appear to authorize the use by Ireland in external affairs of the same King as Britain.

[26] Harrison, THE NEUTRALITY OF IRELAND: WHY IT WAS INEVITABLE 20–21 (1942). "There were no treaties of defensive and offensive alliance that bound them in advance. They were free to make their choice." See also Mansergh, THE COMMONWEALTH AND THE NATIONS 209 (1948).

[27] Harrison, NEUTRALITY OF IRELAND 32. For support of this position, see Irish Association, IRELAND AND THE WAR 30–38 (1940); Mansergh, COMMONWEALTH AND THE NATIONS 207; Matthews, *Neutrality of Eire,* 162 CONTEMP. 148, 152 (September 1942); Smyllie, *Unneutral Neutral Eire,* 24 FOR. AFF. 317 (January 1946).

however, further opposition to the reunification of the Irish Nation on the part of Britain and the Six County Government. With the passage of the Ireland Act 1949, this opposition took legislative form. Instead of fulfilling its responsibility for the good governance of the Six Counties required by Section 75 of the 1920 Act and instead of advancing the cause of Irish unity, Britain tightened "the ligature which was fastened round the body of Ireland by the Government of Ireland Act, 1920."[28] By pledging financial and military support, Britain acted in contravention of the 1920 Act's proscriptions, legislated improperly for Ireland, and placed a new and different guarantee on the "imposed settlement" of 1921, which was "out of accord with the prospect begun by the Truce of establishing permanent relations of friendship between Ireland and Britain based on the unity in independence of Ireland";[29] by pledging that support, Britain made the intransigence of the North a virtue, for the Unionist Government could thus maintain the status quo of opposition to reunification and of discrimination against Catholics.

But guarantees and intransigence do not build viable political units. Despite British aid, the North remained an

---

[28] Mansergh, DOCUMENTS AND SPEECHES ON BRITISH COMMONWEALTH AFFAIRS 1931–1952 827 (1953). In his speech to the Dail Eireann on May 10, 1949, Taoiseach (Prime Minister) Costello added that the ligature "has been pressing upon the body of our nation since that time [1920], preventing the free flow of its life blood, torturing the souls and minds of the people of Ireland, preventing the full development of Ireland as a sovereign State, hindering the people from giving the deepest spiritual and material help that the Irish people would be able to give if we had a united and free Ireland taking its place amongst the nations of the world." Also see generally 826–30; Donaldson, ASPECTS OF IRISH LAW 93–94.

[29] Lynch, SPEECHES AND STATEMENTS ON IRISH UNITY, NORTHERN IRELAND AND ANGLO-IRISH RELATIONS 66 (1972). The language quoted is from a speech made on July 11, 1971. See also Lynch's speech to the Dail on October 20, 1971. *Ibid.*, 92.

Britain's financial support might well be labeled a "subsidy," for it soon exceeded the contribution paid by the North to Great Britain.

artificial quasi unit with neither organic structure as a distinct community nor "antecedent pretensions—no claims based on history or tradition or the inherent right of an ancient community—to colour or to qualify its local and subordinate institutions."[30] While the North had its own Parliament until 1972, Westminster legislated for it; while it had its own financial system, the bulk of revenue came from the Imperial Treasury in London. Moreover, notwithstanding claims that its fifty-odd years of existence had given the Six Counties a type of permanence and acceptability as an international entity, the fact remained that its powers and limitations began and ended in British statutory law.[31]

If there was any doubt about the fallaciousness of Northern claims, that doubt was shaken in August 1971 and shattered on two separate occasions—March 1972 and May 1974. With the introduction of British troops, the suspension of the Stormont Parliament, the retreat to the pre-1920 policy of direct rule by Westminster, the collapse of the embryonic attempt at power-sharing, and the forced return to total British control, the impermanence of the North was revealed for all the world to see. With it, too, the continuing fact of the age-old struggle to free the whole of Ireland from the shackles of British imperialism was again cogently demonstrated.

THE LONDON VIEWPOINT

Northern Ireland occupies a unique position in British affairs. Even though it is a province of the United Kingdom, Ulster has, except for two brief periods, possessed a separate parliament and possesses, anomalously, a written constitution.[32] Northern Ireland's distinctiveness is further en-

[30] Harrison, ULSTER AND THE BRITISH EMPIRE 1939 62–68 (1939).

[31] *Ibid.*, 62–63; Lynch, *The Anglo-Irish Problem*, 50 FOR. AFF. 601, 613 (1972).

[32] The anomaly is that Northern Ireland, part of the United King-

hanced by the fact that, although Britain can intervene directly when necessary, as demonstrated by the imposition of direct rule in 1972 and 1974, Westminster has chosen for the most part to take a hands-off approach to Northern Ireland. For example, the Parliament at Westminster follows the practice of not discussing Northern Irish affairs, except that latitude is permitted in a member's maiden speech, excepted or reserved matters may be discussed, transferred matters for which there is ministerial responsibility at Westminster may be considered, and discussion is proper on any matter on an acceptable motion or a bill.[33] While these exceptions appear quite broad, there was, in fact, little discussion at Westminster of the affairs of Northern Ireland until 1972, when Westminster was forced to exercise its "blockbuster" power under Section 75 of the 1920 Act.

That Britain's hands-off policy is a matter of political choice and not legal prescription is readily established. If Northern Ireland were classifiable as a dominion, the restrictions on Britain of Section 4 of the Statute of Westminster would certainly be applicable, and Britain would be legally prohibited from taking any action affecting Ulster without Stormont's consent. Since, however, Northern Ireland is neither a dominion nor analogous to one, the relevant statute is the 1920 Act, not the 1931 Statute. Accordingly, Section 75 controls, and Westminster's "supreme authority" remains "unaffected and undiminished over all persons, matters, and things" in Northern Ireland.

---

dom, has a written constitution (the 1920 Act), whereas Great Britain does not.

33 See generally Rose, GOVERNING WITHOUT CONSENSUS 115–18; Calvert, CONSTITUTIONAL LAW IN NORTHERN IRELAND 86–103 (1968). As Calvert states at 103, the practice of nondiscussion "operates only within the sphere of questions and other debates and only in relation to matters in respect of which there is, for the time being, no ministerial responsibility at Westminster." See also Donaldson, ASPECTS OF IRISH LAW 136 where the Northern Ireland-Great Britain relationship is called "quasi-federal"; Dicey, INTRODUCTION TO THE STUDY OF THE LAW OF THE CONSTITUTION 175 (1959), where it is labeled "semi-federal."

But Britain did more than adopt a hands-off policy, for, in effect, it was Northern Ireland's protector against *all* threats. When, therefore, the Free State made its claim to "the whole island of Ireland," Britain quickly responded. To begin with, it maintained that the 1921 Treaty froze the Free State's constitutional position with "the status of Canada as it existed in 1921 except in so far as the United Kingdom government, as the other party to the Treaty, agreed otherwise."[34] Secondly, Britain treated the 1937 Constitution, in which the Free State's claim was made, "as not affecting a fundamental alteration in the position of the Irish Free State."[35] Thirdly, it stated that, notwithstanding the Free State's assertions, Articles 2, 3, and 4 of the 1937 Constitution could not affect the position of Northern Ireland as an integral part of the United Kingdom.[36]

Actions always speak louder than words—and while Britain's words were comforting to Northern Ireland, Westminster's policy with regard to the contribution was still more appreciated by Belfast. According to the terms of the 1920 Act, Northern Ireland was obliged to make a contribution to the United Kingdom exchequer representing its share of imperial services, such as defense and the national debt. Within a few years, however, Westminster had agreed to let Northern Ireland draw on "United Kingdom resources to compensate for sub-standard tax revenues."[37] The net effect of this shift in policy was to make Northern Ireland a "beneficiary," since the amount drawn by Belfast far out-

[34] Mansergh, SURVEY: PROBLEMS OF EXTERNAL POLICY 28.

[35] *Ibid.*, 305.   [36] *Ibid.*, 306.

[37] Rose, GOVERNING WITHOUT CONSENSUS 118. To Northern economists the amount drawn was for "the maintenance of parity"; to others it was a "subsidy" (119). In any case, the combined total of special payments and loans was estimated at £300 million for 1972, and, in addition, there was Westminster support for two key industries of Northern Ireland, aircraft and shipbuilding. See THE FUTURE OF NORTHERN IRELAND: A PAPER FOR DISCUSSION 30 (1972) (hereafter cited as 1972 PAPER). And by 1975, the combined total had reached £430 million. See text accompanying note 57 below.

weighed the sum charged for the contribution for imperial services.

The loudest action in support of Northern Ireland was the Ireland Act 1949. After Ireland "left the Commonwealth, it was a natural corollary to declare that Northern Ireland remained part of the Commonwealth,"[38] for if the South was to be accorded the right of self-determination, then, most assuredly, the same right should be granted to the North. In view of the fact, therefore, that Belfast wanted to maintain the British connection, Section 1 (2) of the 1949 Act provided that Northern Ireland would remain part of Britain until Stormont consented to a change of position, for, as Clement Attlee stated in the House of Commons in 1949, "it is quite impossible that [Britain] should take a position which would suggest that Northern Ireland should be excluded from the Commonwealth and the United Kingdom against its will."[39]

Despite Westminster's refusal to alter the Belfast tie without the consent of the Stormont Parliament, it could do so at any time. Suggestions have been made that the need for Stormont approval, in addition to the threefold consent of Queen, Lords, and Commons, has resulted in a partial abdication of Westminster's sovereignty over the Ulster territory.[40] Suggestions have also been made that the 1949 Act was "legislative in effect and not merely declaratory of an intent,"[41] and, as such, it imposed limited conditions on Westminster. The fact remains, however, that no British Parliament can bind its successors. Thus, even if the Parliament of Northern Ireland is viewed as having, in effect, a veto power over any effort to eject Northern Ireland

[38] Donaldson, ASPECTS OF IRISH LAW 94.

[39] Quoted in Mansergh, DOCUMENTS AND SPEECHES 833; see generally 830–36.

[40] See Donaldson, *The Constitution of Northern Ireland: Its Origins and Development*, 11 UNIV. OF TORONTO L. REV. 1, 41–42 (1955–1956).

[41] Mitchell, CONSTITUTIONAL LAW 64 (1964). Mitchell recognizes, though, that the overwhelming body of authority denies that "a Parliament can fetter its successors" 59; see generally 59–65.

from the Commonwealth and to dissolve the British tie, Westminster, since it has the right to make or unmake any law whatever,[42] could repeal the 1949 Act and—assuming the Union with Ireland Act 1800 and the 1920 Act were also repealed—"transfer sovereignty over the province to Eire, or for that matter to Spain or Portugal."[43] Moreover, the 1949 Act, on its face, requires the Ulster Parliament's consent only for union with Ireland and not for a repeal of the act itself. In any case, therefore, Westminster could sever Northern Ireland from the United Kingdom by first repealing the 1949 Act and then passing an act of cession.

Aside from the legal justification for this position, there are other considerations. It may well be argued, for example, that the wishes of the Ulster majority should be taken into account. But equally valid is the view that Belfast is neither the sole judge as to how it shall be governed as part

---

[42] See generally Calvert, CONSTITUTIONAL LAW IN NORTHERN IRELAND 21–22; Dicey, LAW OF THE CONSTITUTION 39–40, 61–70, and 76–85; Lawrence, THE GOVERNMENT OF NORTHERN IRELAND: PUBLIC FINANCE AND PUBLIC SERVICES 1921–1964 75–76 (1965); O'Higgins, *English Law and the Irish Question*, 1 IR. JUR. 59, 64–65 (1966).

Dicey states that an "Act, whatever its terms, passed by Parliament might be repealed in a subsequent, or indeed in the same, session, and there would be nothing to make the authority of the repealing Parliament less than the authority of the Parliament by which the statute, intended to be immutable, was enacted." Dicey, LAW OF THE CONSTITUTION 68 n.1. Indeed, there are but two limitations on Parliament —an external limitation (the possibility that subjects will disobey or resist the law) and an internal one (the nature of the sovereign power itself). *Ibid.*, 76–85.

In addition to being a constitutional expert, Dicey was a staunch Unionist who vehemently opposed Home Rule. In his famous A LEAP IN THE DARK (1911), he attacked Home Rule as "a leap in the dark" and a patchwork affair "made up of shreds and tatters torn from the institutions of other lands." *Ibid.*, 193. Eventually, the constitutionalist Dicey jettisoned the Constitution and pledged himself to armed resistance by the North. See Heuston, ESSAYS IN CONSTITUTIONAL LAW 2–3 (1964).

[43] Newark, *The Constitution of Northern Ireland: The First Twenty-Five Years*, 8 N. IR. L. Q. 52, 59 (1948).

of the United Kingdom, nor a jury that can waive Northern Ireland's obligations. And among the obligations of membership in the United Kingdom is the acceptance of the sovereignty of Westminster over all the people of the United Kingdom.

Nevertheless, Westminster has consistently adhered to the devolution of powers provided by the 1920 Act. Since law and order was not an excepted or reserved matter, it was "transferred" to Stormont. As such, it was not subject to British control. Although London could advise, assist, or influence in this area, it could not take direct action short of exercising the "blockbuster" power of Section 75 of the 1920 Act.

The British Army, therefore, stood behind the RUC and USC. With operational control of the Army in the hands of London, the calling out of the Army would, in effect, result in the transferral of responsibility for law and order to Westminster. Accordingly, the Army was committed in August 1971 only after the Ulster Government had requested its use and after the civil authorities in Northern Ireland had failed to contain the situation through the use of the regular (RUC) and reserve (USC) forces.

Even after the introduction of the British Army, the situation failed to improve significantly. In March 1972, therefore, Prime Minister Edward Heath—a Conservative—proposed the transfer to Westminster of all responsibility for law and order. When Faulkner rejected the idea, Heath exercised the power of Section 75 to institute direct rule, announced that Stormont stood prorogued, and brought the experiment in devolution to a temporary end. Within a week the Northern Ireland (Temporary Provisions) Act 1972 had put Heath's action into legislative form.

In taking this drastic action, Westminster showed its concern that law and order be restored to Northern Ireland. That concern remained of cardinal significance to London, for in the 1973 White Paper Britain stated that there is "no purpose to which the Government is more firmly committed

109

than the restoration of the rule of law in Northern Ireland, and whatever means are necessary to that end will be made available."[44] It was, therefore, not surprising when, in that same document, Westminster made clear that the new Assembly would, like its predecessor, be subject to a delineation of powers along "excepted," "reserved," and "transferred" lines, but that, unlike Stormont, the Assembly would have no responsibility for law and order (a power reserved to the Secretary of State). It was also not surprising that Westminster stated the obvious and provided that although it would rarely legislate in an area where powers had devolved, "there [could] be no room for ambiguity about the right to do so."[45]

The people of Northern Ireland—Catholics and Protestants alike—viewed the Assembly and the "coalition Executive" with great hope. For the first time in Ulster, there were signs that the years of death and destruction were drawing to a close, that the days of partisan strife were numbered. With the passage of time, however, Protestant extremists lashed out at the fragile power-sharing Executive and shattered the hope of the vast majority of the province's citizenry for a lasting peace. With the rejection in the Assembly of a motion by the "loyalist coalition" calling for renegotiation of the constitutional arrangement in Northern Ireland and with the general work stoppage of May 1974, the stage was set for the resignation of the Unionist members of the Executive, the revoking of the warrants of the remaining Executive members, and the proroguing of the Assembly pursuant to Section 27 (6) of

[44] NORTHERN IRELAND CONSTITUTIONAL PROPOSALS (Cmnd. 5259) 7.

[45] Ibid., 14; also 14–16 for an analysis of the legislative powers of the Assembly and 16–18 for an overview of the executive powers of the Northern Ireland Government. In particular, certain powers under the panoply of law and order—ministerial powers in relation to the police and ministerial powers under any legislation concerned with prisons and the treatment of persons in custody—are reserved to the Secretary of State (17–18). The Assembly powers are contained in the Northern Ireland Constitution Act 1973.

the Northern Ireland Constitution Act 1973. And with the collapse of the Assembly and Executive, the significant progress made earlier in the year—both through the optimism that permeated Ulster as a result of power-sharing and through the change in attitude of the Government of the Republic of Ireland, as shown by the Taoiseach's speech before the Dail Eireann in March, which recognized the constitutional status of the province[46]—was shaken.

Even then, however, Westminster continued to search for a solution acceptable to the three sides to the Ulster struggle. Under the terms of the Northern Ireland Act 1974 (which implemented the 1974 White Paper), the Assembly was dissolved, temporary arrangements were made for the governance of Northern Ireland, and a consultative Northern Ireland Constitutional Convention was proposed. While the future of the province remains clouded, it is certain that any decision affecting that future must of necessity await the Constitutional Convention. Any other decision would suit neither the requirements of British democracy nor the wishes of the Northern Ireland citizenry.

THE BELFAST VIEWPOINT

With the creation of the Government of Northern Ireland in 1920, Britain advanced what it considered to be a logical solution to the Irish problem—a solution that neither the North nor the South wanted. The North wanted to maintain a united Ireland in union with Britain; the South wanted a united, republican Ireland. When Britain rejected these alternatives and passed the 1920 Act, the North ac-

---

[46] In that speech Mr. Cosgrave stated that "the factual position of Northern Ireland is that it is within the United Kingdom and my Government accept this as a fact. I now therefore solemnly re-affirm that the factual position of Northern Ireland within the United Kingdom cannot be changed except by a decision of the majority of the people of Northern Ireland." Quoted in THE NORTHERN IRELAND CONSTITUTION (Cmnd. 5675) (cited hereafter as 1974 WHITE PAPER) at 8.

cepted the decision and worked to make the limited self-government prescribed by the 1920 Act viable. Fifty-odd years of self-government has confirmed Northern Ireland as a "separate polity *de facto* and *de jure*."[47] It has also revealed a unique fact: whereas grants of limited self-government throughout the British Empire have generally resulted in demands for greater independence from Britain, the grant to Northern Ireland has not resulted in such a demand but, on the contrary, "has led rather to uniformity, as between Northern Ireland and Great Britain, in respect of laws and social standards."[48]

The support for Northern Ireland's constitutional stand does not, however, rest with the 1920 Act. It goes back to the Acts of Union, for, although those acts are no longer in force with respect to the South, "they retain their full vigour so far as Northern Ireland is concerned."[49] While it can be argued that Westminster may at any time change previously made laws, the fact remains that there are limits to Parliament's sovereignty. Since the Acts of Union "were constituent Acts, establishing legislative bodies with plenary powers subject to certain entrenched clauses which were not amendable or repealable by these bodies,"[50] Westminster remains bound to accept the continued union of Great Britain and Northern Ireland. Moreover, the acts' very wording denies the claim of absolute legislative authority by expressly limiting sovereignty. Finally, the "hiatus in legislative power" created by the expressed limitations on sovereignty means simply and unequivocally that there are certain acts that may not legally be performed.

Despite the soundness of its legal position, the North was faced after World War I with the 1914 Home Rule Act,

[47] Sheehy, DIVIDED WE STAND: A STUDY OF PARTITION 102 (1955), and generally 95–102.

[48] Harrison, ULSTER AND THE BRITISH EMPIRE 63. See also Quekett, 2 THE CONSTITUTION OF NORTHERN IRELAND 71 (1928).

[49] Calvert, CONSTITUTIONAL LAW IN NORTHERN IRELAND 10.

[50] *Ibid.*, 18, and, generally, 17–19.

which was to become effective in 1920. In the hope of partial salvation, the North accepted the 1920 Act, for it "offered at least a temporary escape from the automatic operation of the Home Rule Act."[51] But it viewed the 1920 Act differently from some of its British brethren. The Northern Ireland Government believed, for instance, that it would be unconstitutional for Westminster to exercise its legislative powers in the area of transferred matters, unless Stormont consented to the exercise of those powers. This belief formed the basis for Ulster's acceptance of the 1920 Act; it resulted from the fear of incorporation in a united Ireland under a parliament dominated by the South; and it was based on the knowledge that "the only way to prevent legislation setting up such a Parliament was to have a legislature of [its] own,"[52] thereby requiring that Parliament's consent prior to union with the South. Furthermore, some Ulstermen viewed Section 75 as being far narrower than Britain intended. In 1968, William Craig stated in a speech that the section did not provide Westminster with absolute sovereignty, that it was "merely a reserve of power to deal with an emergency situation," and that it was "difficult to envisage any situation in which it could be exercised without the consent of the Government of Northern Ireland."[53]

A more pressing problem was the contribution required by the 1920 Act. James Craig voiced optimism from the beginning that the contribution would eventually reflect a

[51] Gwynn, THE HISTORY OF PARTITION (1912–1925) 185 (1950). The Suspensory Act 1914 became law on the same day as the Home Rule Bill of 1914. Under its terms, the effective date of the Home Rule Act was to be suspended for six years.

[52] Jennings, THE LAW AND THE CONSTITUTION 153–54 (1943). It is interesting that the 1959 edition of the work does not contain either that language or any similar language.

[53] As a result of his remarks on December 10, 1968, Craig, O'Neill's Minister for Home Affairs, was forced by O'Neill to resign. Craig's remarks are quoted in Wallace, NORTHERN IRELAND: 50 YEARS OF SELF-GOVERNMENT 39 (1971); see generally 34–39 for a discussion of this point.

contribution of British funds to Northern Ireland rather than, as the 1920 Act stated, a contribution to Britain. From the beginning, too, the contribution was examined periodically to determine if any alteration was needed. By 1923 a committee under the leadership of Lord Colwyn had recommended that after 1924 the "imperial contribution should be based on the difference between Ulster's revenue and [its] actual and necessary expenditure [for services], and necessary expenditure was not to include spending or services that did not exist in Britain or that were superior to services there,"[54] but it was to take into account prices, standards, and wages; by 1931 the contribution to Britain virtually disappeared; by 1936, the Unemployment (Agreement) Act (Northern Ireland) had provided Ulster with unemployment assistance; by 1938 the return of Ireland's ports to Dublin meant that Ulster alone could be relied upon and that Ulster's survival as a self-governing body was more than ever in Britain's interest; by 1946 an agreement had been reached under which parity of services and taxation between Britain and Northern Ireland was to be established; by 1949 the Social Services Agreement (1949) had provided that if the cost of social services was higher in Ulster than Britain, Britain would assume eighty percent of the excess cost; by 1951 Britain was making payments for unemployment insurance; by 1961 assistance from Britain to Ulster had reached £45 million a year;[55] by 1972–1973 the special payments and subsidies from Great Britain to Northern Ireland totaled £200 million, and loans from the National Loans Fund provided an additional £100 million to be used for lending to local authorities and other statutory bodies;[56]

---

[54] Lawrence, GOVERNMENT OF NORTHERN IRELAND 45; see generally 37–102 for a detailed discussion of the changing "contribution."

[55] *Ibid.*, 87–88. Indeed, it might well be said that "on the ramshackle foundations of the Act of 1920 he (James Craig) and his colleagues had built, not a half-way house, but a lean-to whose stability depended on the ties that bound it to Britain." *Ibid.*, 61.

[56] See British Information Service, NORTHERN IRELAND 11–13 (1973).

and by 1974–1975 the special payments and subsidies totaled £350 million and the loans an additional £80 million.[57] James Craig had been right.

With the passage of the Ireland Act 1949, "a firm seal [was set] on one of the clearest conventions of the British constitution"[58] and the constitutional status of Northern Ireland under the Acts of Union was reaffirmed. In addition, the 1949 Act acknowledged that Stormont was the voice of Northern Ireland for the purpose of negotiations or agreements amending the Acts of Union. As such, the 1949 Act confirmed that the Acts of Union were "a bilateral treaty, not subject to unilateral amendment . . . [and that] the events of 1921–26, in which the right to speak on behalf of the people of Northern Ireland as to whether or not that territory should opt to remain within the United Kingdom was regarded as having become vested in the Northern Parliament."[59]

The importance of the 1949 Act is heightened by the fact that the act cannot be repealed by Westminster without Stormont's consent. To begin with, the act so transformed parliamentary procedure that any measure affecting Ulster that lacked Stormont's consent would not, in truth, be a valid statute.[60] Secondly, the fact that it is constitutional legislation creates a presumption of statutory interpretation against its repeal. Thirdly, since a basic principle of constitutional law is that one cannot do indirectly that which cannot be done directly, since repeal is a step towards cession, and since cession necessitates Ulster's approval, repeal of the act requires Stormont's consent. Lastly, in view of the

---

See generally NORTHERN IRELAND: FINANCIAL ARRANGEMENTS AND LEGISLATION (Cmnd. 4998) (1972).

[57] 1974 WHITE PAPER 12.

[58] Calvert, CONSTITUTIONAL LAW IN NORTHERN IRELAND 11. "The convention is founded in the Acts of Union." *Ibid.*

[59] *Ibid.*, 24–25. The view expressed by Calvert is advanced not as conclusive but as one "which makes greatest sense."

[60] See Heuston, ESSAYS IN CONSTITUTIONAL LAW 6–7 and 29–30.

115

fact that the act has, in effect, created a fourth estate in addition to the constituent estates of the Queen, Lords, and Commons, repeal is ineffective without consent—"once a new estate is added to Parliament, it is added for all time unless it should itself consent to or acquiesce in . . . an abridgement of its powers"[61] (as did the House of Lords to the Parliamentary Acts).

Following the placing of the Ireland Act 1949 on the Statute Book, Ulster felt safe. It had its long history of successful governance; it had the full backing of Britain and the law. As a result of this feeling of security, the Ulster Government continued to serve all its people well. Even after the so-called civil rights marches began in 1968 and even after the terrorist activities of the subversive IRA made a request for British troops necessary in 1969, the feeling persisted. Although Britain seemed, at times, to be withholding adequate manpower to wipe out the IRA extremists and advocated taking actions, such as the disbanding of the USC, that were clearly deleterious, it always appeared supportive of the Northern Ireland Government.

It came as a rude shock, therefore, when London "ordered" the transfer of the law and order powers from Stormont to Westminster, for a government without such powers is a government in name only. When Belfast quite naturally refused, and London responded by proroguing Stormont and, in rapid succession, imposing direct rule, a weak Assembly and a farcical coalition Executive, and a return to direct rule after the failure of the Executive to deal with IRA murders, Northern Ireland faced its gravest threat since prepartition days. While London was quick to state that its actions would in no way prejudice Ulster's position under the 1949 Act, the fact remains that direct rule must have that effect.

To substantiate this assertion, it is simply necessary to refer to the report of the Ulster Unionist Council in 1936. At a time when there was widespread support for the policy

---

[61] Calvert, CONSTITUTIONAL LAW IN NORTHERN IRELAND 29.

of direct British rule, the report stated that the cry, "back to Westminster," was dangerous because "Northern Ireland without a Parliament of [its] own would be a standing temptation to certain British politicians to make another bid for a final settlement with Irish republicans."[62] The applicability of this rationale to today's situation is all too obvious to require elaboration. Suffice it to say, therefore, that Ulster must reestablish its Parliament at the earliest possible date, for, as the introduction of direct rule indicates, Britain is less concerned with what is constitutional, legal, or right than what is expedient. For that reason, even the powerless Assembly proposed in the 1973 White Paper and created by the Northern Ireland Constitution Act 1973 received the support of responsible Ulstermen. Although the Assembly lacked essential tools such as the power over law and order, it was a weapon with which to defend Northern Ireland's interests. As a result of its demise, it is now critical to fashion a new weapon.

CONCLUSIONS

The answers to the questions posed seem quite clear. Despite Southern claims, Ulster is part of the United Kingdom. In addition, despite Ulster's distinctive position and Northern and Southern views, London has complete legal power over Northern Ireland's fate.

That the political status of Ulster is unique is beyond dispute. Having "proceeded from full integration in 1800, via a sudden extensive measure of legal self-government in the early 1920's and a period of hesitancy thereafter, to a gradual approximation towards its earlier position, at least so far as the substance of political organisation is concerned,"[63] Northern Ireland has, with the assumption of

62 The report is cited in Lawrence, GOVERNMENT OF NORTHERN IRELAND 75.

63 Calvert, CONSTITUTIONAL LAW IN NORTHERN IRELAND 123. As stated earlier, the origin of this status was that Ulster "was obliged in 1920

117

direct rule by Britain, come full circle. As the second cycle begins, it is obvious that the status of Ulster will continue to be, as it has always been, what London determines that it should be.

To admit this fact is not to justify Britain's Northern Ireland policy, which was imperialistic and remains, as Southerners claim, a "giant gerrymander" and a monument to the violation of the principle of self-determination; to recognize the political reality of the situation is not to acknowledge that it is morally right. But, however much the status quo might appear unjustified and immoral, there can be little doubt of the legal soundness of Britain's position in Ulster.

The argument that the Acts of Union cannot be amended or repealed seems, therefore, incorrect. Not only does the weight of legal authority establish that Parliament can at any time change any law, regardless of whether or not the act in question is a constituent act, but also the argument is weakened by the fact that the Acts of Union were really a sham. Since in 1800 Britain had as much control over Ireland as it has over Ulster today, there was never any doubt that, once Britain decided to unite Britain and Ireland, the Irish Parliament would approve the decision. Accordingly, to say that the Acts of Union can legally restrain British action in 1975 is to give a meaning to the acts that was not intended and is not justified.

If a flaw exists in the legality of Westminster's position, it arises from Britain's alleged violations of at least the spirit, if not the letter, of the 1920 Act and the 1921 Treaty. By allowing the 1920 Act's contribution to be reduced and then to become, in effect, a contribution to Northern Ireland, Britain might well be said to have misled the South into accepting the 1921 Treaty, even though, it must be realized,

---

to accept a Parliament that her people did not ask for; and the self-government imposed upon them was the outcome, not of discussion on the abstract merits and demerits of parliamentary devolution, but of the debate on Irish Home Rule." Lawrence, GOVERNMENT OF NORTHERN IRELAND 75.

Britain had the right at any time to change British law; by permitting the Boundary Commission to disband without reaching an agreement, Britain again might be said to have been unfair to the Free State, although, when it appeared that the Boundary Commission was about to make a ruling unfavorable to the South, it was the Free State that proposed the 1925 Agreement. In any case, both contentions are only tangentially relevant to the questions at hand.

What is directly relevant is Section 75 of the 1920 Act. Despite the assertion of William Craig and other Ulstermen that Section 75 was "merely a reserve of power to deal with an emergency situation," Section 75 was not so limited, for under it Britain retained full control in all matters. Ulster was, is, and will remain, until Westminster decides otherwise, "a purely statutory body of limited authority, exercising powers determinable by law, and as unquestionably subject to the British or United Kingdom Government as is the County Council of London."[64] In brief, therefore, Northern Ireland remains a distinct entity—although, since British control over the province is so complete, it might almost be said to be a fictional entity.

Regardless of whether or not Ulster's distinctive existence is fictional, Ireland has no legal claims to the Northern territory. Ireland's claims, as expressed in the 1937 Constitution, are, in light of the years of British rule and the events of the 1920s, historically understandable but legally indefensible. Law and time simply do not lend support to the position that seemed to be espoused by the South until the Taoiseach made his memorable speech in March 1974. To begin with, Ulster is British—as it has been since 1172—and any claim of Ireland to the North would appear to be inferior to Britain's claim. It would seem, moreover, that if Northern Ireland were deemed by London to be separate from Britain, it would be an independent state and not a part of Ireland, for Ulster—with a set population, a defined territory, and a government—already possesses the essentials

[64] Harrison, ULSTER AND THE BRITISH EMPIRE 61.

119

of statehood. Furthermore, the assertion that the demarcation line between North and South was meant to be temporary is immaterial and accords with neither reality nor law, since, as evidenced by the partitions of Germany, Korea, and Vietnam, the passage of time often converts the temporary into the permanent for purposes of international law.

The fact, therefore, that in 1937 Ireland decreed its jurisdiction over "the whole island of Ireland" does not give credence to the Southern claim; the fact that Ulster has chosen to cling to Britain does not, in and of itself, protect the Northern claim to an identity separate from Ireland. Either claim is only as strong as Britain determines it to be. Legally entitled to do as it wishes as a result of eight hundred years of rule, Britain holds all the Ulster cards. If Britain determines that Ireland should control the North, it can repeal the Union with Ireland Act 1800, the 1920 Act, and the 1949 Act and cede the North to Ireland; if Britain determines that Northern Ireland's status as a British province is to be maintained, it can do so; if Britain determines that Ulster should be independent, it can pass legislation that, on top of fifty-five years of quasi self-governance, would fulfill the remaining condition of statehood (Northern Ireland presently lacks only the capacity to enter into relations with other states)[65] and make Northern Ireland a state in all but Southern eyes; and if Britain determines that the people of Ulster should decide their own future in accord with the principle of self-determination that it rejected for Ireland as a whole in 1920, it can do so—as evidenced by the 1973 elections and plebiscite.

While the future status of Northern Ireland is, therefore, undetermined, it is evident that Ulster is, at least for the

[65] The question of statehood is discussed in detail in Bishop, ed., INTERNATIONAL LAW: CASES AND MATERIALS 300–33 (1971); Briggs, THE LAW OF NATIONS 99–132 (1952); H. Lauterpacht, RECOGNITION IN INTERNATIONAL LAW 26–38 (1947). For the application of the criteria for statehood in a modern situation, see Ijalaye, *Was Biafra at Any Time a State in International Law?* 65 AM. J. INT'L L. 551 (1971).

time being, an integral part of the United Kingdom. It is also obvious that even though the Dublin, London, and Belfast actors have title roles on the Northern stage, Britain will continue to have free rein over the status of Northern Ireland.

CHAPTER IV

Uncivil Strife: The Ulster Struggle and the Law of Civil Strife

WITH the status of Northern Ireland as part of the United Kingdom established, the legal aspects of the Ulster conflict can be more readily understood. Since "conflicts between two distinct territorial units which the [world] community expects to be relatively permanent, are, for purposes of policy about coercion, to be treated as conflicts between established states,"[1] the use of force—be it covert or overt—across the North-South line of division constitutes, even if the status of Ulster is questioned, an illegal act; since world order requires that an international entity shall not exercise force across its border except for individual or collective self-defense, such force must be considered illegal whenever the border or line in question has "long been continued and widely recognized."[2] If, indeed, a minimum world ᴵpublic order is to be fact and not illusion, "rational community policy must be directed to the coercive interactions of territorially organized communities of consequential size, whatever the 'lawfulness' of their origin and whatever the prior nice-

[1] McDougal & Feliciano, LAW AND MINIMUM WORLD PUBLIC ORDER 221–22 (1961).

[2] In discussing armistice and cease-fire lines—which the North-South boundary can certainly be called—Quincy Wright stated the position quite concisely: "While hostilities across such a line by the government in control of one side, claiming title to rule the entire state, seems on its face to be civil strife, if such lines have long been continued and widely recognized, as have those in Germany, Palestine, Kashmir, Korea, Vietnam and the Straits of Formosa, they assume the character of international boundaries. Hostilities across them immediately constitute breaches of *international* peace." Wright, *International Law and Civil Strife*, 53 AM. SOC. INT'L L. PROC. 145, 151 (1959).

ties in the presence or absence of the ceremony of recognition."[3]

But the law is not always observed, either in the Ulster conflict or in struggles in other areas of the world. The use of force employed across state or other "relatively permanent" lines is, increasingly, not the classic armed attack of old, but an indirect aggression. By fomenting and abetting indigenous conflicts, hostile foreign states are no less capable of destroying the independent existence of states, territories, and other international entities. And, they are able to do so without suffering depletion of their own human resources or detection by an often undiscerning world—a fact that provides further incentive for the continued commission of vicarious acts of aggression.

Through the medium of third-party groups located within the target entity which it supplies with the requisite support—arms, clothing, food, money, and training—to subvert the governmental structure of the target, the foreign state accomplishes its objective. Even more importantly, it often provides strategic and tactical direction and "specialists in subversion, sabotage, infiltration, fomentation of civil violence, and *coups d'état*."[4]

As the tide of revolution continues to sweep the world,[5]

---

[3] McDougal & Feliciano, LAW AND PUBLIC ORDER 221, n.222.

[4] *Ibid.*, 191. The entire question of coercion is discussed in depth and with real insight, 121–260. Since the matter is largely beyond the purview of this study, this work is highly recommended.

[5] To most Westerners, the concept of revolution is difficult to accept. Westerners have tended to forget that it was often revolution which set them free; and the revolutions of 1688, 1776, and 1789 in Britain, the United States, and France, respectively, demonstrate parallels to the revolutions of today of which Westerners should not remain oblivious. Yet recognition of the "right of revolution" and of certain parallels to our own past need not, does not, mean acceptance of the belief that freedom is found in and through violence and that the "practice of violence binds [the populace] together as a whole, since each individual forms a violent link in the great chain, a part of the great organism of violence which has surged upward in reaction to the settler's violence in the beginning" (Fanon, THE WRETCHED OF THE EARTH

this new medium of aggression becomes more dangerous, and the need to distinguish between this form of aggression and indigenous revolts becomes more acute. While the concept of revolution cannot be embraced, it is, given the feudalistic tyranny that exists in many areas, both understandable and acceptable. The fomentation and abetting of revolution from abroad, though, must be condemned. With the resulting imposition of foreign rule, however subtle it might be, one form of tyranny is merely replaced by another; with the threat of nuclear holocaust and the intensity of existing ideological schisms, aggression in any form is dangerous, for sparks from any part of the world could easily ignite the nuclear fuse. Aggression must, therefore, be divorced from purely internal upheaval.[6]

What makes the distinction particularly difficult is the fact that revolution is so easily exported. Under the guise of resistance to racism or wars of national liberation, exported revolution blends with local conditions to produce a seemingly indigenous conflict. Were such conditions lacking in the target, the hostile foreign state's actions would be both readily discernible and largely ineffective. Since, however, human injustice is prevalent in much of the world,

---

93 [1968]). It also does not require acceptance of the view that to shoot down a European is to kill two birds with one stone, since "there remain a dead man, and a free man; the survivor, for the first time, feels a *national* soil under his foot" (Sartre, *Preface* to *ibid.*, 22).

[6] In the course of their study, McDougal and Feliciano suggest that such a determination can be made by examining "the relation, if any, of the internal disturbance to claimed world revolutionary movements; the differential allegiance of various internal groups to varying competing systems of world public order; the degree of sharing of powers admitted in internal structures of public order; the degree to which internal practices, institutionalized or not, constitute 'provocative conditons' by denial of human rights to minorities or even whole populations. . . ." LAW AND PUBLIC ORDER 193, n.164. Black, in THE DYNAMICS OF MODERNIZATION 264 (1966), predicts that there will be 10 to 15 revolutions a year in the foreseeable future for less-developed countries. The need for this differentiation is, therefore, evident.

those actions are effectively hidden in what ostensibly appears to be "an avenging whirlwind of popular feeling suddenly and spontaneously blowing up against unbearable oppression."[7]

To confuse further an already complex situation, one of the first actions of rebels engaged in a purely internal conflict is to request outside assistance. Where the request is granted, the revolution certainly cannot be said to be exported. But the result is, nevertheless, the same, for once the desired assistance is provided, the conflict is in fact transformed into indirect aggression by the foreign state. At the same time, the rebels often become just as docile and "pawn-like" as their counterparts in cases of exported revolution. And the resulting situation is, from the world perspective, potentially just as dangerous in the case of external assistance to rebellious forces in an ongoing conflict as in the instance of the initiation of strife in a tranquil entity.

In order to facilitate the distinction between indigenous and exported conflict and to balance the countervailing forces that abound in civil struggles, various principles of law have been developed. Unfortunately, however, they have suffered a severe battering over the years. With the upsurge of racial conflicts and wars of national liberation and with the situations that exist in Northern Ireland and in other trouble-spots throughout the world, those principles should be examined carefully to determine their applicability to existing civil struggles and their viability for the future.

[7] Barnet, INTERVENTION AND REVOLUTION: THE UNITED STATES IN THE THIRD WORLD 48 (1968). Barnet also reminds us (49) that, as Aristotle pointed out, " 'insult' is the primary condition that provokes rebellion. Men will put up with egregious exploitation as long as it seems dictated by the natural order. It is only when economic misery can be traced to human injustice that the possibility of a political remedy emerges." See also Gilly, *Introduction* to Fanon, STUDIES IN A DYING COLONIALISM 12 (1965). On the question of resistance to racism, see Nyerere, *Rhodesia in the Context of Southern Africa*, 44 FOR. AFF. 373 (1966); on wars of national liberation, see Barnet, INTERVENTION AND REVOLUTION 60–76.

A cursory review of the literature of civil strife quickly reveals not only a certain amount of doubt about the prescriptions of international law but also a great deal of confusion about the relevant terminology. Whereas one writer will describe the events of a particular conflict in terms of insurrection, revolution, and civil war, another expert will characterize civil strife in terms of rebellion, insurgency, and belligerency in order "to distinguish among conflicts along a continuum of ascending intensity."[8] For purposes of clarity, one set of definitions—rebellion, insurgency, and belligerency—will be used extensively throughout this analysis.

The confused state of the law of civil strife is further demonstrated by the differing views as to what foreign states may do during such conflict. Under one view, civil conflict—which is said to exist "when two opposing parties within a state have recourse to arms for the purpose of obtaining power in the state, or when a portion of the population of a state rises in arms against the legitimate government"[9]—is a domestic issue, and, as such, there can be no foreign interference. Conversely, it has long been maintained that interference in the affairs of another entity may occur by right.[10]

---

[8] Falk, *Janus Tormented: The International Law of Internal War*, in Rosenau, ed., INTERNATIONAL ASPECTS OF CIVIL STRIFE 185, 197. Compare this with Padelford, *International Law and the Spanish Civil War*, 31 AM. J. INT'L L. 226, 277 (1937); see also Hull & Novogrod, LAW AND VIETNAM 73–96 (1968), from which portions of this chapter are adapted.

[9] Thomas & Thomas, NON-INTERVENTION: THE LAW AND ITS IMPORT IN THE AMERICAS 215 (1956). See also Oppenheim, 2 INTERNATIONAL LAW 209 (7th ed., 1952).

[10] "Several reasons are generally advanced for the acceptance of the latter principle. First of all, a state may hold a protectorate which gives it a right to interfere in all external affairs of the protected [entity] and the civil strife is influenced by external forces; secondly, a state or states may interfere to force a delinquent state to submit to the law if that party, in time of war or peace, violates rules which are universally recognized by custom or are laid down in law-making treaties; thirdly, a state that has guaranteed by treaty the form of government of [an entity] may interfere in case of a change in form of the

That interference has, in fact, been the rule rather than the exception is amply demonstrated by centuries of history. From the Roman Empire, to the Middle Ages, to the wars of the sixteenth and seventeenth centuries, to the democratic movements of the nineteenth century, the more powerful political entities of the world have rarely hesitated to interfere in the affairs of the less powerful. To the extent that there has been any hesitancy at all, credit must be given to somewhat imperfect, but widely recognized, principles of law, since, through the years, states have not wanted to be accused of violating those principles.

The Insurgency-Belligerency Doctrine

Under international law, the economic, political, and social structures of a state are entirely within the discretion of the state. Since, therefore, the causes of *pure* civil strife are found in those structures, the outbreak of a rebellion —according to the tenets of this doctrine—does not in any way affect that state's relationship with other states. Even when the conflict spreads and fulfills the requirements of insurgency—effective, organized, and prolonged resistance that either engulfs a definite area or is fairly widespread— the affected state's juridical status remains unchanged. As the intermediate stage between domestic tranquility and all-out war, insurgency does not, for instance, alter the duty of noninterference by other states in its affairs; it does not raise the question of neutrality, since neutrality arises only when war in a technical sense exists, that is, when the insurgency is transformed into belligerency; and it does not create a new relationship between the state recognizing the insurgency and the parties to the conflict, for the recognition of insurgency is nothing more than the mere acknowledgment of high-level insurrection. For these reasons, aid

---

government; and, finally, a state may interfere in a civil struggle to protect its nationals." Hull & Novogrod, LAW AND VIETNAM 74. See generally Oppenheim, 1 INTERNATIONAL LAW 262–67 (4th ed., 1928).

may continue to be given to the established government, and, concomitantly, no assistance may be rendered to the insurgents (who are to be treated as criminals who have violated the laws of the state).[11]

A change is considered to occur, however, when the belligerency of the insurgents is recognized. Belligerency is said to result either when the legitimate government recognizes that status by taking action that elevates the insurgents to the level of belligerents or when a particular civil struggle has reached a certain intensity and affects the interests of the recognizing power.[12] More specifically, insurgency is said

[11] As has been succinctly stated: "Le gouvernement légitime seul représente, après comme avant, le pays devant le droit international et dans toutes occasions. Les insurgés sont toute d'abord traités de criminels qui ont violé le droit pénal de leur propre pays. Ils doivent subir l'effet des lois dans toute sa rigueur. C'est pourquoi, du point de vue du droit international, il ne saurait être question d'un état de guerre." ("As was the case earlier, it is only the legitimate government which represents the country in international law and on all occasions. Insurgents are in the first instance regarded as criminals who have contravened the criminal code of their own country. They should suffer the full effect of the law. That is why, from an international legal viewpoint, it would only be a question of a state of war.") Wehberg, *La Guerre civile et le droit international*, 63 RECUEIL DES COURS (Hague Academy of International Law) 7, 41 (1938). It should nevertheless be recognized that some authorities believe that the continuance of assistance to the established government during insurgency may constitute interference and the denial of the right of the state "to decide for itself—by a physical contest, if necessary, between rival forces—the nature and form of its government. This is so especially when some but not all of the requirements of recognition of belligerency are present. In such cases the formal distinction between the lawful government and the insurgents is particularly undesirable." H. Lauterpacht, RECOGNITION IN INTERNATIONAL LAW 233 (1947). See also Wehberg, *La Guerre civile* 57; Wiesse, LE DROIT INTERNATIONAL APPLIQUÉ AUX GUERRES CIVILES 86 (1898).

[12] Recognition of belligerency may occur either by a formal declaration or, more usually, as it did in the American Civil War, by a government proclamation of a blockade of the insurgents' ports. See H. Lauterpacht, RECOGNITION IN INTERNATIONAL LAW 177; Wilson, *Recognition of Insurgency and Belligerency*, 31 AM. SOC. INT'L L. PROC. 136,

to evolve into belligerency when there exists an armed conflict of a general (as distinguished from a purely local) character, the insurgents occupy and administer a substantial portion of national territory, the hostilities are conducted by organized forces pursuant to the laws of war, and there is a need for outside states to alter their position by recognizing a state of belligerency.[13] Once belligerency has been declared, the recognizing foreign state acquires no new rights in its relations with the "ex-insurgents." It does, however undertake new duties, for, unless it elects to join either the belligerents' or government's forces as a cobelligerent, the foreign state must assume a posture of strict neutrality with respect to each side. Accordingly, the recognition of belligerency is detrimental to the government of the strife-torn state, since it bestows upon the "ex-insurgents" the same rights that the titular government possesses and results, should assistance to that government be continued after belligerency is recognized, in the legalization of aid to the "ex-insurgents" in the same amount as that provided to the titular government.

While the traditional insurgency-belligerency doctrine appears to distinguish quite lucidly among rebellion, insurgency, and belligerency and to provide easily measurable criteria for each phase of civil strife, it has, in fact, been the source of disorder and the object of noncompliance. Indeed, each of the four criteria for ascertaining the existence of a state of belligerency falls prey to these criticisms.

---

141 (1937). See also *The Three Friends*, 166 U.S. 1, 63–64 (1896); Thomas & Thomas, NON-INTERVENTION 219.

13 For additional discussion of these requirements, see Kotzsch, THE CONCEPT OF WAR: CONTEMPORARY HISTORY AND INTERNATIONAL LAW 220–40 (1956); H. Lauterpacht, RECOGNITION IN INTERNATIONAL LAW 176; Oppenheim, 1 INTERNATIONAL LAW 249 (8th ed., 1955); Rougier, *Les Guerres civiles et le droit des gens* 39–41 (1903); Beale, *The Recognition of the Cuban Belligerency*, 9 HARV. L. REV. 406, 407 (1896); McNair, *The Law Relating to the Civil War in Spain*, 53 LAW Q. REV. 471, 477–82 (1937).

To begin with, it is unclear whether a prolonged period of armed violence in a few provinces would constitute belligerency, or whether the entire state must be engulfed in civil conflict before the prerequisite of "an armed conflict of a general character" is fulfilled. It would seem, however, that the conflagration need not consume the state to meet the condition.

Secondly, there are problems concerning the requirement that the insurgents "occupy and administer a substantial portion of national territory." It might, for example, be argued that the insurgents must control a delineated area (as in the American Civil War) rather than mere pockets of the state. It might also be suggested that martial control of the populace would fit within the parameters of "occupy and administer." In each instance, though, the contention would probably fail—and, basically, for the same reason. Since the philosophy behind the belligerency test is the recognition of genuine, widespread opposition to the de jure government, any effort that does not accurately measure popular approval would be in conflict with that philosophy. Both the "designated area" and "martial control" standards are inaccurate measurements. In the former case, the inaccuracy results from the failure to measure opposition that falls short of actual territorial control; in the latter situation, it stems from the erroneous and dangerous conclusion that those individuals who live under forced rule must, of necessity, support their rulers, when, in point of fact, the reverse is more likely to be true. In addition to these points of confusion, doubt exists as to whether the insurgents must either form a government or have merely a "governmental apparatus" at their command. Although in the turmoil of civil strife it would be unreasonable to expect a formal government, it would appear that the insurgents must possess a viable apparatus that constitutes, in effect, a "shadow government," administers the territory under their control, and, following the successful termination of hostilities, may be transformed into an organization capable of assuming governmental operation of the entire country.

Thirdly, there is some disagreement concerning the assertion that the hostilities must be conducted "in accordance with the rules of war." The issue at stake is whether the insurgents must adhere to these prescriptions, or whether they must simply be prepared to meet them. Despite arguments to the contrary, the former proposition is both preferred and preferable. Recognition must be merited; to be merited, the contest must be "carried on with the dimensions and by the method of war and not by the methods of savagery."[14] A contrary conclusion would furnish moral support to forces that oppose the ends of civilization. For that reason, the insurgents must clearly demonstrate their adherence to the rules of war before they will be accorded belligerent status.

Finally, confusion prevails with respect to the circumstances that must exist before outside states recognize belligerency. Several points, however, are beyond question. Of cardinal significance is the principle that recognition is not the granting of a favor. Instead, belligerency is to be recognized only when the relations between the foreign state and the state embroiled in civil strife are seriously disrupted by the conflict, thereby necessitating a definition— or redefinition—of relations between the foreign state and

---

[14] Stowell, INTERNATIONAL LAW 41 (1931). See also *Droits et devoirs en cas d'insurrection*, 18 ANNUAIRE DE L'INSTITUTE DE DROITS INTERNA-TIONAL 217 (1900); Greenspan, THE MODERN LAW OF LAND WARFARE 18–19 (1959); Rougier, LES GUERRES CIVILES 384; Westlake, 1 INTERNA-TIONAL LAW 51 (1910). As Rougier states at 394, "ceux qui prétendent obtenir leur liberté en reversant comme pourraient le faire des sauvages toutes les conquêtes de la civilisation n'ont rien à voir ni avec le droit des gens ni avec l'humanité." ("Those who attempt to attain their liberty in a manner similar to barbarians overturning the achievements of civilization have nothing to do with either international law or with humanity itself.") A discussion of the laws of war will be deferred to Chapter v, "Limits of War."

the participants to the struggle.[15] In the absence of conditions that "force" the foreign state to take such action, its recognition of the insurgents as belligerents would be gratuitous and, as such, would constitute an offense against the de jure government and interference in the domestic affairs of another state.

Even though the insurgency-belligerency doctrine was developed to deal with problems resulting from the effect of civil strife on shipping, its application today is far broader. To some observers it might seem that the older and more restrictive interpretation must still exist, since belligerency is infrequently declared. But this situation results because insurgents generally fail to satisfy fully the necessary requirements, for, even when a civil struggle is of considerable duration and magnitude, one of the other conditions of belligerency may be lacking. In addition, as was the case in the Spanish conflict of 1936 to 1939 and the more recent Vietnam struggle, the direct participation of outside states in an ostensibly civil conflict transforms the struggle into an international contest and, in the process, makes the insurgency-belligerency doctrine inapplicable.

There are, of course, other factors that contribute to the rare invocation of the doctrine. One factor is the amount of discretion reserved to the recognizing state in declaring belligerency. While outside states affected by the struggle should grant the insurgents belligerency status when the factual requirements have been satisfied, it is up to them to determine when the criteria have been met. Although these states are free to determine the existence of the condi-

[15] "Une tierce Puissance n'est autorisée à reconnaître les droits de belligerence que si ses droits et intérêts propres exigent une définition de ses propres rapports avec les Parties aux prises dans la guerre civile." ("A third power is only authorized to recognize in others the rights accorded belligerents if its own rights and self-interests require a definition of its own relations with the parties engaged in the civil struggle.") Wehberg, *La Guerre civile* 88–89. See also Thomas & Thomas, NON-INTERVENTION 220; Wheaton, ELEMENTS OF INTERNATIONAL LAW 34 (1866).

tions of recognition as "promulgated" by international law, their discretion does not extend to an arbitrary liberty of action after these conditions have been clearly ascertained. A state may examine the facts of a particular conflict to determine if those facts warrant the status of belligerency. Once it is apparent that the insurgents have fulfilled the conditions for belligerency, however, the outside state's discretion to recognize that belligerency legally disappears. Concomitantly, it is replaced by a duty to recognize belligerency, for "when recognition is refused notwithstanding the existence of the requirements of belligerency, it amounts, when coupled with discrimination against the insurgents, to intervention denying to a state what is the essence of its sovereignty and independence, namely the right of self-determination."[16] All too often, though, this discretion has been abused; all too often, the discretion has been used "to promote [a state's] policies by recognizing facts not yet established or by refusing to recognize facts which are at the moment established";[17] and all too often, the discretion —a supposedly judicial act based on the application of legal criteria to factual evidence—degenerates into a mere legislative or political act.

Another factor of concern to some is that under the traditional test there is a moral pressure to escalate. It is argued that the standard fails to weigh the relative merits of the participants' positions. It is also asserted that the doctrine, by focusing attention on the external assistance rendered to the insurgents, suggests that the insurgents are simply

16 H. Lauterpacht, RECOGNITION IN INTERNATIONAL LAW 230. See also Phillimore, 1 COMMENTARIES UPON INTERNATIONAL LAW 553 (1879); Thomas & Thomas, THE ORGANIZATION OF AMERICAN STATES 178–79 (1963); Wheaton, ELEMENTS OF INTERNATIONAL LAW 55.

17 Wright, *Some Thoughts about Recognition*, 44 AM. J. INT'L L. 548, 557 (1950). See also Hackworth, DIGEST OF INTERNATIONAL LAW 319 (1940); Wiesse, LE DROIT INTERNATIONAL 20; Falk, *Janus Tormented* 200; Friedmann, *Intervention, Civil War and the Role of International Law*, 59 AM. SOC. INT'L L. PROC. 67, 72 (1965); Garner, *Recognition of Belligerency*, 32 AM. J. INT'L L. 106, 111–12 (1938).

instruments of the foreign power providing the aid. When the struggle is cast in these terms, it is concluded, "acceptance of insurgent victory seems a pusillanimous withdrawal at High Noon."[18]

Yet, despite this problem and despite the elusiveness of the technical formulations that make up the standard, the insurgency-belligerency doctrine does "afford relevant guidance to contemporary decision-makers who must cope with this problem in appraising the genuineness and degree of internal change in authority and effective control."[19] As will be discussed, it remains both the present law and the basis for a more ordered future in the area of civil strife.

Additional Customary Prescriptions

Aside from its rights and obligations under the traditonal insurgency-belligerency doctrine, a foreign state has several affirmative duties under general international law. It has, for instance, the duty to police its frontiers to insure that its territory is not used as a base by armed bands operating against the government of the target state.[20] Since the near impossibility of complete prevention is realized, the law imposes on a state the responsibility to employ "due dili-

---

[18] Farer, *Intervention in Civil Wars: A Modest Proposal*, 67 COLUM. L. REV. 266, 272 (1967).

[19] McDougal & Feliciano, LAW AND PUBLIC ORDER 194, n.164. McDougal and Feliciano do not state the proposition as positively. They assert, instead, that the standard "may possibly afford" the needed guidelines.

[20] See Eagleton, THE RESPONSIBILITY OF STATES IN INTERNATIONAL LAW 88–92 (1928); Kelsen, PRINCIPLES OF INTERNATIONAL LAW 205–206 (1966); Garcia-Mora, INTERNATIONAL RESPONSIBILITY FOR HOSTILE ACTS OF PRIVATE PERSONS AGAINST FOREIGN STATES 15–46 (1962); Brownlie, *International Law and the Activities of Armed Bands*, 7 INT'L & COMP. L. Q. 712, 734 (1958); Curtis, *The Law of Hostile Military Expeditions as Applied by the United States*, 8 AM. J. INT'L L. 1, 36 (1914); Lauterpacht, *Revolutionary Activities by Private Persons against Foreign States*, 22 AM. J. INT'L L. 105, 121 (1928); Thomas & Thomas, *The Civil War in Spain*, in R. Falk, ed., THE INTERNATIONAL LAW OF CIVIL WAR 154–55 (1971).

gence" to prevent such activities from occurring on its soil. Even then, however, the question of culpability arises if the state fails to be duly diligent. Is a state guilty if it merely neglects its duty, or is the state guilty only if there is an intent on its part to affect affairs in another state? Although an argument can easily be made for either view, it is generally conceded that the failure of a state to exercise "due diligence" to deny the use of its territory as a base of operations against the incumbent government of its neighbor is, regardless of motive, an act of interference in the latter's affairs.[21]

A foreign state is, moreover, under the duty not to grant premature recognition to the insurgents. Since the act of recognition bestows benefits on insurgents, premature recognition is definitely an act of interference. Before an external authority is justified in granting recognition, its relations with the incumbent government must be seriously disrupted, and the insurgents must have fulfilled the conditions of belligerency. Similarly, the failure on the part of a foreign state to recognize belligerency after those conditions have been met "would be an imposition of inequality and hardship"[22] upon the insurgents and an unjustifiable interference in the affairs of the strife-torn state.

The most important prescription—and the one most often violated—concerns the granting of assistance. As already noted, assistance to the legitimate government of a state is permissible prior to the recognition of belligerency. Such assistance must be preceded by either the express or tacit consent of the recipient state. Under the doctrine of consent, the request can be made directly in an invitation or indirectly through a prior treaty or arrangement.

In determining the legality of assistance, it is necessary to

[21] See H. Lauterpacht, RECOGNITION IN INTERNATIONAL LAW 233; Thomas & Thomas, NON-INTERVENTION 217; Garcia-Mora, *International Law and the Law of Hostile Military Expeditions*, 27 FORD. L. REV. 309, 320–25 (1958–1959).

[22] Thomas & Thomas, NON-INTERVENTION 220.

examine the so-called legitimate government, for, although it is clearly within the powers of a sovereign state to request aid, "it must be emphasized that sovereignty belongs to the state and not to the government."[23] Only if the incumbent government is still considered to be the representative of the state will assistance to it be lawful. The presumption, though, is in favor of the established government. Until it has been definitely supplanted, the de jure government alone can be regarded and treated as the representative of the state. And until that time, it alone can receive outside assistance.[24]

Significant, too, in assessing the legality of the assistance is the extent to which the request for help was prompted by pressure from the assisting state. If there was no such

[23] Wright, *International Law and Civil Strife*, 53 AM. SOC. INT'L L. PROC. 145, 148 (1959). See also Bluntschli, LE DROIT INTERNATIONAL CODIFIÉ 272 (1874), wherein it is stated that "Lorsque un gouvernement menacé demande à une puissance étrangère d'intervenir, la validité de cet appel dépend de la question de savoir si le gouvernement en question peut encore être considéré comme l'organe et le représentant de l'état. Si le gouvernement a déjà perdu tout pouvoir dans le pays et ne peut trouver dans la nation l'appui nécessaire, il n'a plus de droit de provoquer l'intervention d'un état étranger et de placer ainsi entre les mains d'une armée étrangère l'independance de l'état et la liberté des citoyens." ("When a government that is threatened requests a foreign power to intervene, the validity of this request depends on whether or not the government in question can still be considered as an organ and representative of the state. If the government has already lost all power in the country and is not able to engender the requisite support of the nation, it no longer enjoys the right to call for intervention by a foreign state and in so doing place the independence of the state and the liberty of its citizens within the hands of a foreign army.")

[24] But see Wright, *United States Intervention in the Lebanon*, 53 AM. J. INT'L L. 112, 121 (1959), where he states that "neither faction is competent to speak in the name of the state as long as the results are uncertain." In addition, Wright contends that "there is a presumption that the government in firm possession of the territory, even if not generally recognized, can speak for the state; there is a presumption that even if generally recognized, it cannot speak for the state if not in firm possession of the state's territory" (120).

pressure, support may legally be extended. But should such pressure exist, it would invalidate the invitation, since the "request" would be mere window-dressing to hide an infringement on the requesting state's sovereignty.

It should also be noted in passing that even though assistance is permissible, it is, quite logically, not required. In the absence of an existing treaty, there certainly is no duty on the part of outside states to provide assistance to the legitimate government. While this point is an obvious one, as shown by actions toward regimes in the south of Africa, it obviously is one that is often forgotten by those writers who assert that the insurgency-belligerency standard automatically perpetuates the status quo.

In this connection, it must be reiterated that the legality of assistance is limited to assistance in support of the legitimate government.[25] Since "the enforcement action of the assisting state is, in the last analysis, an action of the assisted state, because authorized by its government,"[26] aid to the government is clearly distinguishable from assistance to the insurgents which cannot be legally justified because it constitutes an act against the de jure government of the besieged state.

In principle, therefore, aid to the incumbent government is permissible until the insurgents have satisfied the condi-

[25] For a fuller discussion, see Kelsen, RECENT TRENDS IN THE LAW OF THE UNITED NATIONS 934 (1951); Wilson, HANDBOOK OF INTERNATIONAL LAW 63 (1910); Baty, *Abuse of Terms: "Recognition": "War,"* 30 AM. J. INT'L L. 377, 398 (1936); Garner, *Questions of International Law in the Spanish Civil War*, 31 AM. J. INT'L L. 66, 68 (1937); Giraud, *L'Interdiction du recours à la force—la théorie et la pratique des Nations Unis*, 67 REVUE GENERALE DE DROIT INTERNATIONAL PUBLIC 501, 522 (1963). But see Falk, *International Law and the United States Role in the Viet Nam War*, 75 YALE L. J. 1109 (1966), for the view that political legitimacy is established by international consensus, rather than by the mere control of the constitutional government, and that factors other than claims to be the constituted government are regularly taken into account in assessing claims of legitimacy. See also text accompanying note 38 below.

[26] Kelsen, RECENT TRENDS 934.

tions of belligerency. This principle, however, is not rigid. If the insurgents are furnished by a foreign state with arms, financial assistance, military supplies, or other support, the traditional doctrine becomes inapplicable. For that reason, the conflict must be closely scrutinized, for "it is a matter of common knowledge that in every social upheaval the party attacked claims that the trouble has been stirred up by outside agents and agitators.[27]

The difficulty is not limited to ascertaining whether such interference exists. There is also disagreement as to the degree of interference that must be present to justify assistance to the established government after the requirements of belligerency have been met. Yet, in spite of disagreement, it would appear that such continued assistance is permitted, even when the interference takes the form of propaganda.[28]

Still, despite the established legality of foreign assistance to the beleaguered government, the danger does exist that other states will, at least to an offsetting degree, counterin-

[27] Edwards, THE NATURAL HISTORY OF REVOLUTION 24 (1927).

[28] While seemingly a low-level form of interference that would not justify abandonment of the traditional doctrine, hostile propaganda is indeed an effective weapon in the process of coercion. As stated in Article 1 of the 1936 Convention Concerning the Use of Broadcasting in the Cause of Peace, states should—and the parties to the Convention undertook to—"stop without delay the broadcasting within their respective territories of any transmission which . . . is of such a character as to incite the population of any territory to acts incompatible with the internal order of the security of a territory of a high contracting party." 186 L.N.T.S. 303. See also Bartlett, POLITICAL PROPAGANDA 5–6 (1940); E. Lauterpacht, *The Contemporary Practice of the United Kingdom in the Field of International Law*, 8 INT'L & COMP. L. Q. 146, 159 (1959); H. Lauterpacht, *Revolutionary Propaganda by Governments*, 13 TRANS. GROT. SOC'Y 143, 145–46 (1928); Novogrod, *Indirect Aggression*, in Bassiouni & Nanda, eds., A TREATISE ON INTERNATIONAL CRIMINAL LAW 198, 217–19 (1973); Preuss, *International Responsibility for Hostile Propaganda against Foreign States*, 28 AM. J. INT'L L. 649, 652 (1934); Whitton, *Aggressive Propaganda*, in Bassiouni & Nanda, eds., A TREATISE ON INTERNATIONAL CRIMINAL LAW 238 (1973); Wright, *Subversive Intervention*, 54 AM. J. INT'L L. 521, 530–35 (1960).

terfere. Given the existing balance of power, the possibility of such interference cannot be taken lightly. Nevertheless, if the desired objective of world order is to be attained, such actions should be rejected and the existing law should be maintained.

Organizational Prescriptions

It is important to realize that the impact of general international law may be quite different from that of particular or organizational law. Whereas the former law is binding upon all members of the world community, the latter prescriptions commonly restrict only the parties to the specified organization. In point of fact, however, the two bodies of law often complement each other.

In Article 10 of the League of Nations Covenant, violations of a state's territorial integrity were proscribed; in Article 11 of the Covenant, the League was empowered to intervene in the event of war, the threat of war, or the rupture of friendly relations between nations. But it was not until 1928, when the American states adopted the Convention on the Duties and Rights of States in the Event of Civil Strife, that the focus of organizational attention was turned to the regulation of interference during civil conflict.[29] According to the terms of the 1928 Convention, the contracting parties agreed to use the means at their disposal to prevent inhabitants within their territory from participating in civil strife in another state; they called upon one another to disarm and intern rebel forces coming into their territory; they forbade traffic in arms, except when those arms were intended for the legitimate government prior to the declaration of belligerency; and they prohibited all arms shipments once the state of belligerency had been recognized.

Shortly thereafter, at the Litvinof Conference of 1933, these concepts were reiterated, and interference, which was

[29] The text of the Convention may be found in *Official Documents*, 22 AM. J. INT'L. L. 159–61 (1928).

defined as "provision or support to armed bands formed in [a state's] territory which have invaded the territories of another state, or refused, notwithstanding the request of the invaded state, to take, in its own territory, all the measures in its power to deprive those bands of all assistance or protection,"[30] was prohibited. Then, in the Charter of the Organization of American States, it was provided that "no State or group of States has the right to intervene, directly or indirectly, for any reason whatever, in the internal or external affairs of any other state."[31] Based upon the assumption that to be genuine a revolution must be the expression of the national will, the foregoing principles prohibited both armed force against and any other form of interference in the strife-torn state. As such, they reinforced the prescriptions of the traditional insurgency-belligerency doctrine.

Further support was provided by the United Nations Charter. Under Article 2 (4), all members are required to "refrain in their international relations from the threat or use of force against the territorial integrity or political independence of any State, or in any other manner, inconsistent with the Purposes of the United Nations." While it might be argued that this provision and the general statement of Article 1 (2) enunciating respect for the principle of self-determination require an embargo on assistance to the legitimate government—and, obviously, to the insurgents—this contention appears to be overly restrictive and to stretch the Charter's meaning by introducing an unintended interpretation. Since such assistance could hardly be

[30] Article II, Subdivision 5 of the Convention. See Pompe, AGGRESSIVE WAR: AN INTERNATIONAL CRIME 52 (1953).

[31] Article 15. Quite obviously, there are many other documents relevant to this discussion. For further examination, see Article 8 of the Convention of Montevideo (1933); Article 1 of the Buenos Aires Protocol Relative to Non-Intervention (1936); Declaration of American Principles (Lima, 1938); Act of Chapultepec (1945); Article 15 of the Bogota Charter of 1948; Charter of the League of Arab States; and Charter of Organization of African Unity.

140

deemed to violate the "territorial integrity or political independence" of the requesting state prior to the fulfillment of the conditions of belligerency and since, as already noted, such assistance constitutes, in effect, an action of the assisted state, the Charter would seem to leave unchanged the pre-United Nations prescriptions that governed the granting of assistance in time of civil strife.

The resolutions promulgated by the United Nations illustrate the prevalent opposition to interference in the affairs of another state. Even though recent developments cast some doubt on the United Nations' earlier resolutions, the United Nations has long condemned such interference. In 1947, the General Assembly passed a resolution "condemning all forms of propaganda, in whatsoever country conducted, which is either designed or likely to provoke or encourage any threat to the peace, breach of the peace, or act of aggression";[32] in 1948, in Article 5 of the Draft Declaration on the Rights and Duties of States, it stated that "no state has the right to interfere in the internal or external affairs of another State";[33] in 1949, in the Essentials of Peace Resolution, it attacked direct or indirect actions aimed at either impairing a state's independence or fomenting civil strife;[34] in 1950, in the Peace through Deeds Resolution, the General Assembly again condemned not only open aggression but also the fomenting of civil strife;[35] in 1954, in the Draft Code of Offences against the Peace and Security of Mankind, it proscribed the organization of armed bands within the territory of one state for incursions into the territory of another state;[36] and in 1965, in the Declaration on the Inadmissibility of Intervention in the Domestic Affairs of

---

[32] Quoted from U.N. WEEKLY BULLETIN 618 (November 11, 1947). See also Wright, *International Law and Ideologies*, 48 AM. J. INT'L L. 616, 623 (1954).

[33] 3 U.N. GAOR 62, U.N. Doc. A/CN.4/2 (1948).

[34] G.A. Res. 290 (IV), 4 U.N. GAOR 13, U.N. Doc. A/1159 (1949).

[35] 5 U.N. GAOR 20, U.N. Doc. A/1775 (1950).

[36] 9 U.N. GAOR, Supp. 9, at 9–12, U.N. Doc. A/2693 (1954).

141

States and the Protection of their Independence and Sovereignty, the General Assembly repeated the prohibitions of the earlier resolutions and condemned efforts to "organize, assist, foment, finance, incite or tolerate subversive, terrorist or armed activities directed toward the violent overthrow of the regime of another state, or interfere in civil strife in another state."[37]

More recently, however, the United Nations has deviated from its firm position of opposition to external assistance to insurgent groups. As a result of Afro-Asian and Soviet support for wars to overthrow racist regimes, the General Assembly has on several occasions urged all states and organizations to provide appropriate moral, political, and material assistance to the inhabitants in the south of Africa in their legitimate struggle for the rights recognized in the Charter. While such pleas are understandable because of the nature of certain African governments and other racist regimes that still dot the globe, they should not be permitted to gain a legal foothold and to further the principle of self-determination at the expense of world order. Yet to reject out of hand these newly advanced legal claims and to waive unhesitatingly the banner of the traditional doctrine would be myopic, if not self-defeating. The doctrine, therefore, must be made to accord with the aspirations of those persons who must adhere to it.[38]

Modifications of the Traditional Standard

Attempts to devise an alternative to the insurgency-belligerency doctrine are not new. In the nineteenth century, the "merits of the cause" position was proposed. Pursuant to the terms of the doctrine, a state ravaged by civil strife

[37] G.A. Res. 2131 (XX), 20 U.N. GAOR, Supp. 14, at 11, U.N. Doc A/6014 (1965).

[38] Lack of adherence could have serious consequences. It has even been stated that "in international law, unlike domestic law, the inability of a rule to control conduct reduces it to the status of a nonrule." Farer, INTERVENTION IN CIVIL WARS 272–73.

was to be deemed two independent "states," and foreign states were justified in assisting that "state" whose cause was thought to be just. But this approach, for obvious reasons, did not and should not today receive much support. Not only does it place the assisting state in the position of passing judgment on matters beyond its capabilities,[39] but the doctrine also constitutes a violation of state sovereignty.

A more widely accepted but equally unacceptable theory is the nonintervention doctrine. In point of fact, there are two versions of the theory. Under one version, military intervention on behalf of the government is permissible until the outcome of the struggle is in doubt; under the other version, all states must assume a posture of neutrality and refuse, in any way, to aid either participant. Whereas the "uncertainty of the outcome" approach is troublesome because standards to determine uncertainty would have to be developed and because only military assistance would be

[39] The "merits of the cause" theory is advanced by Vattel, THE LAW OF NATIONS 626–67 (1867). In his critique of the traditional test, Hall disputes the "merits of the cause" doctrine. The critique merits reproduction: "As interventions, in so far as they purport to be made in compliance with an invitation, are independent of the reasons or pretexts which have already been discussed, it must be assumed that they are either based on simple friendship or upon a sentiment of justice. If intervention on the ground of mere friendship were allowed, it would be idle to speak seriously of the rights of independence. Supposing the intervention to be directed against the existing government, independence is violated by an attempt to prevent the regular organ of the state from managing the state affairs in its own ways. Supposing it on the other hand to be directed against the rebels, the fact that it has been necessary to call in foreign help is enough to show that the issue of the conflict would without it be uncertain, and consequently that there is doubt as to which side would ultimately establish itself as the legal representative of the state. If, again, the intervention is based upon an opinion as to the merits of the question at issue, the intervening state takes upon itself to pass judgment in a matter which, having nothing to do with the relations of states, must be regarded as being for legal purposes beyond the range of its vision." Hall, INTERNATIONAL LAW 287 (1909). This statement is eloquent but, for reasons that have been and will be stated, is shortsighted.

143

barred,[40] the latter test is deficient because of its traumatic effect on embryonic states by leaving the governments of those states without the administrative, economic, and military aid to which they had grown accustomed, and on which they had become dependent. In effect, "an operationally neutral noninterventionary norm would require the prophylactic severance of these umbilical ties, an inconceivable step for states trying desperately to enter the modern section of the world economy."[41]

Of the various alternate theories advanced, the "ASOTS test"—aid short of tactical military support—is the most radical and, accordingly, the one least likely to be accepted. ASOTS "would legitimate assistance short of tactical military support, either to incumbents or rebels, but would proscribe absolutely the commitment of combat troops or battle field advisors (or "volunteers") no matter how few or how negligible their effect."[42] Even though ASOTS would ostensibly help alleviate the possibility of the transformation of civil strife into a great-power conflict, it would not only run counter to the prescriptions of Article 2 (4) of the United Nations Charter but might in fact produce such a conflict. In theory, a clean separation of military from other aid might well work; in practice, the permissibility of assistance to each side under cold war conditions could easily escalate a local conflict and cover both the theoretical division and much of the world with nuclear dust. Still, the basic concept behind the restriction on the use of military forces is a valid one. As history clearly demonstrates, a state engaged in supplying assistance often remains unconcerned about the conflict that is the object of that assistance. But

[40] For further comment on this doctrine, see Wright, *United States Intervention in the Lebanon*, 112.

[41] Farer, *Harnessing Rogue Elephants: A Short Discourse on Foreign Intervention in Civil Strife*, 82 HARV. L. REV. 511, 531 (1969). See also Farer, *Intervention in Civil Wars* 274–75; Moore, *The Control of Foreign Intervention in Internal Conflict*, 9 VA. J. INT'L L. 205, 316–20 (1969).

[42] Farer, *Harnessing Rogue Elephants* 532.

when its troops are killed in combat, the state's interest in the struggle invariably increases, its political forces are unleashed, and its objectives can no longer be limited. As a consequence, the state's ability to extricate itself from the strife decreases.

A more acceptable and practical theory is the "Moore standard" that, aside from United Nations action, there should be no participation by outside states in authority-oriented conflicts.[43] At the same time, however, preinsurgency assistance to the legitimate government would be permitted and could be maintained throughout such conflicts; assistance would be allowed above the preinsurgency limits to offset impermissible aid granted to the insurgents; nonpartisan participation to restore the processes of self-determination would be allowed; and nonauthority-oriented intervention for the protection of human rights would also be permissible. In addition, the "Moore standard" would require (with the African resolutions clearly in mind) that the General Assembly act as the authorizing agency for all partisan intervention.[44]

In the last analysis, though, these modifications of and substitutions for the traditional insurgency-belligerency standard do not seem to do it justice. While in the past the traditional doctrine may well have served "as a Maginot Line for the status quo,"[45] it need not do so in the future. Indeed, with one basic change, the traditional doctrine can be revitalized and made more acceptable, certain, effective, and workable.

If the insurgency-belligerency standard were modified to provide that the Security Council rather than individual states was to determine when a particular civil conflict had been transformed from insurgency into belligerency, or

[43] See Moore, *Control of Foreign Intervention.*

[44] Moore no longer believes that the General Assembly should be the authorizing agency. He advocates, instead, that the Security Council fulfill that function.

[45] Moore, *Control of Foreign Intervention* 315.

when impermissible aid to insurgents warranted continued assistance to the legitimate government, the main pitfalls of the traditional doctrine would be eliminated. While the General Assembly might be a satisfactory authorizing agent, the Security Council would seem to be the more realistic and suitable institution. As a result of the existing big-power struggle and of the fact that under Chapter VII of the United Nations Charter the Security Council already possesses the legal powers to enforce its decisions, the Security Council would appear to be preferable to the General Assembly as the authorizing agent.

If, in addition, the Security Council were also granted the power to determine when aid may be provided to insurgents, the "status quo obstacle" might well be overcome, although the wisdom of such a modification is certainly debatable. Despite arguments to the contrary, the inalienable right of revolution was not affected by the favored treatment of the government under the traditional standard.[46] Admittedly, the existing law of civil strife favors the established government and strong insurgent groups, for to allow the de jure government to receive assistance until the declaration of belligerency is, in effect, to limit the right of revolution to the powerful and, concomitantly, to help maintain the status quo. Admittedly, too, at a time when people are mobilizing to break the shackles of colonialism and to overthrow racist regimes, this result may seem inequitable. When viewed in terms of world order and when juxtaposed with the United Nations Charter's overriding emphasis on peaceful change, however, the traditional standard is certainly reasonable. For that reason, the proposal to permit the Security Council to authorize assistance to insurgents should not be accepted, even

[46] In support of this statement, see H. Lauterpacht, RECOGNITION IN INTERNATIONAL LAW 232. Contra Farer, *Harnessing Rogue Elephants* 526; Moore, *Control of Foreign Intervention* 316; cf. Jessup's discussion of a future world order in which there would be no right to revolt in Jessup, A MODERN LAW OF NATIONS 185 (1948).

though it might well be acceptable if that step were required to obtain Afro-Asian and Soviet support for the modified insurgency-belligerency doctrine.

Either way, though, the institutional weakness of the Security Council is so great that an alternative to the modified insurgency-belligerency doctrine must be developed if some immediate progress in this area is to be made. The "Moore standard" should accordingly be embraced as the logical and realistic first step on the road to the "new," revamped insurgency-belligerency doctrine. Unless and until the United Nations is held in greater esteem by the leading participants in the world's power arena, it would certainly be foolish to think that a doctrine that is dependent on the good faith of those participants and that requires action by the Security Council could possibly succeed, as the United Nations' inaction during the Vietnam and Mideast crises makes patently clear.

Summary

While scholars debate needed changes in the traditional insurgency-belligerency standard and all too often "governments are guided not by fidelity to norms but by their conception of what their interests are,"[47] that standard remains the rod against which a state's actions must be measured. Accordingly, while a foreign state may provide a beleaguered government with assistance during the insurgency stage of civil strife, it must immediately terminate such aid and assume a position of neutrality once belligerency is declared. If the assistance to the de jure government continues after belligerency has been declared, the insurgent forces may receive equivalent aid. Under all other circumstances, however, assistance may not be rendered to the insurgents.

[47] Falk, *Introduction* to Falk, ed., THE INTERNATIONAL LAW OF CIVIL WAR 1, 3 (1971): "Interests have been self-defined by governments in light of their capabilities, foreign policy priorities, and their perception of what others will do in response to provocative action and response."

In addition to refusing aid to insurgents, states may not prematurely grant them belligerent status. When, as evidenced by their control of areas of the state and their government, organized army, and adherence to the rules of war, the insurgent forces have fulfilled the requirements of belligerency, foreign states must recognize the insurgents' belligerency and treat both sides to the conflict equally.

Finally, states must not organize hostile expeditions within their territory directed against a foreign state, encourage the formation of such expeditions by their citizenry, or allow the use of their territory as a sanctuary for insurgents operating in a foreign state. In fact, they are under an affirmative duty to police their borders and to prohibit *all* activities directed against "the territorial integrity or political independence" of any state.

THE DUBLIN VIEWPOINT

To Southerners, the North and South are part of one Ireland, the strife in the Six Counties is a domestic Irish issue that has attained the status of belligerency, and Britain is a foreign state that has long been violating the tenets of international law by aiding the Protestant rebels. However, even if the conflict in the North is viewed as a struggle in an entity separate from the South, the Republic has—by any standard—fulfilled its international obligations. In doing so, though, Dublin has greatly alienated many loyal Irishmen, for the failure of the Republic to take positive action with respect to Article 3 of the 1937 Constitution has been a subject of much discord.

What has made the South's task even more difficult is Ireland's proud history of defiance to injustice. Whether in Pearse's assertion that "bloodshed is a cleansing and a sanctifying thing, and the nation which regards it as the final horror has lost its manhood,"[48] MacSwiney's belief

[48] "We must accustom ourselves to the thought of arms, to the sight

148

that "an authority originally legitimate once it becomes habitually tyrannical may be resisted and deposed,"[49] or Devlin's cry that "if it becomes necessary we will simply make it impossible for any unjust government to govern us,"[50] that tradition has long been and is today important in the Ulster conflict. Yet, despite that tradition, the Dublin Government has maintained a posture which, though politically unpopular, is legally impeccable.

When, for instance, the IRA in the mid-1950s renewed its campaign against the North, Dublin reopened the old internment camp beside the Curragh racetrack. Under the Offenses Against the State Act (1939), it interned suspected IRA members and, when they refused to answer questions posed by military tribunals, sentenced them to prison terms.[51] As a result of one of the arrests that it made, Ireland was brought before the European Commission on Human Rights. Although it won the case when the European Commission determined that "a 'state of emergency' was sufficient reason for a State to violate human rights by

---

of arms, to the use of arms. We may make mistakes in the beginning and shoot the wrong people; but bloodshed is a cleansing and a sanctifying thing, and the nation which regards it as the final horror has lost its manhood. There are many things more horrible than bloodshed; and slavery is one of them." Padraic Pearse, quoted in Lieberson, THE IRISH UPRISING 55 (1966).

49 "Government is just only when rightfully established and for the public good; that usurpation not only may but ought to be resisted; that an authority originally legitimate once it becomes habitually tyrannical may be resisted and deposed; and that when from abuse or tyranny a particular government ceases to exist, we have to re-establish a true one." MacSwiney, PRINCIPLES OF FREEDOM 150 (1964).

50 "We will fight for justice. We will try to achieve it by peaceful means. But if it becomes necessary we will simply make it impossible for any unjust government to govern us. We will refuse to have anything to do with it." Devlin, THE PRICE OF MY SOUL 223 (1969).

51 Bell, THE SECRET ARMY: THE IRA 1916–1970 299 (1971); Coogan, IRELAND SINCE THE RISING 279 (1966); Sunday Times Insight Team, ULSTER 17–18, 20–22 (1972) (cited hereafter as Insight Team, ULSTER).

such expedients as internment without trial,"[52] Dublin was put on notice that in the future the European Commission would determine if such an emergency existed.

Even after the European Commission's "warning," the South remained vigilant. A less conscientious government—especially one faced with the historical and political difficulties that confronted Dublin as a result of still-fresh memories of the Civil War of 1922–1923, and the fact that the party in power (Fianna Fail) had been formed in the 1920s with IRA help—would have folded its arms and let events run their course. Not Dublin. When, for instance, it was revealed that members of the Taoiseach's cabinet were supposedly involved in importing arms and ammunition for use in the North, charges were immediately brought. Although those individuals charged in May 1970 with violating the Firearms Act were found by a jury to be innocent, their trial was further evidence of the Republic's intention to adhere to its apparent international responsibilities.[53]

The Republic thereafter continued to prohibit arms shipments to the Catholics of the North, despite the fact that a strong argument could be made that Northern Catholics had a right, both legally and morally, to arms with which to protect themselves. It immediately stopped the training of Northerners when such training was discovered.[54] It patrolled its border with the North to prevent

[52] Insight Team, ULSTER 20. And for a more detailed discussion of the case—the *Lawless Case*—see Chapter VI, "Human Rights—Human Wrongs."

[53] The Dublin arms trial of Albert Luykx, James Kelly, John Kelly, and Charles Haughey (Minister of Finance) is the subject of MacIntyre's THROUGH THE BRIDEWELL GATE (1971). The related firings of Neil Blaney (Minister of Agriculture and the "South's Ian Paisley") and Haughey, the resignations of Kevin Boland (Minister of Local Government) and Michael O'Morain (Minister of Justice), and the controversy over James Gibbons (Minister for Defense) are also discussed in the work.

[54] The training had been set up under the authority of Defense Minister Gibbons and without the knowledge of Prime Minister Lynch.

the crossing of armed bands. And it even went so far as to ban the playing over Radio Eireann of "Over the Wall," a record which described various escapes from Belfast's Crumlin Road jail.

In the spring of 1972, the Republic took still more drastic action. To curtail terrorist activities that either originated or terminated in the South, it again revived the Offenses Against the State Act (1939). Unhappy over the increased use of Southern soil as a base of operations, the Republic also established a special criminal court on the grounds that the ordinary courts were inadequate to secure the effective administration of justice and the preservation of public peace and order. Within a short period of time, it had begun its crackdown on both wings of the IRA, a crackdown that included the arrest, conviction, and imprisonment of Sean MacStiofain, the leader of the Provisionals. Moreover, in December 1972, the Offenses Against the State (Amendment) Bill—which many people feel is more extreme than the obnoxious Special Powers Act of the North—was passed. Among its provisions, the new law provides for fines and prison sentences for participation in an unlawful demonstration, meeting, or procession and for the jailing of suspected IRA members on the sworn statement of a ranking officer of the Garda Siochana "that he believes that the accused was at a material time a member of an unlawful organization."[55]

At the same time, though, that the Republic was exercising great diligence in assuring that the Northern conflagration was not fed in any way by the South, the British and Northern Governments were delinquent in fulfilling their international legal obligations. As evidenced by re-

---

When he was informed of the exercise, he stopped it. At the time the training came to an end, nine men had completed the course. See Insight Team, ULSTER 190–91.

[55] Section 3 (2) of the act. The Garda Siochana is the Republic's police force.

peated British incursions into the Republic to capture IRA terrorists, the failure of British and Northern authorities to prevent terrorist activities from the North by Protestant extremists, and the continued repression of Northern Catholics in violation of all international standards, Britain and the North were constantly demonstrating their inability to resolve peacefully the Northern conflict.

THE LONDON AND BELFAST VIEWPOINTS

While the death and destruction in Northern Ireland are great, the struggle remains—for purposes of international law—low-level civil strife within the confines of the United Kingdom. Since the IRA "controls" no terrain, has no government, is not an organized army, and does not adhere to the rules of war, the conflict most assuredly cannot be viewed as belligerency; since, in fact, the IRA has little impact and less support, it cannot in truth even be deemed an insurgent force. The struggle—the rebellion—presents in terms of the law of civil strife, therefore, but one question: is Dublin fulfilling its international obligations with respect to the prohibition of assistance to the IRA terrorists? That question, regrettably, must be answered most emphatically in the negative.

The Republic's infidelity to international prescriptions is amply demonstrated by the fact that the Official and Provisional branches of the IRA have their headquarters in Dublin, the IRA has training camps throughout the South, cross-border gun battles rage constantly, raiding parties from the Republic strike into Ulster and then return to the sanctuary of the South, the police watched while terrorists burned the British Embassy in Dublin, and gelignite—which is used in the bombs of the IRA—can be readily obtained in the Republic.[56] Yet these actions, reprehensible

[56] Support for these allegations comes from a wide variety of sources. See generally Rose, GOVERNING WITHOUT CONSENSUS 167–68 (1971) (train-

as they are, and violating the basic tenets of international law as they do, are insignificant when juxtaposed against other, more affirmative Southern acts.

By far the most serious of these acts was the infamous gun-running episode of 1969–1970. In a complex series of events that culminated in the Dublin Arms Trial whitewash of 1970, several members of the Lynch Government attempted to underwrite the cost of IRA operations in the North. Although Lynch pushed through his divided cabinet a policy that Dublin "would not *officially* supply the northern Catholics with arms,"[57] he also capitulated, following the Bogside uprising of August 12, 1969, to pressure from his "Northern" cabinet members and placed Messrs. Blaney, Boland, and Haughey in charge of Ulster policies in an effort to forestall their threatened resignations.[58] Once they were in a position to dictate Dublin's Northern policy, the three men toyed with the idea of an Irish Army invasion of Ulster—an invasion that would be occasioned by a

---

ing camps and the lethargy of the Dublin police in combatting the IRA); Scarman, VIOLENCE AND CIVIL DISTURBANCE IN NORTHERN IRELAND IN 1969 (Cmd. 566) 239–40 (1972) (a description of the IRA raid on the Crossmaglen RUC station); Kramer, *Letter from Ireland*, 48 NEW YORKER 46, 61 (February 19, 1972) ("Southern terrorists stand at the frontier, two feet into the sanctuary of the Republic, and bombard the British soldiers on the other side with bombs and rifle fire in a kind of insane border war that leaves them free from any retribution"); "Liar Lynch Protects I.R.A.," 6 PROTESTANT TELEGRAPH 1, December 21, 1971 (each of the above allegations is made—"According to . . . Jack Lynch, the Irish Republic is 'not a haven for the IRA.' If he believes that he is a liar; also he must not only be blind and deaf, but totally devoid of all mental processes to understand plain and indisputable fact").

[57] Insight Team, ULSTER 182 (emphasis supplied). The machinations of this period are described in some detail at 178–91.

[58] Two of these three cabinet members—Blaney and Haughey—had strong family ties to the North. Boland, on the other hand, was a man with impeccable Republican credentials, since his father had founded Fianna Fail with DeValera, his uncle had worked with Collins, and his brother had helped create Taca, Fianna Fail's fund-raising club. *Ibid.*, 178–79.

153

phoney border incident.[59] When that idea proved unacceptable, they immediately turned to more covert means to increase tensions, and, at the same time, Lynch went on television to call for a United Nations peacekeeping force and to announce that the Irish Army was erecting four field hospitals along the border.

Those covert means consisted of financing and of training at the hands of Southern soldiers. As was revealed during the Dublin Arms Trial, £200,000 was promised to the IRA if a Northern command was established and all IRA political involvement south of the border ceased.[60] Eventually, a total of £175,000 was made available to the people of the North— £75,000 for propaganda purposes and the rest for the "general relief of suffering" (a euphemistic expression for guns); eventually, too, most of the remaining £100,000 made its way circuitously from the Dublin Government to the Irish Red Cross, to a series of banks, and to the Northern IRA (although some of the funds evaporated in the attempt to import the arms and ammunition, which led directly to the Dublin Arms Trial of September-October, 1970).[61]

[59] The proposed bogus incident would have involved a call from Londonderry for an ambulance from the Republic, firing on the ambulance as it crossed the border, and the taking of Londonderry by an "outraged" Irish Army. *Ibid.*, 180. See also Smyth, THE AXIS AGAINST ULSTER 5 (1972), where the author states that the Republic would seize a border area and "under cover of this 'international incident' the United Nations would be introduced to superintend the last hours of Ulster, and the caesarean and bloody birth of a new Ireland."

[60] Insight Team, ULSTER 186–87. There were those persons among the IRA who felt that the entire financial effort was merely a scheme to divorce the northern wing of the IRA from the southern, Dublin-based organization. If this was indeed the objective of the Republic's offer to provide financial assistance, it was successful, as the subsequent Official-Provisional split demonstrates. Yet, it seems fairer to say that the South was genuinely interested in aiding the North, but that it wanted to protect itself from the embarrassment that would result from IRA actions emanating from the Republic. Accordingly, Dublin proposed the plan that would serve both objectives at once.

[61] The maze of transactions to disguise the operation is described

While the financial problems were being resolved, a training center for Northerners was established in County Donegal. To circumvent the obvious difficulties that would arise if Dublin were discovered supporting an illegally armed force, "civilians" were not to be given arms training. Instead, all Northern Catholics desirous of such training were required by Dublin to enlist for one week in the Forsai Cosanta Aitula, the Irish Army Territorials.[62] Shortly after this ruse was commenced, however, it was discovered and revealed to the world, and Dublin was forced to abandon the program.

A more subtle but equally illegal Dublin interference in Ulster affairs was (and is) the barrage of subversive broadcasting beamed to the people of Northern Ireland. During the Bogside unrest of August 1969, for instance, Lynch's inflammatory broadcast "strengthened the will of the Bogsiders to obstruct any attempt by the police to enter their area and to harass them by missile and petrol bomb attack whenever they appeared on the perimeter."[63] Undoubtedly, too, that broadcast heightened tensions in other areas of Ulster, and, in the opinion of most observers, directly led to attacks on a Belfast police station.[64] Indeed, it would be naive to conclude that Lynch's broadcast—which proclaimed "that the Stormont Government is no longer in control of the situation . . . [which] is the inevitable outcome of the policies pursued for decades by successive Stormont Governments . . . [and] that the Irish Government can no longer stand by and see innocent people injured and perhaps worse"[65]—was not a provocation and an encourage-

---

ibid., 189–90. A second source of funds for the IRA is the Irish-American community. Although the magnitude of the funds provided by Irish-Americans is unknown, it is thought to be great.

[62] *Ibid.*, 190.

[63] Scarman, VIOLENCE AND CIVIL DISTURBANCE 79.

[64] *Ibid.*, 88.

[65] Scarman, 2 VIOLENCE AND CIVIL DISTURBANCE 44. The text of Lynch's August 13, 1969 speech may be found *ibid.* 43–44, and Lynch, SPEECHES

ment to Catholic activists. And it would be equally naive to conclude that Lynch's August 12, 1971 "call on all Irish people, North and South, who are opposed both to repression and violence to join together in political action aimed at"[66] bringing the Stormont regime to an end was not violative of the prescriptions of customary international law and of Article 2 (4) of the United Nations Charter.

These violations are not made less serious by periodic Dublin statements decrying the use of Irish soil by terrorists, the curtailment, as a result of world pressure, of the training of Northern Catholics, and the fabricated display of the Dublin Arms Trial. Yet it is through the passage of unenforced antiterrorist legislation that the bad faith of the Republic is most clearly revealed. Although the reinstatement of the Offenses Against the State Act and its 1972 amendment provide Dublin with the legislative means to fulfill its international obligations, the mere passage of legislation—without more—is not enough. Now the Republic must enforce the legislation, an action which it has to date either refused to do or, in those few instances in which it has invoked the legislation, it has done with respect to "people whose connections with violence are fairly remote—people on the open political official Sinn Fein movement—while leaving untouched notorious military leaders of the Provisional IRA."[67] Until it is enforced, the passage of antiterrorist legislation will be as empty a ges-

---

AND STATEMENTS ON IRISH UNITY, NORTHERN IRELAND AND ANGLO-IRISH RELATIONS AUGUST 1969-OCTOBER 1971 1–3 (1972).

[66] Lynch, SPEECHES AND STATEMENTS 76. In his response to the Lynch statement of August 12, 1971, which was repeated in a telegram from Lynch dated August 19, 1971, Prime Minister Heath stated that "supporting the policy of passive resistance now being pursued by certain elements in Northern Ireland [is] calculated to do maximum damage to the co-operation between the communities in Northern Ireland which it is our purpose, and I would hope would be your purpose, to achieve." *Ibid.*, 79.

[67] Conor Cruise O'Brien, quoted in Stone, *Ireland: "The Killing Sickness,"* 214 NATION 390, 392 (1972).

ture as Dublin's prior efforts to fulfill its international duties; until that time, too, the Republic will remain in default of those duties.

CONCLUSIONS

Civil struggles usually raise several interesting legal questions. In the case of the uncivil strife raging in Northern Ireland, however, all but one of those questions—the question of granting assistance to rebel forces—is inapplicable. Although other issues could be made applicable by twisting historical and political facts, they would only be of theoretical interest, for the North is part of the United Kingdom, and the conflict is a rebellion or, perhaps, an insurgency. Even if the struggle were deemed to be a belligerency— which would be conceding a great deal, since it would mean accepting sporadic fighting in Belfast, Derry, and occasionally elsewhere as a struggle of a general nature, the IRA command as a viable governmental apparatus, and the rebels' terror tactics as being in accord with the rules of war—that belligerency would affect only third-party assistance to the legitimate government; Britain—as the legitimate government—is not a third party; and no state other than Britain is providing aid to or on behalf of the Ulster authorities. Consequently, the sole issue concerns assistance to the rebels.

While, parenthetically, British incursions into the Republic and Protestant extremist forays south of the border must be deemed in violation of international law, the real question that must be answered is whether the Republic is, in any way, aiding the Northern rebels, since neither of the above violations would justify such assistance. Given the fact that, despite some contrary scholarly opinions, both customary and organizational international law clearly condemn such assistance as an infringement upon the target state's sovereignty, any aid to Northern rebels would constitute illegal conduct on the part of Ireland.

157

While Dublin points to the passage of strong legislation, the banning of arms shipments to the North, the immediate end to the training of Northern Catholics when that training was brought to the Taoiseach's attention, the banning of an emotional and provocative record, and the patrolling of its border to prevent the use of the South as a terrorist sanctuary as proof of its good-faith intention to abide by international prescriptions, the fact remains that in each instance it had to be prodded by world opinion to take the action in question. In addition, the fact also remains that having gone on record with each of the above actions, Dublin has, for the most part, done nothing more.

Certainly, Dublin is not responsible for the troubles in the North; certainly, too, it is difficult for Southern leaders —many of whom are the sons of Republican gunmen—in whom the concept of armed nationalism is ingrained, to crack down on the IRA. Rather than contain the Northern conflagration, though, Dublin has fanned the flames of the uncivil strife by financing and training Northern rebels, by urging the peoples of the North to resist the legal governmental authorities of Northern Ireland, and by omitting to take the requisite action to curb the effectiveness of the IRA. While "difficulty" might well explain how Dublin can commit or omit these actions—how it can bring the proceedings of the Dublin Arms Trial but not press in earnest for conviction on charges of supplying arms, how it can pass legislation without adequately enforcing it, and how it can brazenly broadcast to the North about the need to resist—"difficulty" cannot excuse actions that, under the existing state of international law, are definitely illegal. Accordingly, the Republic's two-pronged actions of commission and omission, although readily understandable, must be condemned.

CHAPTER V

Limits of War: The Applicability of the Laws of War to the Ulster Conflict

To say that war is as old as man is trite; to assert that the laws or rules of war always control the actions of men during conflicts is naive. Yet the prescriptions of war have long been one factor in the conduct of armed struggles. At least since the days of Grotius, some people have believed not only that all laws are not held in abeyance in war but that, "on the contrary, war ought not to be undertaken except for the enforcement of rights; when once undertaken, it should be carried on only within the bounds of law and good faith."[1] And at least since the time of Rousseau, some people have held that "the object of war being the destruction of the enemy State, a commander has a perfect right to kill its defenders so long as their arms are in their hands: but once they have laid them down and have submitted, they cease to be enemies, or instruments employed by an enemy, and revert to the condition of men, pure and simple, over whose lives no one can any longer exercise a rightful claim."[2]

What these laws were and are intended to do is to modify

[1] Grotius, Prolegomena to the Law of War and Peace 18 (1957). Grotius admits that "nothing is more common than the assertion of antagonism between law and arms" (4), and adds that "throughout the Christian world I observed a lack of restraint in relation to war, such as even barbarous races should be ashamed of; I observed that men rush to arms for slight causes, or no cause at all, and that when arms have once been taken up there is no longer any respect for law, divine or human" (21). The laws of war predate Grotius, for they were born in the medieval days of knightly chivalry. See T. Taylor, Nuremberg and Vietnam: An American Tragedy 20 (1972).

[2] Rousseau, *The Social Contract*, in E. Barker, ed., Social Contract: Essays by Locke, Hume, and Rousseau 177 (1962).

the brutality and inhumanity of war. What they do is to provide guidelines for "humanizing" international armed struggles by outlawing "needless cruelties, and other acts that spread death and destruction and are not reasonably related to the conduct of hostilities."[3] Despite the vast gap between promise and performance, however, the laws of war are of great—and increasing—importance. Based on man's natural sense of reason and justice and founded on custom and usage, the works of scholars, the decisions of military courts and jurists, and innumerable treaties, the laws of war have gradually obtained universal recognition.[4]

One of the first attempts to codify the rules of war was Lieber's Code, which, in 1863, became the law by which the armed forces of the United States were governed.[5] In addition, Lieber's Code served as the foundation for the United States Law of Land Warfare of 1917 and 1940 and for the Declaration of the International Conference at Brussels in 1874, the Manual of the Institution of International Law in 1880, the Hague Conventions of 1899 and 1907, and the Geneva Conventions of 1929 and 1949.[6]

[3] Taylor, NUREMBERG AND VIETNAM 20. The laws of war deal with the issue of human rights in a war setting. Since, however, they have "grown up" separately, they are treated in this chapter, and other issues of human rights are dealt with in Chapter VI, "Human Rights—Human Wrongs."

[4] See generally Greenspan, THE MODERN LAW OF LAND WARFARE 4–5 (1959); JUDGMENT OF THE INTERNATIONAL MILITARY TRIBUNAL FOR THE TRIAL OF MAJOR GERMAN WAR CRIMINALS (Misc. No. 12 [1946] Cmnd. 6964) Sessional Papers XXV (1946/47) at 40.

[5] As noted in note 1 above, the laws of war are quite old. Even though the rules were not codified until the nineteenth century, they were in effect long before that time, since "the customs themselves, even if they are not themselves written down as rules, have the same binding force as the written norms." Trainin, *Questions of Guerrilla Warfare in the Law of War*, 40 AM. J. INT'L L. 534, 536 (1946).

[6] See generally Hall, INTERNATIONAL LAW 469 (8th ed., 1924); Hull & Novogrod, LAW AND VIETNAM 79 (1968); Oppenheim, 2 INTERNATIONAL LAW 336–96 (7th ed., 1952); Wright, *The American Civil War*, in R. Falk, ed., THE INTERNATIONAL LAW OF CIVIL WAR 30, 55 (1971). A more

Until the adoption of the Geneva Conventions of 1949, though, the laws of war were not made specifically applicable to civil conflicts such as the Ulster "troubles." Although those laws did apply to civil strife prior to 1949, they had no effect on a struggle before the insurgents attained the status of belligerency. Moreover, even the recognition of belligerency by foreign states did not impose on governments the obligation to bestow on insurgents the benefits of the laws of war. In an attempt to provide individual states with adequate security to meet the danger posed by insurgents, "customary law in effect conceded [to] the constitutional government a large freedom to restore and maintain its effective control, a freedom practically unregulated save, perhaps, by amorphous doctrines on 'humanitarian intervention' on the part of third states, and more recently by broad human-rights commitments and standards."[7]

As a result of this line of reasoning, two points were quickly obvious. First of all, it was soon clear that the availability of the laws of war to civil strife was in fact meaningless, for, with the dearth of "belligerent" civil struggles, the law remained largely inapplicable. Secondly, it was also evident that there was no acceptable justification for treating noncombatants in domestic conflicts differently from their counterparts in international struggles. When the delegates to the postwar conference met in Geneva, therefore, their attention was directed, albeit in an off-hand fashion, to the problem of civil strife. Thus, while the 1949 conventions emanating from that conference "do not purport to be applicable as such to civil wars, they set forth [through Article 3, which is common to each of the four

---

detailed discussion of the code devised by Francis Lieber may be found in Taylor, NUREMBERG AND VIETNAM 21–24, and Wright, *American Civil War* 54–56.

[7] McDougal & Feliciano, LAW AND MINIMUM WORLD PUBLIC ORDER 536 (1961). The doctrine of "humanitarian intervention" is discussed in Chapter VII, "The Internationalization of Civil Strife."

conventions] minimum standards to be observed by each party to an 'armed conflict not of an international character occurring in the territory of one of the High Contracting Parties.' "[8]

Article 3 of the Geneva Conventions of 1949

Before arriving at what was to become Article 3 of the Geneva Conventions of 1949, the delegates at Geneva debated long and hard about the merits and demerits of three propositions dealing with civil strife: that the conventions were to apply in *all* cases of internal armed conflicts; that they were not to apply in *any* such struggles; and that they were to apply only when the strife had reached certain proportions and had certain characteristics. In attempting to resolve the opposing viewpoints, delegates were confronted with two divergent histories. On the one hand, they were faced with the thirty-year effort of the International Committee of the Red Cross to extend the Hague and Geneva Conventions to victims of civil wars;[9] on the other hand,

[8] *Ibid.*, 73 n.174 and, generally, 72–73. The Geneva Conventions of 1949 consist of the Geneva Convention for the Amelioration of the Condition of the Wounded and Sick in Armed Forces in the Field (T.I.A.S. 3362), the Geneva Convention for the Amelioration of the Condition of Wounded, Sick and Shipwrecked Members of Armed Forces at Sea (T.I.A.S. 3363), the Geneva Convention Relative to the Treatment of Prisoners of War (T.I.A.S. 3364), and the Geneva Convention Relative to the Protection of Civilian Persons in Time of War (T.I.A.S. 3365). They may also be found in United States, Department of the Army, TREATIES GOVERNING LAND WARFARE (1956).

[9] At the Tenth International Red Cross Conference in 1921, a resolution was passed "affirming the right to relief of all victims of civil wars or social or revolutionary disturbances in accordance with the general principles of the Red Cross." Pictet, COMMENTARY ON THE GENEVA CONVENTION FOR THE AMELIORATION OF THE CONDITION OF THE WOUNDED AND SICK IN ARMED FORCES IN THE FIELD 40 (1952). At the Sixteenth IRC Conference in 1938, a resolution was adopted that supplemented and strengthened the 1921 resolution by requesting Red Cross societies to endeavor to obtain the application of both the 1907 Hague Convention and the 1929 Geneva Convention to all struggles. *Ibid.*, 40–41. And at the Seventeenth IRC Conference in Stockholm, a draft was adopted

they encountered their own traditions and inclinations, which viewed rebels as traitors who were to be dealt with as common criminals and which resented "any attempt by outside bodies, including the International Committee of the Red Cross, to intercede on behalf of such rebels."[10] As is usually the case in such situations, a balance was struck— a balance in this instance between the safety of the state and humanitarianism—and a compromise Article 3 was promulgated.

Rather than make specific provision for civil strife, as some delegates proposed, or restrict the availability of the laws to international struggles, as many delegates hoped, Article 3 was created as "a Convention in 'miniature' applicable to non-international conflicts only."[11] It was also

---

that served as the basis for the 1949 Geneva Conference and that advocated that the principles of the earlier conventions be made obligatory on each of the adversaries in all conflicts. *Ibid.*, 42–43.

[10] Draper, THE RED CROSS CONVENTIONS 14 (1958). See also Bond, *Protection of Non-Combatants in Guerrilla Wars*, 12 WM. & MARY L. REV. 787, 800–801 (1971); Draper, *The Geneva Conventions of 1949*, 114 RECUEIL DES COURS (Hague Academy of International Law) 63, 83 (1965). The position of the United States exemplifies this point of view. In effect, the United States held that every government had the right to put down a rebellion within its borders and to punish insurgents in accordance with its penal laws. It also held that a premature recognition of belligerency would be a tortious act and constitute a breach of international law. Moreover, the United States claimed that a state should not be expected to abandon sound principles of law to apply the Conventions. And even though it agreed that the Conventions should apply when civil strife had reached a certain level, the United States restricted the Conventions' application merely to belligerencies, for it asserted that the requisite level was attained when the insurgents had de facto authority over persons within a determinate territory, possessed armed forces that were under the direction of an organized civil authority and adhered to the customary rules of war, and agreed to the Conventions. See Yingling & Ginnane, *The Geneva Conventions of 1949*, 46 AM. J. INT'L L. 393, 395 (1953).

[11] Draper, RED CROSS CONVENTIONS 15. The text of Article 3 reads as follows:

In the case of armed conflict not of an international character oc-

created with "the advantage of not being based upon the principle of reciprocity and it [had] an automatic application once such a conflict [had] broken out."[12] Of still greater import, though, was the fact that, since Article 3 represented a compromise, it stood a better chance of being effective. Indeed, if the provisions of Article 3 had been made obligatory on each adversary in all conflicts, the article would probably have been a dead letter, for the legitimate

---

curring in the territory of one of the High Contracting Parties, each Party to the conflict shall be bound to apply, as a minimum, the following provisions:

(1) Persons taking no active part in the hostilities, including members of armed forces who have laid down their arms and those placed *hors de combat* by sickness, wounds, detention, or any other cause, shall in all circumstances be treated humanely, without any adverse distinction founded on race, colour, religion or faith, sex, birth or wealth, or any other similar criteria.

To this end, the following acts are and shall remain prohibited at any time and in any place whatsoever with respect to the above-mentioned persons:

(a) violence to life and person, in particular murder of all kinds, mutilation, cruel treatment and torture;

(b) taking of hostages;

(c) outrages upon personal dignity, in particular humiliating and degrading treatment;

(d) the passing of sentences and the carrying out of executions without previous judgment pronounced by a regularly constituted court, affording all the judicial guarantees which are recognized as indispensable by civilized peoples.

(2) The wounded and sick shall be collected and cared for.

An impartial humanitarian body, such as the International Committee of the Red Cross, may offer its services to the Parties to the conflict.

The Parties to the conflict should further endeavour to bring into force, by means of special agreements, all or part of the other provisions of the present Convention.

The application of the preceding provisions shall not affect the legal status of the Parties to the conflict.

Throughout this chapter, there appear quoted passages without citations. All such passages are taken from the text of Article 3.

12 *Ibid.*

government's activities would have been restricted in so many spheres that the article's doom would have been sealed with its birth.

In analyzing the prescriptions of Article 3, one is immediately struck by the ambiguity of seven controversial words —"armed conflict not of an international character." Although a persuasive argument might well be advanced that these words make Article 3 applicable to any noninternational armed conflict, it is generally accepted that the article does not apply to acts of banditry or even to shortlived insurrections. Article 3 is, in addition, said to envisage a "situation where the normal criminal processes cannot be applied to the persons who are the opposing Party to the conflict,"[13] where the insurgents possess an organized military force, the ability to act authoritatively within a determinate territory, and the means of respecting and ensuring respect for Article 3, and where the legitimate government must employ its regular military forces to quell the disturbances. However, despite both this viewpoint and the fact that "nations have been all too reluctant to acknowledge the application of Article 3 to conflicts in which they find themselves involved,"[14] the better view appears to be that

[13] Draper, RED CROSS CONVENTIONS 89. In that connection Draper adds that Article 3 is "in existence whenever sustained troop action is undertaken against rebels, even though the rebel organisation and control of any area is minimal, and the situation is such that the police are not able to enforce the criminal law in a particular area by reason of rebel action" (94).

[14] Higgins, *International Law and Civil Conflict*, in E. Luard, ed., THE INTERNATONAL REGULATION OF CIVIL WARS 169, 183 (1971). For instance, Britain refused to acknowledge that it was under any obligation to apply Article 3 in the Cyprus, Kenya, and Malaya conflicts, and France denied the applicability of Article 3 to the Algerian struggle. *Ibid.*; Farer, *Humanitarian Law and Armed Conflicts: Toward the Definition of "International Armed Conflict,"* 71 COLUM. L. REV. 37, 5𝟮 (1971). See also Draper, RED CROSS CONVENTIONS 15 n.47 for the observation that "the refusal of France and the United Kingdom to recognise that these conflicts fall within Art. 3 has, it is thought, been determined by political consideration and not by any objective assessment of the facts."

165

Article 3 "should be applied as widely as possible [and that] however useful, therefore, the various conditions stated above may be, they are not indispensable, since no Government can object to respecting, in its dealings with internal enemies, whatever the nature of the conflict between it and them, a few essential rules which it in fact respects daily, under its own laws, even when dealing with common criminals."[15]

Doubt exists, too, concerning the words "each Party to the conflict shall be bound to apply." Are the insurgents bound by Article 3 or do the prescriptions of Article 3 apply only to the High Contracting Parties who signed the Geneva Conventions of 1949? While few if any scholars would deny that insurgents are in fact required to adhere to the prohibitions of Article 3, many writers offer diverse—and often weak or even contradictory—reasons for this conclusion.

To begin with, it is argued that insurgents are bound because treaties bind states, not merely the governments that negotiate the treaty,[16] even though balking insurgents might assert that they only "claim to represent the people [and] do not necessarily assent to the obligations of a government."[17] Secondly, it is believed that Article 3 sets forth established law independently of contractual obligation, although this view—which might be supported by "the very

[15] Pictet, COMMENTARY ON THE GENEVA CONVENTION 50. Pictet continues: "If an insurgent party applies Article 3, so much the better for the victims of the conflict. No one will complain. If it does not apply it, it will prove that those who regard its actions as mere acts of anarchy or brigandage are right. As for the *de jure* Government, the effect on it of applying Article 3 cannot be in any way prejudicial; for no Government can possibly claim that it is *entitled to* make use of torture and other inhumane acts prohibited by the Convention, as a means of combating its enemies" (52).

[16] See Kelly, *Legal Aspects of Military Operations in Counterinsurgency*, 21 MIL. L. REV. 95, 117 n.85 (1963).

[17] *The Geneva Convention and the Treatment of Prisoners of War in Vietnam*, 80 HARV. L. REV. 851, 857 (1967) [hereafter cited as *The Geneva Convention*].

content of the article, as well as the fact that the weight of world opinion subscribes to these provisions"[18]—is open to question, since the laws of war traditionally govern only hostilities between states or civil strife that has attained the state of belligerency and since the practice of states dating from 1949 would suggest otherwise.[19] Thirdly, it is claimed that rebels are bound because the binding of the legitimate government binds all of its subjects,[20] even though this position is hardly convincing in view of the fact that, traditionally, rebels were bound only when belligerency had been declared.[21] Finally, and most persuasively, it has been suggested that all participants in civil strife are obligated to conform to the tenets of Article 3 because the alleged necessities of war are not in any way compromised and because the drafters of Article 3 took into account the special requirements of rebellion "by the separate treatment of civil war and the imposition of more limited duties."[22]

When taken together, these viewpoints, however imprecise and imperfect, lead one to conclude that insurgents are included in the words "each Party." Such a conclusion is, however, not just legally sound. It is also practically and theoretically required. Indeed, "by definition, insurgents cannot adhere to a treaty prior to the commencement of

[18] See Greenspan, MODERN LAW OF LAND WARFARE 624.

[19] See *The Geneva Convention* 856–57.

[20] See Greenspan, MODERN LAW OF LAND WARFARE 623–24. Parenthetically, the irony of this position—which does not suggest its invalidity—is that insurgents are bound by the actions of the government that they are attempting to overthrow. See generally Hooker & Savaster, *The Geneva Convention of 1949: Application in the Vietnamese Conflict*, 5 VA. J. INT'L L. 243, 251 (1965).

[21] See *The Geneva Convention* 857.

[22] *Ibid.*, 858. See also McNair & Watts, THE LEGAL EFFECTS OF WAR 31 (1966); Schwarzenberger, INTERNATIONAL LAW AS APPLIED BY INTERNATIONAL COURTS AND TRIBUNALS 718 (1968). To the extent that the aforesaid theories fail to deal adequately with civil strife, the reason may be attributed to the fact that they were "concepts originally developed solely to regulate the affairs of nation-states." *The Geneva Convention* 857.

167

hostilities, and if the applicability of Article 3 were made to turn on accession afterwards, there would be too great a risk of non-adherence merely as a short-sighted response to pressures of the moment."[23] For this reason, it hardly seems unjust to bind insurgents without their consent to a treaty to which states of all ideologies have become signatories and from which the insurgents derive great benefit.

Both the legitimate government and insurgents are therefore required, "as a minimum," to treat humanely, "in all circumstances," all "persons taking no active part in the hostilities." By condemning, inter alia, "cruel treatment and torture," "humiliating and degrading treatment," and summary justice,[24] the drafters left the parties to the conflict with sufficient flexibility to conduct hostilities and, at the same time, advanced the cause of humanitarianism through the protection of noncombatants as human beings. By making the proscriptions applicable "in all circumstances," they removed "the eroding effect of military necessity"[25] as a factor in a participant's decision to apply the article, and they clearly indicated that the failure of a participant to fulfill its obligations under Article 3 would justify a subsequent charge of war crimes by the other participant, but not a concomitant violation of Article 3 by that party. And, by extending the protection of the article to "members of the armed forces who have laid down their arms and those placed *hors de combat* by sickness, wounds, detention, or

[23] *The Geneva Convention* 858.

[24] Only summary justice is prohibited outright. "No sort of immunity is given to anyone under this provision. There is nothing in it to prevent a person presumed to be guilty from being arrested and so placed in a position where he can do no further harm; and it leaves intact the right of the State to prosecute, sentence and punish according to the law." Pictet, COMMENTARY ON THE GENEVA CONVENTION 54. But cf. Oppenheim, 2 INTERNATIONAL LAW 372, for the view that "the indiscriminate carrying out of executions for acts other than war crimes proper may strain to the breaking point the humanitarian obligations of Article 3."

[25] Draper, RED CROSS CONVENTIONS 97.

any other cause," the drafters did what both justice and reason dictate; for while the battlefield logically suggests "that a soldier act differently toward a combatant than toward a non-combatant . . . no [such] reason requires that the soldier initially treat one non-combatant differently from another."[26]

Of import, too, in "humanizing" civil strife is the provision in Article 3 that permits an "impartial humanitarian body, such as the International Committee of the Red Cross, [to] offer its services to the Parties to the conflict." Prior to the adoption of this provision, humanitarian initiatives were often looked upon by the legitimate government as an unfriendly act; with its adoption, such an interpretation became unjustified. Unfortunately, however, some of the mistrust and resentment from the pre-1949 period has carried over into the present. As evidenced by resistance to Red Cross offers of assistance in the Algerian, Kenyan, and Tibetan struggles,[27] states are fearful that acceptance of those offers will result in the application to the conflict of the protections of Article 3, which, as stated earlier, they are at best reluctant to accord insurgents.

While the contracting parties have not been anxious to acknowledge the applicability of Article 3—and at this point it might be well to state that Article 3 binds only the signatories of the Conventions, unless, of course, Article 3 is viewed as having become customary law during the past twenty-six years—they have at times done so. What they have not done, however, is implement the suggestion in paragraph 3 of the article that they "should further endeavour

26 Bond, *Protection of Non-Combatants* 794. He adds, quite correctly, that "the non-combatant poses no immediate threat. He has surrendered or is offering no resistance or . . . is in 'the hands of' the soldier. What action the soldier may take against a non-combatant during the conduct of military operations should depend on a balancing of military necessity against the human rights of the individual—and not be dependent upon an individual's status as a citizen, enemy alien, guerrilla sympathizer, or loyal supporter."

27 See Draper, RED CROSS CONVENTIONS 91.

to bring into force, by means of special agreements, all or part of the other provisions" of the Geneva Conventions. Since the provision would serve to secure increased benefits for persons affected by the strife, it is indeed regrettable that to date the suggestion has been "overlooked." In addition, since the governments of the states bound to adhere to Article 3 continue, despite paragraph 4, to be fearful that an agreement with insurgents will elevate the insurgents' position in the eyes of the world, it is doubtful that the "special agreements" envisioned in Article 3 will ever become a reality.

In an effort to dispel fears and to garner support for Article 3, the drafters provided in paragraph 4 that "the application of the preceding provisions shall not affect the legal status of the Parties to the conflict." Indeed, without the addition of that language, there seems little doubt that, given the desire of governments to retain their inherent powers over rebels, Article 3 would have been rejected by the states represented at Geneva.[28] Accordingly, it is universally accepted in theory that the extension of the benefits of Article 3 to insurgents does not in any way change their status, although the hesitancy of states to apply the article would in practice seem to dictate a different conclusion.

This hesitancy, albeit unjustified, can perhaps be explained by the fact that once a conflict is said to be within the confines of Article 3, any contracting party has the right to demand compliance from another contracting party engaged in civil strife. To some extent, therefore, "armed conflicts of a non-international character have been effectively internationalised"[29]—or at least they would be if Article 3 were applied. In light of the fact that governments jealously guard their powers under the cloak of domestic jurisdiction,

[28] See generally *ibid.*, 17; Pictet, COMMENTARY ON THE GENEVA CONVENTION 60–61; Siotis, LE DROIT DE LA GUERRE ET LES CONFLITS ARMÉES D'UN CARACTÈRE NON-INTERNATIONAL 217–18 (1958) "les auteurs de ce texte voulaient desarmer toute opposition à son adoption" ("the authors of this text wished to block all opposition to its adoption").

[29] Schwarzenberger, INTERNATIONAL LAW 719.

they are loathe in any way to relinquish that jurisdiction. In light of the fact, too, that Article 3 is deemed to involve such a relinquishment, states are less than enthusiastic about acknowledging the article's applicability.

It has been said that Article 3 is deficient because it guarantees only minimum substantive rights and "because its failure to guarantee supervision by a neutral body makes the implementation of its substantive provisions necessarily speculative";[30] it also has been said that Article 3 is inadequate, since "the slaughter of prisoners with or without legal proceedings can hardly satisfy humanitarian conscience."[31] While these conclusions are factually beyond dispute, they overlook the main deficiency, namely, the unwillingness of governments to concede the application of the proscriptions of Article 3 to conflicts within their borders. In that regard, a call for a neutral body—a body under the overall supervision of the Security Council could play such a role—might well be in order. Such a body would first decide if Article 3 applies and then concern itself with supervision of the article's substantive rights. Until such a body is created, until the organs of the United Nations exercise their condemnation and enforcement powers, or until states voluntarily accept Article 3 in all struggles above the level of banditry, solace must be found in the knowledge that "the establishment of a legal norm may precede its regular enforcement, but the existence of such a norm is a value in itself."[32]

Additional International Prescriptions

Important norms are also set forth in the European Convention for the Protection of Human Rights and Fundamental Freedoms and in the Universal Declaration of Hu-

[30] Farer, *Humanitarian Law and Armed Conflicts* 39.

[31] Veuthey, *The Red Cross and Non-International Conflicts*, 113 INT'L REV. OF RED CROSS 411, 416 (1970). For the purpose of developing a more acceptable and adequate treaty to protect people caught in "armed conflict not of an international character," the International Red Cross has, since 1953, held both meetings of experts and general conferences of national Red Cross representatives. See *ibid.*, 414.

[32] Draper, RED CROSS CONVENTIONS 100.

man Rights. More specifically, Article 2 of the European Convention and Article 3 of the Universal Declaration state that everyone has a right to life and personal security, although Article 2 of the European Convention provides that in certain instances—including the effecting of a lawful arrest and the quelling of a riot or insurrection—a resulting deprivation of life will not be deemed to be in contravention of the articles. Article 3 of the European Convention and Article 5 of the Universal Declaration furthermore prohibit torture or cruel, inhuman, or degrading treatment or punishment. And Article 15 of the European Convention strengthens the proscriptions of Articles 2 and 3, for, while it permits derogations from the obligations imposed by the European Convention, it denies the right of derogation from Article 2 (except in respect of deaths emanating from lawful acts of war) and Article 3.

Other provisions of these instruments will be discussed in the chapter that follows.[33] Suffice it to say at this point that signatories of the instruments are required to treat humanely all persons under all circumstances.

Related Matters

Before measuring the actions of the participants in the Ulster conflict against the standards of Article 3 of the Ge-

[33] For a detailed analysis of Articles 2 and 3 of the European Convention, see Fawcett, THE APPLICATION OF THE EUROPEAN CONVENTION ON HUMAN RIGHTS 28–41 (1969). Articles 6 and 7 of the International Covenant on Civil and Political Rights (GA Res. 2200A) provide, respectively, that all peoples have an "inherent right to life" and that "no one shall be subjected to torture or to cruel, inhuman or degrading treatment or punishment." The Covenant has not yet attained the force of law because it has not been signed by the required thirty-five states. However, Britain signed the Covenant on September 16, 1968. See Schwelb, *The United Kingdom Signs the Covenants on Human Rights*, 18 INT'L & COMP. L. Q. 457 (1969). See also U.N. Doc. A/RES/3218 (XXIX) (A/c.3/L.2106/Rev.1) (1974) for the text of a U.N. resolution on torture and other cruel, inhuman, or degrading treatment or punishment in relation to detention and imprisonment. The vote on the resolution was 125 to 0 with one abstention.

172

neva Conventions, Articles 2 and 3 of the European Convention, and Articles 3 and 5 of the Universal Declaration, two other areas must be studied. First of all, guerrilla warfare in general and the use of terror in particular must be analyzed. Secondly, the permissibility of employing nontoxic riot gas to bring civil disorders under control must be examined. Since the IRA is waging guerrilla warfare and since nontoxic riot gas has been employed by the Ulster authorities to contain demonstrators and marchers, both areas are of import.

GUERRILLA WARFARE AND THE USE OF TERROR

To be sure, guerrilla warfare is not a new weapon. In 1808, for instance, the Spanish effectively used guerrilla warfare against Napoleon. Not until the twentieth century, however, when Mao Tse-tung, Vo Nguyen Giap and Che Guevara developed the strategy of guerrilla warfare, did it become the effective weapon that it is today. Under their aegis, guerrillas formed into armed bands that became "the fighting vanguard of the people"[34] in a "war of the broad masses of an economically backward country standing up

[34] Guevara, GUERRILLA WARFARE 17 (1961). As Guevara states:

The guerrilla band is an armed nucleus, the fighting vanguard of the people. It draws its great force from the mass of the people themselves. The guerrilla band is not to be considered inferior to the army against which it fights simply because it is inferior in fire power. Guerrilla warfare is used by the side which possesses a much smaller number of arms for use in defense against oppression.

The guerrilla fighter needs full help from the people of the area. This is an indispensable condition. This is clearly seen by considering the case of bandit gangs that operate in a region. They have all the characteristics of a guerrilla army, homogeneity, respect for the leader, valor, knowledge of the ground, and, often, even good understanding of the tactics to be employed. The only thing missing is support of the people; and inevitably, these gangs are captured and exterminated by the public force.

See also Bindschedler-Robert, *A Reconsideration of the Law of Armed Conflicts*, in Carnegie Endowment, THE LAW OF ARMED CONFLICTS 1, 38 (1971).

173

against a powerfully equipped and well trained army of aggression."[35] At their suggestion, moreover, the guerrillas (the fish) sought the help of the people (the water), for, just as fish die without water, so the guerrillas, according to the three masters of this form of warfare, cannot succeed without popular support.[36]

Yet conditions and times change. One such change concerns the guerrillas themselves. Although the Mao-Giap-Guevara analysis has stood the test of time and conquered many a powerful foe, it seems somewhat dated in the 1970s. Indeed, while there can be little doubt that guerrillas can be more successful with popular support, there can also be no doubt "that insurgencies can and do develop without popular support and that apathy can be as beneficial to the insurgent as actual support."[37] If, therefore, Mao's fish-water analogy is to be retained, it should perhaps be "modified" to include catfish—a hardy fish that, as people in the southern United States have learned, can survive without water for long periods of time.

A second change concerns the locale of the guerrillas, a change that makes it easier for catfish to live without water.

[35] Giap, PEOPLE's WAR PEOPLE's ARMY 48 (1962). Giap adds: "Is the enemy strong? One avoids him. Is he weak? One attacks him. To his modern armament one opposes a boundless heroism to vanquish either by harassing or by annihilating the enemy according to circumstances, and by combining military operations with political and economic action; no fixed line of demarcation, the front being wherever the enemy is found."

[36] In the words of Mao Tse-tung: "Many people think it impossible for guerrillas to exist for long in the enemy's rear. Such a belief reveals lack of comprehension of the relationship that should exist between the people and the troops. The former may be likened to water and the latter to the fish who inhabit it. How may it be said that these two cannot exist together? It is only undisciplined troops who make the people their enemies and who, like the fish out of its native element, cannot live." Mao, ON GUERRILLA WARFARE 92–93 (1961).

[37] Paust, *My Lai and Vietnam: Norms, Myths and Leader Responsibility,* 57 MIL. L. REV. 99, 135 (1972).

Whereas traditional guerrilla theory looks to the rural population for support and awaits the fulfillment of revolutionary conditions, the guerrillas of the 1970s—as exemplified by Uruguay's Tupamaros—can at any time find the requisite revolutionary conditions in the slums of cities. In "inadequate housing, poor sanitation, boredom, unemployment, corrupt landlords, and little educational opportunity are but a few of the conditions that can be exploited by a smooth-talking agitator";[38] in the stores of the cities are the food, money, and weapons that guerrillas require; and in the urban ghettos are the anonymity that is the urban guerrilla's lifeblood and the opportunities to blend the smoke of incinerator fires with the emissions of arms factories.

What has not changed, however, is the guerrilla's strategy. Fighting in dispersed and mobile groups, the guerrilla continues to employ ambushes, surprise attacks, and sabotage and, as a rule, to avoid pitched battles. Never losing "sight of the main objective of the fighting that is the destruction of the enemy manpower,"[39] he seeks above all to eliminate losses—even at the cost of losing ground—to insure the realization of that goal and the complete liberation of the country.

While sabotage is a legitimate and important weapon in the guerrilla's arsenal, "it is necessary to distinguish clearly between sabotage, a revolutionary and highly effective method of warfare, and terrorism, a measure that is generally ineffective and indiscriminate in its results, since it often makes victims of innocent people and destroys a large number of lives that would be valuable to the revolution."[40]

---

[38] R. Black, *A Change in Tactics?: The Urban Insurgent*, 23 AIR UNIV. REV. 50, 53 (1972). But Guevara, as evidenced by his development of suburban warfare that would paralyze the commercial and industrial life of a country, saw the need to adapt the traditional theory to changing times. See Guevara, GUERRILLA WARFARE 37–39.

[39] Giap, PEOPLE'S WAR PEOPLE'S ARMY 48.

[40] Guevara, GUERRILLA WARFARE 26. He also points out that "it is ridiculous to carry out sabotage against a soft drink factory, but it is

175

Although it has been argued that terror may be a valuable tactic[41] and that it may be employed against people occupying administrative positions, since those individuals "assume a common risk in time of civil war whether they wear a three piece suit or a uniform,"[42] there is no question that, legally speaking, acts of terror against the civilian population or against "members of armed forces who have laid down their arms [or have been] placed *hors de combat*" violate the prescriptions of Article 3 of the Geneva Conventions.[43] At the same time, therefore, that ambushes of the military and the blowing up of military barracks (or key industrial complexes so long as civilian life or limb is not threatened) are

---

absolutely correct and advisable to carry out sabotage against a power plant" (27).

On the subject of the use of terror, see generally Crozier, The Rebels 159 (1960) ("terrorism is the weapon of the weak"); Feldman, *Violence and Volatility: The Likelihood of Revolution*, in H. Eckstein, ed., Internal War: Problems and Approaches 111–29 (1964); Janos, *Authority and Violence: The Political Framework of Internal War*, in Eckstein, ed., Internal War 130–41; and Thornton, *Terror as a Weapon of Political Agitation*, in Eckstein, ed., Internal War 71–99.

[41] Guevara states that it "should be considered a valuable tactic when it is used to put to death some noted leader of the oppressing forces well known for his cruelty, his efficiency in repression, or other quality that makes his elimination useful. But the killing of persons of small importance is never advisable, since it brings on an increase of reprisals, including deaths." Guevara, Guerrilla Warfare 26.

[42] Caflisch, *Summary Record of the Conference*, in Carnegie Endowment, The Law of Armed Conflicts 65, 79 (1971). The basis for this position is that one should not discriminate "in favor of the local official who uses the police to enforce his policies or those of the central regime and the police captain who responds to the orders of the administrative official. In many civil wars, the whole issue is which administrative structure, including the police and army, shall govern." *Ibid.*, 78–79.

[43] See generally Bindschedler-Robert, *Reconsideration of the Law*, 91; Lawrence, *The Status under International Law of Recent Guerrilla Movements in Latin America*, 7 int'l lawyer 405, 418–22 (1973); Paust, *My Lai and Vietnam* 139–46. It would also be instructive to see G.A. Res. 2444, 23 u.n. gaor, Supp. 18, at 50, U.N. Doc. A/7218 (1969).

permissible, assassination, indiscriminate warfare which results in attacks on the civilian population, massacres, and wanton destruction of nonmilitary objectives are clearly illegal actions. At the same time, too, that these prohibited acts might be said to be effective weapons in the guerrilla arsenal, it must be remembered that effectiveness and legality are not synonymous, and that the policy of Article 3—and all laws of war—is to balance military necessity and humanitarianism.

RIOT GAS AND THE LAWS OF ARMED CONFLICT

To combat both guerrillas and nonviolent opponents, governments often employ nontoxic riot gases. In doing so, they raise the question of the legality of their actions. Even though the only actions to date—the 1925 Geneva Protocol[44] and a 1969 General Assembly resolution[45]—speak of the use of gases in *international* armed conflicts, they are important in an analysis of noninternational armed conflicts because they may shed some light on whether the community of nations deems the usage of nontoxic riot gases inhumane treatment. If, indeed, such usage were proscribed internationally as being inhumane, it naturally would follow that the domestic employment of nontoxic riot gases would violate Article 3 of the Geneva Conventions, Article 3 of the European Convention, and Article 5 of the Universal Declaration.

Unfortunately, the 1925 Protocol is less than clear on the issue of nontoxic riot gases. While tear gases producing poisonous fumes are definitely prohibited by the Protocol, the confusion resulting from the English use of the word "other" and the French resort to "similaires" has continued without

[44] Protocol for the Prohibition of the Use in War of Asphyxiating, Poisonous or Other Gases, and of Bacteriological Methods of Warfare, June 17, 1925, 94 L.N.T.S. No. 2138, at 64 (1929).

[45] G.A. Res. 2603A, 24 U.N. GAOR, Supp. 30, at 16, U.N. Doc. A/7630 (1969). The resolution prohibited "chemical agents of warfare—chemical substances, whether gaseous, liquid or solid—which might be employed because of their direct toxic effects on man, animals or plants."

abatement since 1925;[46] and while the debate will undoubtedly continue for some time, it is interesting to note—especially in view of the implications for Northern Ireland—the ostensible shift in the British position. Although Britain maintains that its posture is unchanged and that all gases, including lachrymatory (tear) gas, are prohibited, it argues, in a somewhat tortured fashion, that "modern technology has developed CS smoke which, unlike the tear gases available in 1930, is considered to be not significantly harmful to man in other than wholly exceptional circumstances and [that it] regard[s] CS and other such gases accordingly as being outside the scope of the Geneva Protocol."[47]

The resulting confusion about the international use of nontoxic riot control agents provides little guidance for the internal application of such gases. In any case, however, it is obvious that there are limits to the usage of such agents in civil strife. Admittedly, the use of temporary gases is less cruel than bombs or bullets and greatly reduces the physical suffering of combatants and noncombatants alike; admitted-

---

[46] For detailed discussions of riot control agents and the Protocol—which the United States finally ratified in December 1974—see Bunn, *Banning Poison Gas and Germ Warfare: Should the United States Agree?* 1969 WISC. L. REV. 375, 394–406; and J. N. Moore, *Ratification of the Geneva Protocol on Gas and Bacteriological Warfare: A Legal and Political Analysis,* 59 U. VA. L. REV. 419, 454–65 (1972). See also Thomas & Thomas, LEGAL LIMITS ON THE USE OF CHEMICAL AND BIOLOGICAL WEAPONS 74–76 (1970).

[47] 795 PARL. DEB., H.C. 18 (Written Answers by Sec. of State for For. & Comm. Affairs to Questions). "CS is referred to as a super tear gas whose effects are felt almost immediately. It causes extreme burning of the eyes accompanied by a copious flow of tears, coughing, difficulty in breathing and chest tightness, involuntary closing of the eyes, stinging sensation of moist skin, running nose, and dizziness or swimming of the head. In addition, heavy concentrations will cause nausea and vomiting." Thomas & Thomas, LEGAL LIMITS 11. See also Bothe, DAS VÖLKERRECHTLICHE VERBOT DES EINSATZES CHEMISCHER UND BAKTERIOLOGISCHER WAFFEN 348 (1973); Whiteman, 10 DIGEST OF INTERNATIONAL LAW 473 (1968); J. N. Moore, *Ratification of the Geneva Protocol* 464–65.

ly, too, the possible effect of nontoxic gases on certain classes of people—the young, infirm, and old—seems less significant than the impact of such agents on the broad masses of society.[48] Yet the fact remains that the indiscriminate resort to irritants that are deemed permissible would certainly appear to make cruel that which might otherwise be considered humane and, in the process, to violate the tenets of Article 3 of the Geneva Conventions, Article 3 of the European Convention, and Article 5 of the Universal Declaration.

Summary

Whenever civil strife—armed conflict not of an international character and in excess of mere acts of banditry—occurs in the territory of a contracting party to the Geneva Conventions of 1949, the European Convention, or the Universal Declaration, the parties to the conflict are, at a minimum, bound to treat humanely all persons taking no part in the hostilities. In particular, each party—regardless of whether that party is the legitimate government or insurgents engaged in guerrilla warfare—is prohibited from taking any action that would constitute an outrage upon personal dignity. Furthermore, in the case of the Geneva Conventions, each party agrees to permit impartial humanitarian bodies to offer their services and to endeavor to bring into force more extensive protections than are embodied in Article 3.

Insofar as the use of nontoxic riot control agents is concerned, the better view appears to be that they may be employed in the type of conflicts envisioned by Article 3. Care must be taken, though, that they are used humanely, for if such agents are employed indiscriminately, they would produce results prohibited under international law.

[48] See generally Bindschedler-Robert, *Biological and Chemical Weapons*, in Bassiouni & Nanda, eds., A TREATISE ON INTERNATIONAL CRIMINAL LAW 351, 355 (1973). There are suggestions that nontoxic riot control agents may have a negative effect on certain members of these classes.

179

THE DUBLIN VIEWPOINT

Just as Britain's attempt to solve the "English problem" represents a low point in its long history, so its efforts to deal with opponents of British rule establish a modern nadir in the application of the laws of war to civil strife. Be they before or after 1949, those efforts make this dark British page of history still blacker.

The pre-1949 actions were vividly and painfully exemplified by the notorious Black and Tans, who, in response to Irish attempts to break the British connection, unleashed a wave of terror across Ireland reminiscent of the campaign of Cromwell; the post-1949 actions are summarized in the indiscriminate use of CS smoke and firepower during the August 1969 riots and in the death of a single unarmed man —Harry Thornton—who, because his van unavoidably backfired before a British Army post, was mercilessly shot down in direct contravention of Article 3 of the Geneva Conventions, Article 2 of the European Convention, and Article 3 of the Universal Declaration. Yet it is in the inhumane treatment of detainees and internees and the brutal onslaught of the British Army in Derry on January 30, 1972 that these condemnable and illegal acts are most glaringly revealed.

Following complaints by concerned Irishmen of the repressive treatment accorded those individuals deprived of their liberty by the internment policy of the British, Britain convened the Compton Committee to inquire into allegations against the security forces of physical brutality made by persons arrested on August 9, 1971.[49] Despite obvious

[49] See Compton, REPORT OF THE ENQUIRY INTO ALLEGATIONS AGAINST THE SECURITY FORCES OF PHYSICAL BRUTALITY IN NORTHERN IRELAND ARISING OUT OF EVENTS ON THE 9TH AUGUST, 1971 (Cmnd. 4823) (1971) (hereafter cited as Compton Report). The Compton Report considered the cases of eleven men who had been submitted to "interrogation in depth" from August 11 to August 17, 1971; the second Compton Report (not available to the public) considered the case of three other men who had been so interrogated from October 11 to October 18, 1971. The con-

tortures—lack of sleep, forced standing in a spreadeagled position, repeated beatings, cursings, hooding, required physical exercises, noise, lack of food and drink, and denial of attendance at religious services[50]—the Compton inquiry "denied their meaning by Alice-in-Wonderland logic, by obscure and hypocritical phrases that whitewashed the brutality and spoke only of 'ill-treatment' and 'deep interrogation' —rhetoric seeking to justify obviously barbarous means by resort to a worthy end."[51] For the Compton Committee, ill-treatment and brutality were distinguishable; for the rest of the world—as evidenced by Article 3 of the Geneva Conventions, Article 3 of the European Convention, and Article 5 of the Universal Declaration—they are synonymous.[52]

Not only was the Compton investigation a ludicrous mockery of common sense, but also it was a perversion of justice. Indeed, instead of the legal protections on which the British pride themselves, the Compton inquiry was de-

---

clusions of the second report were that there was no ill-treatment in two of the three cases; the report did state, however, that hooding, wall-standing, deprivation of sleep, and bread-and-water diets were employed. See "One Allegation Upheld and Two Rejected in Second Inquiry," *The Times* (London); November 17, 1971, at 5, col. 6.

50 See generally TORTURE: THE RECORD OF BRITISH BRUTALITY IN IRELAND 2–39 (1972) (hereafter cited as TORTURE). As told by one of the tortured internees, "the obvious reason for making us face the wall and look straight ahead was to ensure that no 'prisoner's' eyes witnessed an assault on any other 'prisoner'" (27). Quite obvious, too, was the fact that the techniques employed were "intended to produce mental disturbance and disorientation in order to persuade the victim to become compliant in supplying information" (39). See also Faul & Murray, BRITISH ARMY AND SPECIAL BRANCH RUC BRUTALITIES 9–10 (1972); Sunday Times Insight Team, ULSTER 293–97 (where the authors state that the inquiry reported without comment the official reasons for the procedures concerning detainees).

51 Kennedy, *Ulster is an International Issue*, 11 FOREIGN POL. 57, 62 (1973).

52 See Compton Report 23, where brutality is defined as "an inhuman or savage form of cruelty, and that cruelty implies a disposition to inflict suffering, coupled with indifference to, or pleasure in, the victim's pain."

181

fective on several grounds. It was held in private (ostensibly to protect soldiers and their families from the risks of IRA reprisals); it consisted solely of Englishmen (who could not possibly be objective in assessing the guilt of their fellow countrymen); it lacked the statutory power to compel witnesses to attend; it excluded cross-examination of witnesses by lawyers; and it limited itself to an examination of physical methods of torture, when, in fact, "much of the suffering of internees [was] due to specifically contrived methods of psychological torture."[53] Is it any wonder then that internees refused to subject themselves to this mock inquiry and to cooperate in an investigation by persons who "represented" their torturers, thereby leaving the Compton inquisition to depend for its information on newspaper clippings and hearsay?

So blatantly inadequate was the Compton investigation that London immediately ordered an inquiry into authorized procedures for the interrogation of persons suspected of terrorism. While the majority of the three-man committee appointed to consider those procedures—the Parker Committee—"vindicated" Compton, the minority report of Lord Gardiner took issue with Compton's findings. Although Gardiner stated that the Parker Committee was not a court of appeal from the Compton investigation, he pointed out that the records upon which Compton relied were incomplete and that under Compton's definition of brutality there would be no logical limit to the ill-treatment permissible so long as the ill-treatment proved "to be necessary to get

[53] Campaign for Social Justice in Northern Ireland, NORTHERN IRE-LAND—THE MAILED FIST: A RECORD OF ARMY & POLICE BRUTALITY FROM AUGUST 9–NOVEMBER 9, 1971 61 (1972). Apropos the question of torture, it might well be argued that doctors examining men prior to subjecting them to acts of torture were violating the 1948 Geneva Declaration, which stated that doctors, even under threat, "will not use [their] medical knowledge contrary to the laws of humanity." TORTURE at 62. See also AMNESTY INTERNATIONAL REPORT OF AN ENQUIRY INTO AL-LEGATIONS OF ILL-TREATMENT IN NORTHERN IRELAND 46 (1972) for the view that "ill-treatment is illegal, immoral, and inexpedient."

182

the information out of [a man]."[54] In addition, Gardiner revealed that the British Army failed to adhere to the regulations of the Joint Directive on Military Interrogation in Internal Security Operations Overseas, which require that "military personnel are to acquaint themselves with the laws of the country concerned, and . . . not act unlawfully under any circumstances whatever";[55] for, although British law permits "anything which is reasonably necessary to keep [a man] in custody,"[56] it prohibits hooding (a tort and a crime), wall-standing, and deprivation of diet ("unless duly awarded as a punishment under prison rules")[57] or sleep. Finally, he concluded that the procedures followed "were secret, illegal, not morally justifiable and alien to [British] traditions."[58]

While Gardiner's condemnation of British methods of interrogation was based on British, not international, law, he would undoubtedly have concluded, had he been the man heading the tribunal, that British Army actions in Derry on January 30, 1972 violated international law. Instead of Gardiner, however, the inquiry into the Bloody Sunday massacre was headed by Lord Widgery. And, in lieu of an objective investigation, more British whitewash was spread on the prison walls of Ulster.

[54] Parker, REPORT OF THE COMMITTEE OF PRIVY COUNSELLORS APPOINTED TO CONSIDER AUTHORISED PROCEDURES FOR THE INTERROGATION OF PERSONS SUSPECTED OF TERRORISM (Cmnd. 4901) 20 (1972) (hereafter cited as Parker Report). Earlier, Lord Gardiner exclaimed that "under this definition, which some of our witnesses thought came from the Inquisition, if an interrogator believed, to his great regret, that it was necessary for him to cut off the fingers of a detainee one by one to get the required information out of him for the sole purpose of saving life, this would not be cruel and, because not cruel, not brutal." *Ibid.*, 13.

[55] Paragraph 6 of the Joint Directive. It may be found in the appendix to the Parker Report 23–24. For a caustic attack on the Joint Directive, see Brownlie, *Interrogation in Depth: The Compton and Parker Reports*, 35 MODERN L. REV. 501, 507 (1972).

[56] Parker Report 13.   [57] *Ibid.*

[58] *Ibid.*, 22.

To say that "the style and language of the Derry report is not that of a learned Judge"[59] is to state the obvious. To assert that Widgery's decision to restrict his tribunal's reference to the actual scene of violence and to the period when the violence began on January 30, 1972 is to avoid "raising questions about political decisions taken in relation to the march and to protect those politicians who took them from accountability for the horrible events that followed those decisions."[60] And to believe that "there would have been no deaths in Londonderry on 30 January if those who had organized the illegal march had not thereby created a highly dangerous situation in which a clash between demonstrators and the security forces was almost inevitable"[61] is to place murder and illegal marching in the same criminal category

[59] *Did Widgery Write Widgery?*, 1 CIVIL RIGHTS 3 (April 28, 1972). "All through it is dominated by the propagandist and the question which now falls to be answered is not whether Widgery wrote the report but 'what person or persons wrote the report to which Lord Widgery appended his name?' "

[60] Boyle, WIDGERY—A CRITIQUE 2 (1972). "If he had been as rigorous in excluding evidence on behalf of the Army concerning events prior to that day, as he was in preventing attempts by the next-of-kin's lawyers to have political decisions prior to the march examined, criticism *might* have been muted." *Ibid.*, 3 (emphasis added). See also Barritt & Booth, ORANGE AND GREEN 66 (1972).

[61] Widgery, REPORT OF THE TRIBUNAL APPOINTED TO INQUIRE INTO THE EVENTS ON SUNDAY, 30TH JANUARY 1972, WHICH LED TO LOSS OF LIFE IN CONNECTION WITH THE PROCESSION IN LONDONDERRY ON THAT DAY (H.L. 101, H.C. 220) 38 (1972) (hereafter cited as Widgery Report). But see Boyle, WIDGERY 5–8; Commission of Human Rights, *Government of Ireland Against the Government of the United Kingdom* (Appl. Nos. 5310/71 & 5451/72), 41 COLLECTION OF DECISIONS 1, 38 (1973); Kennedy, *Ulster is an International Issue* 63; "Bloody Sunday Laid to British in U.N. Report," *Washington Post*, June 8, 1972, Section A, 20, col. 1. The most critical and detailed attack on Widgery may be found in Dash, JUSTICE DENIED: A CHALLENGE TO LORD WIDGERY'S REPORT ON "BLOODY SUNDAY" (1972), where the author concludes both that "the record of the Inquiry justifies a finding that in all of the cases of the known dead and wounded, the soldiers fired either deliberately or recklessly at unarmed civilians" (14) and that "an official Inquiry which began with promise did not fulfill that promise" (85).

184

and to reject out of hand the international standards of Article 3 of the Geneva Conventions, Article 2 of the European Convention, Article 3 of the Universal Declaration, and the regulations of the British Army itself.

Those regulations state that "to enforce law and order no one is allowed to use more force than is necessary"[62] and that "any excess in the use of force constitutes a crime."[63] Although the use of arms against a mob may constitute justifiable force, "the firing on a mob can only be excused by the necessity of self-protection, or by the circumstance of the force at the disposal of the authorities being so small that the commission of some outrage—such as the burning of a building, or the breaking open of a prison, or the attacking of a barrack—cannot be otherwise prevented."[64] Moreover, since the actual display of armed force "may provoke a mob and thus do more harm than good,"[65] meetings and processions "should be interfered with as little as possible and no exhibition of force should take place until some violent crime has been or is about to be committed."[66]

Even though these regulations condemn the British Army's Derry actions on their face, however, they are not as damning as the "Yellow Card instructions." Since the aforesaid regulations are contained in a manual, an argument—albeit a weak one—might be made that troops in the field were unaware of its contents; since the "Yellow Card instructions" were issued to each soldier on a small card that he was required to carry with him, ignorance of those instructions would be even less defensible than ignorance of the manual regulations.

The "Yellow Card instructions" are, indeed, strong evidence against the British Army's actions. In brief, they provide that only minimum force may be used; that all crises should, if possible, be handled without firing; that, if firepower is required, only aimed shots should be fired; that a

---

[62] Great Britain, MANUAL OF MILITARY LAW, Part II, 501 (1968).
[63] *Ibid.*, 508.   [64] *Ibid.*, 506.
[65] *Ibid.*, 508.   [66] *Ibid.*, 507.

warning should be given before firing occurs unless "hostile firing is taking place in [the soldier's] area, and a warning is impracticable, or when any delay could lead to death or serious injury to people whom it is [the soldier's] duty to protect or to [the soldier himself]";[67] and that, after the warning is given, a soldier may fire against a "person carrying what [he] can positively identify as a firearm [which is defined to include grenades, nail bombs, and gelignite bombs], but only if [he has] reason to believe that [that person] is about to use it for offensive purposes and [that person] refuses to halt when called upon to do so, and there is no other way of stopping him."

When the British Army's actions on Bloody Sunday are measured against these standards, it is obvious that they were murderously criminal. One need go no further than the testimony of a British officer who said that he fired two rounds into a wall to scare off rioters—a clear violation of the "Yellow Card instruction" that only aimed, not warning, shots be fired—and the accompanying statements of other soldiers who fired into a crowd—another violation—after hearing two shots "which they *presumed* to be directed at them from the main body of rioters."[68]

With his sieve-like logic, Widgery thus earned his rightful place along Compton. Other than contempt, however, that is all he earned. Unable and unwilling to apply British law to British actions, he succeeded not in covering those actions with his whitewash but in highlighting them.

THE LONDON VIEWPOINT

During the recent Algerian War, "the use of torture in the conduct of interrogations of suspects was a deliberate

---

[67] The quotations in this paragraph are from the Yellow Card, which is more formally known as the Instructions by the Director of Operations for Opening Fire in Northern Ireland (Revised November 1971).

[68] *Widgery Waives the Rules*, 83 NEW STATESMAN 547 (April 28, 1972).

policy adopted by the French military authorities 'to save lives' and to assist in ferreting out those responsible for the terrorism in the city of Algiers.''[69] In view of the death and destruction wrought by the IRA on the inhabitants and cities of Belfast, Londonderry, and, occasionally, other areas, such drastic methods of interrogation might well be justified. Still, the British Government has long opposed the use of torture and has constantly endeavored to develop humane arrest, interrogation, and detention procedures for suspected terrorists.[70] As the 1965 Joint Directive clearly states, "apart from legal and moral considerations, torture and physical cruelty of all kinds are professionally unrewarding since a suspect so treated may be persuaded to talk, but not to tell the truth."[71]

When charges were made, therefore, concerning brutality on the part of the Army and RUC, Britain—despite the fact that it was under no international compulsion to do so— immediately ordered an investigation. Under the supervision of Sir Edmund Compton, the inquiry found "that the security forces [had] discharged their onerous duties with the utmost restraint despite the provocations"[72] which were —and are—daily forthcoming.

[69] Fraleigh, *The Algerian Revolution as a Case Study in International Law*, in Falk, ed., THE INTERNATIONAL LAW OF CIVIL WAR 179, 200 (1971). For the observation that terrorists, who by definition have violated the rules of war, cannot hide behind the laws of war, see Trinquier, MODERN WARFARE 21–23 (1964).

[70] See generally Bowen, REPORT BY MR. RODERIC BOWEN, Q.C., ON PROCEDURES FOR THE ARREST, INTERROGATION AND DETENTION OF SUSPECTED TERRORISTS IN ADEN: 14 November 1966. (Cmnd. 3165, 1971 reprint) (hereinafter cited as Bowen Report).

[71] Parker Report, appendix 23. The legal considerations referred to are, in British eyes, domestic considerations. Since the fighting in Northern Ireland is viewed as nothing more than acts of banditry on the part of terrorists, the prescriptions of Article 3 of the Geneva Conventions and other international documents are deemed inapplicable.

[72] Maudling, *Introduction by the Home Secretary*, in Compton Report iii, vi.

187

By the time that the Compton Committee first met on August 31, 1971, 105 persons of the 342 suspects that had been arrested on August 9 had been released, while the remaining 237 persons had been placed in detention in the Crumlin Road jail and on board the *Maidstone*.[73] At the start of the proceedings, a public announcement was made and a letter mailed or delivered to each of the 342 persons arrested on August 9 requesting him to appear before the Compton Committee to substantiate supposed allegations of brutality. Only one such person appeared. For that reason, the investigation was somewhat hampered, and the Compton Committee was forced to rely on personal inspection of the sites where the events took place, oral evidence of officials, hearsay information (mainly in the form of press reports), and written statements purported to be signed by complainants.

More specifically, the Compton Committee examined the complaints of eleven men arrested on August 9, questioned from August 11 to August 17, and placed in the area specified in the detention order after that date. Following review of these complaints and of the general rules governing the custody of detainees and the processes of interrogation as described by British officials,[74] the Compton Committee concluded that, despite certain conflicts that could not be resolved, ill-treatment of detainees had occurred as a result of forced wall-standing, hooding, continuous noise, deprivation of sleep, and a bread-and-water diet and that a measure of ill-treatment and unintended hardship had resulted from other practices.[75] Yet it also concluded, most emphati-

[73] Compton Report 3. The *Maidstone*, a ship moored on the Belfast harbor, was used as a detention center.

[74] *Ibid.*, 12–13. Government testimony stated that wall-standing provides security and imposes discipline which aids the interrogation, that hooding protects the detainee from identification by other detainees and "isolates" them, that the noise to which detainees were subjected prevents their overhearing and being overheard, and that a bread-and-water diet imposes discipline. *Ibid.*, 13.

[75] The Compton Committee found that a measure of ill-treatment

cally, that ill-treatment was not brutality, for "brutality is an inhuman or savage form of cruelty, and that cruelty implies a disposition to inflict suffering, coupled with indifference to, or pleasure in, the victim's pain [and that it did] not think that [had] happened."[76]

Not willing to let matters rest, Westminster, within two weeks of the release of the report of the Compton Committee, set up the Parker Committee to study "whether, and if so in what respects, the procedures . . . authorised for the interrogation of persons suspected of terrorism and for their custody while subject to interrogation require[d] amendment."[77] The Parker Committee determined that the procedures did not require amendment. Although it admitted that long-term mental injury could not scientifically be ruled out, the Parker majority concluded that there was no real risk of such injury if proper safeguards were applied. In short, it stated that, although the end did not justify the means, new and valuable information could be obtained from in-depth interrogations. However, it added that these interrogations "should only be used in cases where it [was] considered vitally necessary to obtain information"[78] and where proper safeguards that conformed to the Joint Directive (and hence to Britain's international obligations under the Geneva Conventions, European Convention, and Universal Declaration) were employed.

While the Parker Committee was still deliberating, Britain established a tribunal to inquire into "the events on Sunday 30 January [1972] which led to loss of life in connection with the procession in Londonderry on that day."[79] That

---

existed in the deception of making detainees think that they were being pushed from an airborne helicopter (*ibid.*, 24–26), that the obstacle course over which they were forced to run resulted in "unintended hardship from the rough going" (*ibid.*, 30), and that the special exercises they were made to perform also produced hardship (*ibid.*, 36).

[76] *Ibid.*, 23.　　　　　　　　[77] Parker Report v.

[78] *Ibid.*, 7 and, generally, 7–9.

[79] Widgery Report 1. See also Commission of Human Rights, *Gov-*

tribunal—the Widgery Tribunal—quickly disputed the allegations of British Army criminality.

To begin with, Lord Widgery observed that in view of the fact that no marches had been permitted since August 9, 1971, the decision of NICRA to hold a march on January 30, 1972 caused a good deal of consternation among various government and army officials. Despite fears that the march would get out of control and that "to allow such a well publicized march to take place without opposition . . . would bring the law into disrepute and make control of future marches impossible,"[80] British Army orders provided that if the march "took place entirely within the Bogside and Creggan it should go unchallenged,"[81] except that scoop-up operations were to be launched to arrest as many hooligans and rioters as possible.

Secondly, Lord Widgery questioned the wisdom of the arrest operation. While he stated, however, "that if the Army had maintained its 'low-key' attitude the rest of the day would have passed off"[82] with only a minimum of rioting, he also recognized that "the Army had been subjected to severe stoning for upwards of half an hour . . . and [that] the future threat to law and order posed by the hard core of hooligans in Londonderry made the arrest of some of them a legitimate security objective."[83]

Thirdly, he concluded, after "listening to evidence and watching the demeanour of witnesses under cross-examination,"[84] that "the first firing . . . was directed at the soldiers."[85] In that connection, he found that the British Army's return of fire was permissible, that the "Yellow Card instructions" were both satisfactory and satisfactorily fol-

---

ernment of Ireland Against the Government of the United Kingdom (Appl. Nos. 5310/71 & 5451/72), 41 COLLECTION OF DECISIONS 1, 37 (1973).

[80] Widgery Report 6.   [81] *Ibid.*, 7.
[82] *Ibid.*, 12.   [83] *Ibid.*
[84] *Ibid.*, 21.   [85] *Ibid.*

lowed, and that additional "restrictions on opening fire would inhibit the soldier from taking proper steps for his own safety and that of his comrades and unduly hamper the engagement of gunmen."[86]

Finally, Lord Widgery stated that none of the deceased or wounded was conclusively proven to have been shot while handling a firearm or bomb and that some were acquitted of any complicity in such action. But he added—in language vindicating the Army—that "there is a strong suspicion that some others had been firing weapons or handling bombs in the course of the afternoon and that yet others had been closely supporting them."[87] Accordingly, in opening fire on the rioters, the soldiers not only did not suffer a general breakdown in discipline but acted in a manner required by their orders.[88]

The Compton-Parker-Widgery reports are clear evidence of the propriety of British actions in Northern Ireland and the compliance of those actions with the requirements of both domestic and, assuming its applicability, international law. For those persons who remain critical or at least skeptical, it might be well to recognize the thin line that exists in areas of this nature between legality and illegality and between right and wrong. Indeed, that thinness is apparent when it is realized that in interrogation the choice is often between questioning that borders on hardship[89] and allowing information that results in death and destruction to be "overlooked." Similarly, that thinness is obvious when it is recognized that in antiguerrilla warfare the choice is often between shooting too early and killing an innocent civilian or shooting too late and getting killed.

[86] *Ibid.*, 38. [87] *Ibid.*
[88] *Ibid.*, 39.
[89] See Parker Report 2: "Discomfort and hardship are clearly matters which any persons suspected of crime, under ordinary conditions, will suffer and that is accepted as not only inevitable but permissible. Equally, everyone would agree that torture, whether physical or mental, is not justified under any conditions."

The Belfast Viewpoint

Insofar as compliance with the norms and laws of war that pertain to the interrogation of suspects is concerned, the Belfast and London positions are the same; insofar as the events of January 30, 1972 are concerned, they affect only the British Army. Before turning, however, to the use of CS smoke—a matter in which Belfast had a definite interest, it might be well to note the obvious restraint on the part of the RUC. Given the terror that the IRA has brought to Northern Ireland, that restraint in interrogating known members of that illegal and murderous organization is even more remarkable than the restraint shown by the British Army, for, after all, the British Army is only a "temporary" visitor to Ulster. Given, too, the countless "violence to life and person, in particular murder of all kinds, mutilation, cruel treatment and torture" wrought by IRA bombs and bullets, the occasional hardships endured by known terrorists during interrogation pale into insignificance when measured against the guerrilla's wholesale attack on the foundations of Article 3 of the Geneva Conventions, Articles 2 and 3 of the European Convention, and Articles 3 and 5 of the Universal Declaration.

Just as charges are wildly and incorrectly made against the RUC in connection with the interrogation of terrorists, so they were improperly hurled in 1969, when the RUC had to employ CS smoke to put down the Bogside riot. In absorbing endless verbal abuse and torrents of paving stones before using CS smoke to extricate itself from a difficult situation, the RUC demonstrated the calm that was to stand it in good stead in the days to come. Yet when the RUC at last was forced to rely on CS smoke to battle the "harmless," rock-throwing Bogsiders, it was quickly accused of having violated Article 3 of the Geneva Conventions.

That accusation had no validity. Not only was the use of CS smoke the most humane means available to restore law

192

and order, but also the Geneva Conventions did not at that time—if they ever did—apply to the Ulster strife. Since Article 3 is inapplicable to acts of banditry and small-scale riots, there was absolutely no justification in August 1969 to make reference to the Article. In point of fact, the RUC adhered to the prescriptions of Article 3; in point of law, it was not required to do so.

Rather than engage in mental gymnastics to try to prove RUC violations of law, it would be more relevant to look to the underlying cause for both the interrogation procedures and the use of CS smoke: terrorism. If, indeed, the prescriptions of domestic and international law can be said to have any meaning, they must condemn the murderous tactics of the IRA; and if, indeed, those tactics—assassination, mutilation by bombing, and rule by threats of violence—are juxtaposed with the laws of war, they must be deemed in violation of that body of law.

CONCLUSIONS

The question as to the standard to be applied in Ulster is made somewhat moot by the fact that the Joint Directive incorporates the main tenets of Article 3 of the Geneva Conventions of 1949, Article 3 of the European Convention, and Article 5 of the Universal Declaration. Nevertheless, it would appear that the international prescriptions are indeed applicable, since they come into play whenever a conflict within the borders of a contracting party (Britain is a signatory of all three documents) escalates beyond the limits of banditry. Although Britain might well consider IRA members to be mere bandits, such a conclusion at this stage of the conflict does not accord with reality. Moreover, the fact that Britain "can no longer maintain order through the normal application of its internal common law and is thus obliged to adopt a special code beyond its common laws . . . signifies the existence of a grave 'internal con-

193

flict' "[90]—a grave internal conflict justifying and warranting the application of international humanitarian standards that attempt to put an end to the "growing brutalization of civilians in armed conflicts."[91]

A determination that international prescriptions apply does not, of course, affect only Britain. The IRA must adhere to the same standards. Unfortunately, rather than follow them, it has consistently violated those basic humanitarian rules.

Since the IRA is obviously greatly outmanned, it has adopted the hit-and-run tactics of the guerrilla. First employed successfully in Ireland by Michael Collins,[92] guerrilla warfare is, regardless of whether the weapon is a bomb or bullet, an acceptable and "legal" means of conducting hostilities. What is unacceptable and illegal, however—and what has alienated the IRA from the vast majority of the Northern Catholic community, thereby forcing this new breed of "catfish" to live without the water of popular support and to adapt to the firm ground of Ulster's ghettos in which it can feed on and breathe amid apathy and despair —is violence directed against individuals "taking no active part in hostilities." And that is precisely what the countless assassinations, indiscriminate gelignite explosions in civilian centers, and scorched-earth tactics constitute.

[90] Jabhat al-Tahrir al-Quami, WHITE PAPER ON THE APPLICATION OF THE GENEVA CONVENTIONS OF 1949 TO THE FRENCH-ALGERIAN CONFLICT 19 (1960). Although the author was speaking of France's adoption of emergency administrative and legislative measures to deal with the Algerian struggle, he might just as well have been writing of Britain's adoption of measures for Northern Ireland.

[91] Gottlieb, *International Assistance to Civilian Populations in Armed Conflicts*, 4 N. Y. U. J. INT'L L. & POL. 403 (1971).

[92] See generally Younger, IRELAND'S CIVIL WAR 75 (1968) for a description of the 1919 Soloheadbeg episode in which two Irish policemen were killed. See also *ibid.* 124 for an IRA man's views on guerrilla tactics. Although the discussion that follows is limited to the IRA, indiscriminate acts of violence by Protestant extremists are equally condemnable.

In order to combat the vicious and sustained IRA campaign of terror, the decision was made by Britain to institute internment. Once it was made and civilians were arrested, Britain was obligated, in spite of repeated and murderous IRA attacks, to conform its methods of interrogation to the prescribed standards of domestic and international law. This action, despite the "strained" reasoning of the Compton Report, it clearly did not take. While on paper—witness the Joint Directive—certain procedures were proscribed, those methods were in fact followed. Although the Compton Report changed "cruel treatment and torture" to "ill-treatment" to protect the guilty and although the Parker majority attempted to approve of the illegal methods by retroactively anointing them with safeguards, Britain clearly violated the minimum standards of human decency.

To contain demonstrators and marchers, the decision was also made to use force. That decision may or may not accord with the prescriptions of law. For instance, the use of CS smoke seems justifiable and humane, even though the justifiability and humanitarianism of the CS usage during the August 1969 Battle of the Bogside evaporated as the RUC indiscriminately covered the Bogside with a blanket of choking smoke.

The decision, however, to employ armed force against unarmed civilians on January 30, 1972 in Derry was neither justifiable nor humane at any point. In fact, given the British *Manual of Military Law* and the "Yellow Card instructions," it was criminal under British law. Although Widgery found that part of the "Yellow Card instructions" pertaining to firing without warning confusing,[93] he failed to conclude—as he most certainly should have—that no soldier should have been faced with the ostensibly confusing instruction, because no soldier should have been involved in "scoop-up" operations, or, if so involved, no soldier should have used live ammunition. Furthermore, al-

[93] Widgery Report 34.

195

though the marchers were clearly wrong to taunt British soldiers and to hurl stones at them, the idea that unruly marchers should be shot for throwing nonexplosive objects is incomprehensible and definitely in violation of British law and the prescriptions of the Geneva Conventions, European Convention, and Universal Declaration.[94]

To those persons who would answer—as indeed Widgery did[95]—that a soldier not only may be unable to understand and apply the *Manual* and "Yellow Card instructions" but also may be incapable of distinguishing a rock from a bomb, the retort is simple. While soldiers on police-type duty "are bound to use such force as is reasonably necessary . . . to prevent serious crime or riot . . . they must not use lethal weapons to prevent or suppress minor disorder or offenses of a less serious character, and in no case should they do so if less extreme measures will suffice."[96] Thus, while "a person, whether a magistrate or a peace officer, who has the duty of suppressing a riot, is placed in a very difficult situation . . . if by his acts he causes death, he is liable to be indicted for murder or manslaughter . . . if he does not act he is liable to an indictment or an information for neglect; he is therefore bound to hit the precise line of his duty, and . . . difficult as it may be, he is bound to do" so.[97]

Naturally, it is difficult for a person to find fault with

94 While Article 2 of the European Convention permits governmental organs to take lives during the quelling of a riot, it requires that the deaths be the result of an "action lawfully taken." The deaths in Derry on January 30, 1972 were not the result of an "action lawfully taken." See generally Draper, *Human Rights and the Law of War*, 12 VA. J. INT'L L. 326, 338 (1972).

95 Widgery Report 34.

96 Great Britain, MANUAL 511–12 (Opinion of Law Officers, August 18, 1911).

97 *Ibid.*, 509 (quoting from Mr. Justice Littledale's opinion in *R.V. Pinney*). Were murder charges to be instituted against British armed forces members, they would have to be brought in civil court. See Kiralfy, THE ENGLISH LEGAL SYSTEM 308 (1967); Walker & Walker, THE ENGLISH LEGAL SYSTEM 170–72 (1970).

his own country; naturally, too, there are few persons—as the Compton-Parker-Widgery reports demonstrate[98]—that have the requisite courage to do so. Yet if justice is to be done, if an open and humane society is to rise phoenix-like from the Ulster ashes, and if the Geneva Conventions, European Convention, and Universal Declaration are to have their intended effect, that courage must be developed, for only in that way will the world's military and political perversions be effectively exposed and eliminated.

[98] Quite obviously, this condemnation excludes Lord Gardiner. The British commissions, inquiries, and tribunals have acted in such a self-serving, subjective manner that perhaps the time has "now come for an inquiry into British official inquiries." See *Widgery Waives the Rules*, 83 NEW STATESMAN 547 (1972).

CHAPTER VI

Human Rights—Human Wrongs:
An Examination of the Leading Issue
of the Ulster Struggle

OF THE many legal questions raised by the conflict in Northern Ireland, the one which must of necessity be singled out concerns human rights. In a sense, it is *the* legal question, for, when the civil rights demonstrations began in 1968, the sole issue revolved around purported discriminatory practices directed against Catholics. As is the case with other Ulster questions, however, the factual and legal origins of this issue date not from 1968 but from a far earlier period.

The concern for human rights may be traced back to the political philosophy of the Greeks and Romans.[1] Or, to shorten the voyage, that concern may be found in the political tradition of freedom enunciated by Locke and Blackstone. From these men sprang the English doctrine of fundamental rights. From them emerged the belief that although Parliament was nearly supreme, it could neither do the unnatural nor pass statutes that were immune from the overriding law of nature. From them arose the idea that "nobody has an absolute arbitrary power over himself, or over any other to destroy his own life, or take away the life or property of another."[2] And from them flowed the concepts

---

[1] See H. Lauterpacht, AN INTERNATIONAL BILL OF THE RIGHTS OF MAN 16–40 (1945).

[2] Locke, *An Essay Concerning the True Original, Extent and End of Civil Government*, in E. Burtt, ed., THE ENGLISH PHILOSOPHERS FROM BACON TO MILL 403, 457 (1939). Locke's statement on legislative power reads: "It is not nor can possibly be absolutely arbitrary over the lives and fortunes of the people. For it being but the joint power of every member of the society given up to that person, or assembly, which is

198

that formed the basis for, to name but two documents, the United States' Declaration of Independence and France's Declaration of the Rights of Man and of the Citizen.

In practice, however, human rights remained through the centuries what individual states determined them to be. Unable to claim the protection of other states, unless otherwise provided by international agreement, individuals remained subject to the whims and caprices of their own governments.

THE CHARTER OF THE UNITED NATIONS

Not until the United Nations Charter was promulgated were human rights afforded recognition in an international instrument. Article 1 (3) of the Charter asserts that one of the purposes of the United Nations is to solve problems of a humanitarian character; Article 55 states, inter alia, that the United Nations shall promote "universal respect for, and observance of, human rights and fundamental freedoms for all without distinction as to race, sex, language, or religion"; and Article 56 provides that "all Members [of the United Nations] pledge themselves to take joint and separate action in cooperation with the Organization for the achievement of the purposes set forth in Article 55."[3]

---

legislator; it can be no more than those persons had in a state of nature before they entered into society, and gave it up to the community. For nobody can transfer to another more power than he has in himself; and nobody has an absolute arbitrary power over himself, or over any other to destroy his own life, or take away the life or property of another." See also H. Lauterpacht, INTERNATIONAL BILL OF RIGHTS 54–65; H. Lauterpacht, INTERNATIONAL LAW AND HUMAN RIGHTS 127–41 (1950) for an overview of British law and theory. For a survey of the law of human rights, see Chakravarti, HUMAN RIGHTS AND THE UNITED NATIONS 3–25 (1958); Jessup, A MODERN LAW OF NATIONS 68–93 (1948); Schwelb, HUMAN RIGHTS AND THE INTERNATIONAL COMMUNITY 11–25 (1964).

[3] In addition, Article 13 1.(b) provides that the General Assembly shall initiate studies and make recommendations to assist in the realization of human rights and fundamental freedoms for all, and Article

These provisions, though vague, would appear legally to obligate all member states. There are, however, scholars who argue that "a frame for a picture must not be mistaken for the picture itself, and [that] the United Nations may need to be protected against some of its more ardent friends."[4] In the view of these scholars, the Charter of the United Nations merely sets forth policies, principles, and purposes, which some day will be given the force of law. In their view, too, not only does the Charter not bind members to adhere to the aforesaid provisions, but also any attempt so to bind them would have a negative effect by making states reluctant "to assume further commitments."[5]

While no one can argue with the proposition that—aside from the tenets of customary international law—states should only be bound by the terms of the instruments to which they have consented, it would indeed seem that the member states of the United Nations have agreed to be so bound as respects the human rights provisions. Although the effectiveness of the prescriptions is greatly weakened both by the absence of a definition of what is meant by "human rights and fundamental freedoms" and by the lack of even the most rudimentary enforcement powers, the fact remains that neither of these omissions destroys the legal obligations of the Charter. In short, "the cumulative legal result of all these pronouncements cannot be ignored."[6]

---

76 (c) states that one of the basic objectives of the trusteeship system is "to encourage respect for human rights and for fundamental freedoms without distinction as to race, sex, language, or religion."

4 Hudson, *Integrity of International Instruments*, 42 AM. J. INT'L L. 105, 107 (1948).

5 "If Governments cannot have confidence that the instruments by which they bind themselves will not be made to serve unintended purposes, if respect is not paid to the terms and tenor of the obligations imposed by such instruments, the result may be a reluctance to assume further commitments and the progressive development of international law may be seriously retarded." *Ibid.,* 108.

6 H. Lauterpacht, INTERNATIONAL LAW AND HUMAN RIGHTS 148. As the author states, "The legal character of these obligations of the Char-

The Universal Declaration of Human Rights

The battle of scholars over the effect of the United Nations Charter on member states is a mere skirmish compared to the war over the legal position of the Universal Declaration of Human Rights. When the Universal Declaration was adopted in 1948 by the General Assembly of the United Nations, it was widely accepted as a declaration that would awaken the consciences of men and women throughout the world and just as widely rejected as a legal instrument. It was viewed as setting "out a legislative program in municipal and international law to be attained by joint and separate action of the Member States of the United Nations";[7] it was recognized as the first half step on the road to an effective and legally binding Bill of Rights; it was regarded as marking "no advance in the enduring struggle of man against the omnipotence of the state";[8] and it was stated to have the effect of moral persuasion and to be in fact a moral code of conduct. Yet the Universal Declaration was not—with the noticeable exception of the Belgium and French judgments—held to be a legally obligatory instrument.[9]

---

ter would remain even if the Charter were to contain no provisions of any kind for their implementation. For the Charter fails to provide for the enforcement of its other numerous obligations the legal character of which is undoubted." See generally *ibid.*, 147–59; Ganji, International Protection of Human Rights 116 (1962); Schwelb, *The International Court of Justice and the Human Rights Clauses of the Charter*, 66 am. j. int'l l. 337, 341–46 (1972).

[7] Drost, Human Rights as Legal Rights: The Realization of Individual Human Rights in Positive International Law 33 (1951).

[8] H. Lauterpacht, *The Universal Declaration of Human Rights*, 25 brit. y.b. int'l l. 354, 372 (1948).

[9] See Chakravarti, Human Rights 70–74; Drost, Human Rights as Legal Rights 32–38; Moskowitz, The Politics and Dynamics of Human Rights 102 (1968); Cohen, *Human Rights under the United Nations Charter*, 14 law & contemp. prob. 430, 432–33 (1949); S. Fawcett, *A British View of the Covenant*, 14 law & contemp. prob. 438, 439

201

That was 1948. In the years since the adoption of the Universal Declaration, it has undergone a metamorphosis, a metamorphosis that lends force to the assertion that "the moral norms of today may very well become the legal norms of tomorrow."[10] While not all jurists and scholars agree on the precise limits of that change, they are in agreement that the Universal Declaration has "probably exceeded the most sanguine hopes of its authors"[11] and that it has indeed acquired some legal status.

These scholars generally believe that "what has taken place has been the operation of a fundamental law of physics: nature abhors a vacuum."[12] Since the Universal Declaration and the Covenants on Human Rights were together to form an International Bill of Rights, since the Covenants were only recently adopted,[13] and since the Covenants are presently not in force, the Universal Declaration, they assert, has filled the gap resulting from the failure to provide effective Covenants. Moreover, they seem to reject—of necessity—the traditional division between "binding" treaties

---

(1949); Kunz, *The Universal Declaration of Human Rights*, 43 AM. J. INT'L L. 316, 316–22 (1949); H. Lauterpacht, *Universal Declaration* 356–72; McDougal & Leighton, *The Rights of Man in the World Community: Constitutional Illusions versus Rational Action*, 14 LAW & CONTEMP. PROB. 490, 497 (1949). Belgium claimed that the General Assembly was a juridical organ and that any recommendations made by it had an undeniably legal character; France believed that the Universal Declaration was a complement to the United Nations Charter. See H. Lauterpacht, INTERNATIONAL LAW AND HUMAN RIGHTS 402–407.

[10] Ganji, INTERNATIONAL PROTECTION; see generally 141–66.

[11] Robertson, HUMAN RIGHTS IN THE WORLD 28 (1972). See also Warren, *It's Time to Implement the Declaration of Human Rights*, 59 A.B.A.J. 1257 (1973).

[12] Schwelb, HUMAN RIGHTS AND THE INTERNATIONAL COMMUNITY 37.

[13] The International Covenant on Civil and Political Rights and the International Covenant on Economic, Social and Cultural Rights [G.A. Res. 2200 (XXI); 61 AM. J. INT'L L. 861 (1967)] set forth individual rights that are to have the force of law. Adopted by the General Assembly on December 16, 1966, the Covenants will go into effect after they have been ratified by thirty-five states.

and "non-binding" pronouncements and to accept that pronouncements, "if approved without substantial dissent by the overwhelming majority of Governments of sovereign States and acquiesced in by the rest, acquire an authority which takes them out of the category of 'non-binding' pronouncements."[14] Accordingly, they conclude that in view of the tendency on the part of the United Nations General Assembly to speak of the Universal Declaration in the same breath as the Charter—as evidenced by the statements in the 1960 Declaration on the Grant of Independence to Colonial Countries and Peoples and the 1963 Declaration on Racial Discrimination admonishing all states faithfully to observe the Charter *and* the Universal Declaration—the Universal Declaration has become clothed in the character of customary law.[15]

Although this new "law" lacks machinery to enforce its provisions, it nevertheless sets forth standards that not only should, but some day will, be followed. For these reasons, the Universal Declaration is germane to all conflict and nonconflict situations. Of particular relevance to a discussion of the human rights issue in the Ulster struggle are the

[14] Schwelb, HUMAN RIGHTS AND THE INTERNATIONAL COMMUNITY 74. "A strict distinction between law-making in the formal sense and the recognition of new rules of international intercourse short of formal adoption by international treaty . . . is neither possible nor desirable in contemporary international society." Friedmann, THE CHANGING STRUCTURES OF INTERNATIONAL LAW 137 (1964).

[15] See generally Robertson, HUMAN RIGHTS IN THE WORLD 26–28; Schwelb, HUMAN RIGHTS AND THE INTERNATIONAL COMMUNITY 34–74; Waldock, *Human Rights in Contemporary International Law and the Significance of the European Convention,* INT'L & COMP. L.Q. SUPP. NO. 11 1, 13–16 (1965).

The Assembly for Human Rights, which met in Montreal in March 1968, and the International Conference on Human Rights, which met in Teheran in April and May 1968, stated that the Universal Declaration constituted an authoritative interpretation of the United Nations Charter and that over the years it had become a part of customary international law. See generally Sohn & Buergenthal, INTERNATIONAL PROTECTION OF HUMAN RIGHTS 518–20 (1973); U.N. Doc. A/Conf. 32/41, U.N. Pub. E. 68 XIV. 2 (1968).

following provisions of the Universal Declaration:[16] Article 1, which states that all people "are born free and equal in dignity and rights"; Article 7, which makes all persons equal before the law and entitled to the equal protections of the law; Article 9, which prohibits arbitrary arrest or detention; Article 12, which protects all persons from arbitrary interference with their homes and privacy; Article 18, which grants the right of freedom of religion; Article 20, which states that "everyone has the right to freedom of peaceful assembly and association"; Article 21, which provides for participation in government, equal access to public service, and universal suffrage; Article 23, which holds that everyone has the right to work; Article 25, which provides for adequate housing;[17] and Article 26, which states that "education shall be directed to the full development of the human personality and to the strengthening of respect for human rights and fundamental freedoms" and which allows parents to "choose the kind of education that shall be given to their children."

The European Convention for the Protection of Human Rights and Fundamental Freedoms

Aside from its significance in its own right, the Universal Declaration has fulfilled the important function of serving as the model for various covenants and constitutions. Most notable of these, and most pertinent to the Northern Ireland strife, is the European Convention for the Protection of Human Rights and Fundamental Freedoms. Signed in 1950 and in effect since 1953, the European Convention provides both implementation machinery and, for the first time, the opportunity for aggrieved individuals to bring

16 G.A. Res. 217A, 3 U.N. GAOR 71, 7 U.N. Doc. A/810 (1948).

17 The right to work and the right to adequate housing are also provided in Articles 6 and 11, respectively, of the Covenant on Economic, Social and Cultural Rights, which was signed by Britain on September 16, 1968. See Schwelb, *The United Kingdom Signs the Covenants on Human Rights*, 18 INT'L & COMP. L.Q. 457 (1969).

complaints to an international body of a quasi-judicial nature.[18]

Pursuant to the terms of the European Convention, the European Commission of Human Rights may—after domestic remedies have been exhausted (Article 26)—receive petitions "from any person, non-governmental organization or group of individuals claiming to be the victim of a violation by one of the High Contracting Parties of the rights set forth in [the] Convention" (Article 25). If a friendly settlement of the matter cannot be obtained (Article 28), the European Commission draws up "a Report on the facts and state[s] its opinion as to whether the facts found disclose a breach by the State concerned of its obligations under the Convention" and transmits the report, together with such proposals as it thinks fit, to the Committee of Ministers (Article 31). If the question is not referred to the European Court of Human Rights in accordance with the terms of Article 48, the Committee of Ministers decides by a two-thirds vote of its members if there has been a violation and, if the vote is affirmative, the measures required to be taken by the contracting party concerned (Article 32). And if the European Commission, a contracting party whose national is alleged to be a victim, a contracting party that referred the case to the European Commission, or a contracting party against which the complaint has been lodged brings a case before the European Court (Article 48), the European Court decides the matter (Article 50), states its reasons for the judgment (Article 51)—which is final (Article 52) and with which the contracting parties agree to abide (Article 53)—and transmits the judgment to the Committee of Ministers, which supervises its execution (Article 54).

In substance, the rights protected by the European Convention clearly reflect the influence of the Universal Decla-

18 See Ganji, INTERNATIONAL PROTECTION 229–71; Robertson, HUMAN RIGHTS IN THE WORLD 72–75; Greenberg & Shalit, *New Horizons for Human Rights: The European Convention, Court and Commission of Human Rights*, 63 COLUM. L. REV. 1384, 1388 (1963).

ration. To begin with, Article 5 states that everyone has the right to liberty and that no one will be deprived of his liberty, except, inter alia, that a "lawful arrest or detention of a person [may be] effected for the purpose of bringing him before the competent legal authority on reasonable suspicion of having committed an offence or when it is reasonably considered necessary to prevent his committing an offence or fleeing after having done so"; Article 5 also provides that everyone arrested will be promptly informed of the reasons for the arrest and of any charges against him, quickly brought before a judge or other authorized official and entitled to a trial within a reasonable time or to release pending trial, and empowered "to take proceedings by which the lawfulness of his detention [will] be decided speedily by a court and his release ordered if the detention is not lawful." Secondly, Article 6 affirms that everyone will be given "a fair and public hearing within a reasonable time by an independent and impartial tribunal established by law," that he will be presumed innocent until proven guilty, and that he will have certain minimum rights, among them, the right to have adequate time and facilities to prepare a defense, the right to legal assistance, and the right to cross-examine witnesses. Thirdly, Article 8 states that all persons have the right to respect for their private and family lives, homes, and correspondence. Fourthly, Article 9 establishes the right to freedom of thought, conscience, and religion. Fifthly, Article 11 provides for the right to freedom of peaceful assembly and of association with others. And, finally, Article 14 affirms that the rights and freedoms of the European Convention are to be secured without discrimination of any kind.

After setting forth these rights and duties, the European Convention establishes a "loophole" for contracting states. Under the terms of Article 15, any contracting state may, "in time of war or other public emergency threatening the life of the nation," derogate from its obligations under the European Convention "to the extent strictly required by the exigencies of the situation, provided that such measures are not inconsistent with its other obligations under international law" (Section 1). In addition, the article prohibits derogation in certain instances (Section 2)—the two instances applicable to the Ulster conflict being the requirements of Articles 2 and 3 discussed in the preceding chapter. Furthermore, the article provides that any contracting party that avails itself of the right of derogation must "keep the Secretary-General of the Council of Europe fully informed of the measures which it has taken and the reasons" for those measures (Section 3).

In effect, therefore, the contracting states have reserved to themselves a "measure of discretion." This "measure of discretion" with respect to all but the most fundamental provisions of the European Convention allows the parties to make a favorable estimate of the situation in time of emergency. But the latitude established by the article is not unlimited. Even though at one time the contracting parties may well have believed that a state declaration derogating from the requirements of the European Convention was conclusive proof that the arrest or detention had been effected under emergency conditions, they were rudely disabused of that belief in 1961. As the *Lawless Case*[19] clearly evidenced, the European Court is the final arbiter concerning the legitimacy of a contracting state's derogation under Article 15.

The facts of the *Lawless Case* are strikingly similar to situations that have occurred countless times since the in-

[19] The decision of the Supreme Court of Ireland in *The State (O'Laighleis) vs. O'Sullivan & Min. for Justice* may be found in 2 YEARBOOK OF EUROPEAN CONVENTION 608 (1958–1959); the decisions of the European Commission in 2 YEARBOOK OF EUROPEAN CONVENTION 308 (1958–1959) and 3 YEARBOOK OF EUROPEAN CONVENTION 492 (1960); and the decision of the European Court in 2 YEARBOOK OF EUROPEAN CONVENTION 474 (1960) and 4 YEARBOOK OF EUROPEAN CONVENTION 430 (1961). The Gaelic form of Lawless is O'Laighleis. In proceedings before Irish courts, O'Laughleis was used; in proceedings before the European Commission and European Court, Lawless was employed.

ternment policy of August 9, 1971 was set in motion in Northern Ireland. Following the start of a new wave of IRA terror in 1956, the Republic of Ireland revived the Offenses Against the State Act (1939). Under the provisions of the act, the Irish Government arrested a large number of known and suspected IRA members. One of those arrested and detained without trial (from July 13, 1957 to December 11, 1957) was Gerard Lawless. He promptly filed suit—first in Ireland and then, after his action was dismissed, before the European Commission.

Specifically, the European Commission had to determine whether the 1939 Act was in conflict with Ireland's obligations under Articles 5 and 6 of the European Convention and, if it was in conflict with those provisions, whether Lawless' detention was justified by the right of derogation provided for in Article 15 of the European Convention. Although the European Commission concluded, by a nine-to-five vote, that Ireland had not exceeded its authority under Article 15 and, by an eight-to-six margin, that the facts of the case did not disclose a breach of Ireland's obligations under the European Convention, it referred the case to the European Court because of the large number of minority votes. Even though the European Court found that Lawless' detention conflicted with the protections afforded by Articles 5 and 6, the Court nevertheless decided that the Irish Government was justified in declaring that an emergency existed that threatened the life of the nation, that Lawless' detention without trial was a measure strictly required by the exigencies of the situation and clearly within the limits of Article 15 (1), and that the facts of the case did not therefore disclose a breach by the Irish Government of its obligations under the European Convention.[20]

While Lawless certainly lost his case, he might also, paradoxically, be said to have won it. In fact, his case was a milestone in the effort to protect fundamental freedoms, for

[20] See 4 YEARBOOK OF EUROPEAN CONVENTION 486 (1961).

"never before had an international tribunal entertained the petition of an aggrieved individual who summoned his own country to the bar to answer a charge that it had denied him a fundamental human right."[21] In fact, too, his case represented a victory because the European Court refused to accept as conclusive the state's declaration that the arrest and detention had been effected under the emergency provisions of Article 15.[22]

One ground, however, on which Lawless clearly failed was in arguing before the Supreme Court of Ireland that the European Convention was part of the municipal law of Ireland. In rejecting his argument, the Irish High Court stated that "when the domestic law makes its own provisions it cannot be controlled by any inconsistent provisions in international law"[23] and that the High Court accordingly could not "accept the idea that the primacy of domestic legislation is displaced by the State becoming a Party to the Convention for the Protection of Human Rights and Fundamental Freedoms."[24] Since the European Convention had not been made the subject of an Irish statute, neither Lawless nor any other Irishman could rely upon the European Convention before an Irish Court.

21 Greenberg & Shalit, *New Horizons* 1387.

22 For a more detailed discussion of the *Lawless Case*, see Kelly, FUNDAMENTAL RIGHTS IN THE IRISH LAW AND CONSTITUTION 85–88 (1968) (the author incorrectly states, at 88 n. 38, that O'Laighleis—Lawless—took his complaint to the European Court; an individual may bring an action before the European Commission, but he cannot take an action to the European Court); Morrisson, THE DEVELOPING EUROPEAN LAW OF HUMAN RIGHTS 161–73 (1967); Robertson, HUMAN RIGHTS IN EUROPE 112–39 (1963); Weil, THE EUROPEAN CONVENTION ON HUMAN RIGHTS 72–75 (1963); Buergenthal, *Proceedings against Greece under the European Convention of Human Rights*, 62 AM. J. INT'L L. 441, 444–45 (1968); Mosler, *The Protection of Human Rights by International Legal Procedure*, 52 GEO. L. J. 800, 808 (1964); O'Higgins, *The Lawless Case*, 16 CAMBRIDGE L. J. 234 (1962).

23 *The State (O'Laighleis) vs. O'Sullivan & Min. for Justice*, 2 YEARBOOK OF EUROPEAN CONVENTION 608, 622 (1958–1959).

24 *Ibid.*, 624.

In light of Britain's refusal to take "action to incorporate the provisions of the European Convention into [its] law,"[25] the "precedent" of the Irish High Court's decision is revealing. Quite obviously, an Irish court cannot bind a British court.[26] Equally obvious, however, is the conclusion that an action before a British court based on the European Convention would be dismissed as quickly as was the *Lawless Case* before the Irish High Court.

Legislation in Northern Ireland

Although many legislative acts have had an impact on human rights, four pieces of domestic legislation are of particular significance in the Ulster struggle. Those acts are the 1920 Act; the Civil Authorities (Special Powers) Act (Northern Ireland) 1922 (hereafter called the Special Powers Act);[27] the Detention of Terrorists (Northern Ireland) Order 1972 (hereinafter called the 1972 Order);[28] and the Northern Ireland (Emergency Provisions) Act 1973 (hereinafter called the 1973 Emergency Powers Act).[29]

Aside from providing the constitutional basis for the existence of Northern Ireland, the 1920 Act stated that the Northern Ireland Parliament would not make any law that directly or indirectly establishes, endows, or gives a preference, privilege, or advantage to any religion or that

[25] Ezejiofor, PROTECTION OF HUMAN RIGHTS UNDER THE LAW 158 (1964).

[26] See *Chung Chi Cheung v. The King*, A.C. 160 (1939); Mosler, *Protection of Human Rights* 816; Weil, *The Evolution of the European Convention on Human Rights*, 57 AM. J. INT'L L. 804, 823–24 (1963).

[27] 12 & 13 Geo. 5, C.5 (N.I.); 23 & 24 Geo. 5, C.12 (N.I.)

[28] 1972 STAT. INSTR. No. 1632 (N.I. 15). The order is, in effect, an act. Pursuant to the terms of Section 1 (3) of the Northern Ireland (Temporary Provisions) Act 1972, the Queen has the "power by Order in Council to make laws for any purpose for which the Parliament of Northern Ireland has power to make laws." Such orders have the same validity and effect as an act passed by Stormont.

[29] Eliz. 2, C.53 (July 25, 1973).

affects "prejudicially the right of any child to attend a school receiving public money without attending the religious instruction at that school" [Section 5 (1)]. In addition, it swept the statute books clear of all enactments imposing any penalty, disadvantage, or disability on an individual or order on account of religious beliefs [Section 5 (2)].[30]

Even though the 1972 Order whittled away some of the Special Powers Act's provisions and even though the 1973 Emergency Powers Act repealed the remaining provisions of that act, the Special Powers Act has long been, is, and will long be on the lips and in the minds of Ulster's inhabitants. For that reason and despite the fact that it is no longer law, the Special Powers Act must be examined in some detail.

Section 1 of the Special Powers Act granted to the Minister of Home Affairs or any RUC officer designated by him the power to "take all such steps and issue all such orders as may be necessary for preserving the peace and maintaining order"; Section 2 provided that an individual was guilty of violating the act if he took certain actions that were prejudicial to the preservation of peace, even if those actions were not provided for in the regulations contained in the Schedule to the act; Section 10 gave the Minister of Home Affairs the power to prohibit the holding of inquests; and the Schedule contained the far-reaching regulations for peace and order referred to in Section 1. For instance, Regulation 4 gave the Army and police the authority to enter, without a warrant, any home believed to be used or kept for any illegal purpose; Regulation 6 enabled the Army and police to search and seize from any person "firearms, ammunition, explosive substances or any article or document" which the searching party believed to be used

[30] For a detailed discussion of the effect of this important section on religious liberty, see Calvert, CONSTITUTIONAL LAW IN NORTHERN IRELAND 253–72 (1968).

211

for any purpose prejudicial to the peace; Regulation 8 allowed the Minister of Home Affairs to prohibit the publication or distribution of any newspaper, periodical, book, or other printed matter; Regulation 10 permitted the RUC to arrest an individual without a warrant and to detain him for up to 48 hours for purposes of interrogation; Regulations 11, 12, and 13 provided for the detention and internment of any person suspected of having acted, acting, or being about to act in a manner prejudicial to the preservation of peace and maintenance of order in Northern Ireland; Regulation 19 established curfew powers; Regulation 24A deemed various organizations—including the IRA and Sinn Fein—unlawful associations; and Regulation 38 stated that certain members of the RUC could order any assembly of three or more persons to disperse, if the officer making the demand believed that the assembly might lead to a breach of the peace.

With the passage of the 1972 Order, Regulations 11, 12, and 13 were repealed. In brief, the 1972 Order called for commissioners appointed by the Secretary of State for Northern Ireland and a Detention Appeal Tribunal, whose members were also appointed by the Secretary of State (Section 3); provided for an interim custody order under which a person could be detained for no more than twenty-eight days, unless during that period the case was referred to a commissioner for determination, in which event he could be detained until the case was decided (Section 4); set forth that, in those instances where a case was referred to a commissioner, the commissioner must determine if the individual in question had committed or attempted to commit a terrorist act, and if his detention was necessary to protect the public (Section 5); allowed an individual to appeal from a detention order within twenty-one days to the Detention Appeal Tribunal (Section 6); and held that the Secretary of State could at any time direct the discharge of a person detained under an interim custody order or the release under certain conditions of an individual detained under a detention order (Section 9).[31]

In an effort to devise additional legal procedures to deal with terrorist activities, Britain enacted the 1973 Emergency Powers Act. Based on recommendations made by the Diplock Commission, which Britain had established the previous year, the 1973 Emergency Powers Act provided for, inter alia, nonjury trials for scheduled offenses (Section 2); bail to be set by judges of the High Court in cases of scheduled offenses (Section 3); acceptability of written statements in trials involving scheduled offenses if the statement was made in the presence of a constable, and if the person who made the statement was dead, unfit to attend the trial, outside Northern Ireland, or missing (Section 5); shifting the burden of proof to the defendant in certain instances (Section 7); arrest and detention, by a constable and without a warrant (Section 11); detention, by the Army and for no longer than four hours, of a person suspected "of committing, having committed or being about to commit any offence" (Section 12); power to search for munitions (Section 13); imprisonment of individuals belonging to proscribed organizations (Section 19); and banning the collection of information concerning the Army or police that would be helpful to terrorists (Section 20).

Summary

The state of the law within the world community and the boundaries of Northern Ireland is fairly clear. Despite some rejection of the legal effect of the Universal Declaration, the better view is that it does have legal weight. Accordingly, the Universal Declaration must, together with the United Nations Charter and the European Convention,

---

31 A detailed discussion of the 1972 Order may be found in Rauch, *The Compatibility of the Detention of Terrorists Order (Northern Ireland) with the European Convention for the Protection of Human Rights*, 6 N. Y. U. J. INT'L L. & POL. 1 (1973).

form the human rights yardstick against which the facts and laws of Ulster are measured.

THE DUBLIN VIEWPOINT

The human wrongs perpetrated in the Six Counties are classifiable into two categories: first, those wrongs arising by dint of law; and second, those wrongs emanating from individual or group actions. In each instance, however, the harm done to the Catholic population is deep and violates international standards of law and decency.

When the Special Powers Act was passed in 1922, it was intended as a temporary measure. Supposedly enacted to deal with the violence between North and South, it was renewed annually until 1933, when, despite the fact that that violence had never materialized, it was made permanent. Until its repeal, the Special Powers Act remained an embarrassment to Britain; until its repeal, an ostensibly emergency act was made into a societal norm, which blandly assured to Catholics "that they [had] the fullest of powers to correct the legislation if they so desire[d]—when they [became] a majority";[32] and until its repeal, the North was committed to a policy of government by decree, since the Minister of Home Affairs or any RUC man he appointed had a blank check to do as he deemed necessary in the field of law and order.[33]

[32] Edwards, THE SINS OF OUR FATHERS: ROOTS OF CONFLICT IN NORTHERN IRELAND 104 (1970).

[33] See generally *ibid.*, 105; Harrison, ULSTER AND THE BRITISH EMPIRE 1939 94–96 (1939); Sunday Times Insight Team, ULSTER 33 (1972) (cited hereafter as Insight Team, ULSTER); Wallace, NORTHERN IRELAND: 50 YEARS OF SELF-GOVERNMENT 92–95 (1971); Edwards, *Special Powers in Northern Ireland*, CRIM. L. REV. 7, 10–16 (1956). The basis for the statement that Stormont surrendered its powers and opted for government by decree is that under Section 1 (4) of the Special Powers Act both Houses of Stormont were limited to petitioning the Governor to annul a regulation promulgated by the Minister of Home Affairs.

Of the many prejudicial provisions of the Special Powers Act, Regulation 24A stood out as a monument to irrationality, arbitrariness, and sectarianism. By proscribing various Republican clubs and organizations that were established to propagate the concept of union *within* the parameters of the law, the regulation in effect made normal political life impossible and, concomitantly, fostered attempts to effectuate change by other than legal means. Indeed, as Lord MacDermott's well-reasoned dissent in *Forde v. McEldowney* stated, the power that was embodied in Regulation 24A was "too sweeping and too remote on any rational view,"[34] for it labeled as unlawful any organization that described itself as a Republican club or that was a "like organisation howsoever described."

Even more arbitrary, however, were the provisions of Regulations 11 and 12. Designed by Unionists to leave power in the hands of the Executive, since they feared that fair trials were impossible because of IRA intimidation of prosecution witnesses, the regulations provided for internment [Regulation 12] and detention of an individual "where his presence [was] required in the interest of justice and . . . for such time as his presence [was] so required" [Regulation 11 (5)]. In truth, though, the regulations were nothing more than tools with which to silence all political opponents of the Unionist system. As such, they clearly violated the prescriptions of international law in general and Articles 5 and 6 of the European Convention and Article 9 of the Universal Declaration in particular.

With the introduction of internment on August 9, 1971, Regulation 12 was once again brought to the center of the

[34] *Forde v. McEldowney*, N. IR. L. R. 11, 24 (1972). The case involved the trial of a member of a club outlawed by Regulation 24A. Although the club was not a threat to peace, law, or order, the court held that the prohibition against the club was intra vires.

In passing, it should be noted that Britain proscribed the IRA in November 1974. See Prevention of Terrorism (Temporary Provisions) Act 1974 c.56.

215

Northern stage. In the process, the baseness of this so-called "system of law" was revealed for all the world to see; in the process, too, Britain was forced to derogate from its obligations under the European Convention, as it had previously been required to do in 1957 and 1969.

The results of internment and the accompanying practice of "rearrests"—arrests that were made after the individuals arrested were found to be not guilty, after directed verdicts were ordered when the judge concluded that there was insufficient evidence to allow the case to go to the jury, and after charges were withdrawn because there was a lack of the requisite evidence with which to proceed—were truly horrifying. Yet to the repressed Catholic minority of the North, they were merely further "deplorable evidence of the political poverty of the policies which [had] been pursued there for some time"[35] and of the Protestant need constantly to tip the scales of justice against the Catholic community.

Among the many results of internment, perhaps the most infamous was the effect that internment had on the families of those individuals deprived of their freedom. Nerves were shattered; physical ailments developed; and children missed school, wet beds, and became fearful of soldiers. In addition, to add injury to injury, harassment by the Army—kicking doors, requiring homes to be left open, and smashing furniture—of many an internee's family was practiced while the internee awaited his fate.[36]

---

[35] Lynch, *Statement on Internment of 9th August 1971*, in SPEECHES AND STATEMENTS ON IRISH UNITY, NORTHERN IRELAND AND ANGLO-IRISH RELATIONS 73 (1972). See generally Northern Ireland Civil Rights Association (cited hereinafter as NICRA), INNOCENT EQUALS GUILTY UNDER THE SPECIAL POWERS ACT 1–5 (1972).

A glaring example of Regulation 11 "at work" was the McElduff Case. McElduff had been arrested, tried, and released (because he had been improperly arrested). Immediately upon his release, he was re-arrested. See Boyle, *The McElduff Case and the Law of Arrest under the Special Powers Act*, 23 N. IR. L. Q. 334 (1972) for a detailed discussion of the case.

[36] See Ragg, SURVEY OF INTERNEES' FAMILIES 3 (1972).

That fate was determined by procedures that were just as perverted and inequitable as internment itself, procedures that revolved around the Minister of Home Affairs and an advisory committee. Created by Regulation 12 (1) of the Special Powers Act, the advisory committee—the Brown Committee—was empowered to consider "representations which a person in respect of whom [an internment] order [was made] made against the order." While at first blush this procedure might not seem unjust, its true nature is quickly revealed. Indeed, when it is recognized that the Brown Committee required each internee to prove his innocence, lacked executive power and could merely advise the Minister of Home Affairs to confirm or rescind his original decision, refused to give an internee any indication of the suspicions which led to his internment, denied an internee the services of a lawyer in making his presentation before the committee (an attorney was permitted to help prepare a written statement to be submitted to the committee), and required each internee to take an oath concerning his future behavior, it is obvious that the Brown Committee was simply a Protestant ploy to make an inequitable policy appear just.[37]

Partly because the only remedy to obvious breaches of Articles 5 and 6 of the European Convention was to make representations to the Brown Committee, partly because the Special Powers Act itself constituted a failure by Britain to comply with the obligations in Article 1 of the European Convention to secure to all persons within its jurisdiction the rights and freedoms of the European Convention, and partly because of the repeated violations of Articles 2 and 3 of the European Convention, Ireland filed an application with the European Commission in December 1971.[38] Al-

[37] Campaign for Social Justice in Northern Ireland, NORTHERN IRELAND—THE MAILED FIST: A RECORD OF ARMY & POLICE BRUTALITY FROM AUGUST 9–NOVEMBER 9, 1971 62–63 (1972) (cited hereinafter as THE MAILED FIST); Stewart, THE CIVIL RIGHTS CASE 5 (1972).

[38] Commission of Human Rights, Government of Ireland against the

217

though the European Commission has not to date rendered its findings other than to state that the application, despite Britain's objections, is admissible, it most assuredly cannot fail to find that Britain's actions clearly violate the European Convention. When that finding is made, it will also be apparent that Britain's conduct in the Six Counties violates the prescriptions of the Universal Declaration, since the purpose of the European Convention, as set forth in its preamble, is "to take the first steps for the collective enforcement of certain of the Rights stated in the Universal Declaration."[39]

In an effort to remove some of the weight of world opinion, Britain in 1972 passed the 1972 Order and established the Diplock Commission. Both actions represented mere window-dressing and a legal facade for the continuance of special powers and internment.[40] In the case of the 1972 Order, the repressive policies of Regulations 11 and 12 of the Special Powers Act were supposedly removed from the Northern scene, but in fact they are retained under the improved, but still inhuman, legislation; in the case of the Diplock Commission, as evidenced in both the Diplock Report and the 1973 Emergency Powers Act emanating from the report, the powers of search, arrest, interrogation, interference with private property, and complete or partial closure of clubs, pubs, and places of entertainment are even more widespread than under the evil, ostensibly repealed, Special Powers Act. Furthermore, the Diplock Report recommended and the 1973 Emergency Powers Act provides for the admission of statements unless the victim can prove that he was tortured, the permissibility of statements on the uncorroborated word of police officials, and a range of

Government of the United Kingdom (Appl. Nos. 5310/71 & 5451/72), 41 COLLECTION OF DECISIONS 1 (1973) (hereinafter cited as EUROPEAN COMMISSION).

[39] See *ibid.*, 30 for support of this statement.

[40] See generally *The Diplock Report*, 2 CIVIL RIGHTS 3 (January 14, 1973).

"scheduled" offenses for which, as determined by a director of public prosecutions in a decision that is wide open to political abuse and that will undoubtedly be used to suit British needs, there will be trial without jury.[41]

This effort to hide discriminatory and inhuman treatment beneath the mantel of law is hardly novel to Britain's Irish policies. Be it in the eighteenth-century Penal Laws, the one-sided internment policies of the Special Powers Act,[42] or the empty commissions, inquiries, reports, and tribunals, Britain has long sought to make the illegal appear legal. In the past, Britain has fairly successfully covered up both its activities and those of its Northern henchmen; in the future, it will be hard-pressed to do so. As a result of the European Commission's inquiry and a United Nations investigation recently demanded by three civil rights organizations,[43] the eyes of the world will be focused on the Six Counties, thereby forcing Britain to take meaningful action, to enact just laws, and to right obvious wrongs.

Those wrongs have also long been manifested in the actions of the Protestant majority and their government. Although those actions date back to the plantation of 1607, it is unnecessary to turn the clock back much more than

[41] See *Special Powers and Internment to Continue*, 2 CIVIL RIGHTS 1 (April 19, 1973).

[42] Another example of British "justice" occurred in 1972. After Section 38 (1) of the Special Powers Act was held to conflict with Section 4 (1) of the 1920 Act, which prohibits the North from legislating on any matters affecting the Army, the British House of Commons rushed through—on the same day that the Northern Ireland High Court decided that Section 38 (1) was illegal—the Northern Ireland Act 1972, which gave the Ulster puppets full power to direct Army operations. See Boyd, BRIAN FAULKNER AND THE CRISIS OF ULSTER UNIONISM 75 (1972).

[43] The National Council for Civil Liberties, the Northern Ireland Civil Rights Association, and the Association for Legal Justice filed a sixty-page communication with the United Nations in July 1973. See *Britain Indicted*, 2 CIVIL RIGHTS 1 (November 1973); " 'Violation of Rights' Dossier Sent to Dr. Waldheim," *The Times* (London), August 31, 1973, at 2, col. 2.

forty years to understand fully the depth of Protestant discrimination towards the Catholic community. Indeed, the 1933 statement of Sir Basil Brooke that many people "employ Catholics, but I have not one about my place" and his 1934 remark recommending to "people who are loyalists not to employ Roman Catholics, ninety-nine percent of whom are disloyal" accurately reflect the average Protestant's view of his Catholic brethren, a view that has remained unchanged for centuries.[44]

Unfortunately, Brooke's advice was followed in both the public and private sector. Even though Protestant employers often cited lack of education and skill rather than religion as the reason for their discriminatory policies, the fact remained—and remains—that Catholic unemployment is twice as high, percentagewise, as it should be.[45] Moreover, the situation is unlikely to change greatly. While public contracts now require an antidiscrimination clause, sectarianism has reigned for so long that, to take but one example, "even if fair appointment and promotion procedures are now operated in both central and local government it will be ten

[44] The former Brooke comment may be found in Edwards, THE SINS OF OUR FATHERS 70, and in Wallace, NORTHERN IRELAND 70; the latter comment is quoted in Wallace, NORTHERN IRELAND 70. Brooke, later Lord Brookeborough, was Prime Minister of Northern Ireland from 1943 to 1963.

[45] See generally Harris, PREJUDICE AND TOLERANCE IN ULSTER 214 (1972); Harrison, ULSTER AND THE BRITISH EMPIRE 87; Hastings, BARRICADES IN BELFAST: THE FIGHT FOR CIVIL RIGHTS IN NORTHERN IRELAND 32 (1970) (citing the 20 percent unemployment rate in predominantly Catholic Derry in 1967); Hawkins, THE IRISH QUESTION TODAY: THE PROBLEMS AND DANGERS OF PARTITION 32–33 (1941). A different, but related, form of discrimination involved appointments to various positions. During one period (1937–1939), for instance, "of the 27 umpires, deputy umpires and chairmen of courts of referees only two were Catholics. Of 22 recent appointments to the Commission of the Peace in Belfast only one was a Catholic. Different Ministries made nominations to Boards constituted under Acts of Parliament and did not nominate a solitary Catholic." Campbell, FIFTY YEARS OF ULSTER, 1890–1940 328 (1941).

to fifteen years before Catholics are available in sufficient numbers inside these services for promotion to senior posts."[46]

As a direct result of these discriminatory policies, Catholics are constantly forced to emigrate from the Six Counties. Unable to find employment in the North, they are driven from their homes in search of a means to support themselves. In this manner, the Protestant majority is able to remain the majority. Without discrimination, the higher birth rate among Catholics would eventually make the Catholics the majority; with discrimination and its accompanying emigration, the Catholic-Protestant proportions in the Six Counties have remained "virtually static" over the years.[47]

To accelerate that emigration, life has been made as unpleasant as possible for Catholics. In that regard, Catholics are continuously awarded poor housing in ghettos from which they are—except when they emigrate—rarely able to extricate themselves. For example, when a new house becomes vacant, it is almost invariably awarded to Protestants, despite the fact that a Catholic family may have been on a waiting list long before and require better housing much more than the Protestant family that receives the house. Such was the case in Dungannon in 1968, in the instance which sparked the first civil rights demonstration; and such is still the case today, in spite of the advent of an ostensibly impartial points system.

However, discomfiture in hopes of encouraging Catholic emigration is only part of the reason for housing discrimination and for the concomitant failure to develop new housing estates. An equally pernicious ground is to prevent tipping

46 COMMENTARY UPON THE WHITE PAPER (COMMAND PAPER 558) ENTITLED "A RECORD OF CONSTRUCTIVE CHANGE" PUBLISHED BY THE GOVERNMENT OF NORTHERN IRELAND ON 20 AUGUST, 1971 25–26 (1971); see generally 25–28.

47 See THE MAILED FIST at 7; NICRA, DISCRIMINATION: THE FACTS 2 (1972); Wyatt, *Battle of the Boyne II*, 94 COMMONWEAL 162, 163 (April 23, 1971).

the voting balances in Protestant wards, since banning discrimination in housing and "creating new estates causes population movement and therefore alteration of the political composition of electoral wards within local authorities."[48] Moreover, even if for some reason too many Catholics "infiltrate" a Protestant section, the governmental constituency is quickly changed or "gerrymandered."[49] Nowhere has this practice been more evident than in Derry where, through constant changes in ward size, numbers of seats, and voting qualifications, a heavily Catholic community has been controlled over the years by Protestants.[50] Although the sectarian Derry Borough Council was replaced in 1969 with a Development Commission, which more fairly represents the composition of the local population, gerrymandering remains today a powerful Protestant weapon in Derry and throughout the North.

To entrench themselves still further, Protestants established a system of voting based on taxes. Until it was abolished in 1969, the system, contrary to the democratic principle of one man, one vote, provided that only ratepayers had the franchise in local council elections. Consequently, the local government franchise was not available to nearly one-quarter of those persons entitled to vote at Stormont elections.

Yet even here the Protestant attack on the Catholic minor-

---

[48] NICRA, DISCRIMINATION 5. See also Barritt & Booth, ORANGE AND GREEN 25 (1972).

[49] See Gallagher, THE INDIVISIBLE ISLAND: THE HISTORY OF THE PARTITION OF IRELAND 226 (1957). Gerrymandering was the name applied by Boston editor Ben Russel to the rearrangement of the electoral areas of Essex County, Massachusetts by Governor Elbridge Gerry in the eighteenth century after Russel saw a drawing of the area to which artist Gilbert Stuart had added wings, beak, and claws.

[50] For various examples of Northern gerrymandering, see *ibid.*, 225–65; Bestic, THE IMPORTANCE OF BEING IRISH 174–75 (1969); O'Neill, ULSTER AT THE CROSSROADS 172 (1969); Stetler, THE BATTLE OF BOGSIDE 145 (1970). See Insight Team, ULSTER 29 for a description of the Fermanagh County Council.

ity did not—does not—abate, for it also extended to the education system. As early as the 1920s, the Unionist majority attempted to merge the Protestant and Catholic schools into a single, state-controlled education system. When both communities took issue with the plan—a plan that would only have provided "an agreed syllabus Christianity, watered down to the lowest common denominator of different persuasions and taught by persons who may not even [have been] believing Christians themselves"[51]—it was abandoned. Still, the fact that it was discarded officially does not mean that it was forgotten, for it is clear that the failure of the Government to finance adequately Catholic schools is a sub rosa effort to drive Catholic schools out of business or, alternatively, to further the Catholic's plight by undermining his education.

That discrimination existed and exists in violation of Britain's international obligations is apparent. That the elimination of discrimination through legislative reforms is not enough is equally apparent, since legislation can only "attack the obvious symptoms but do little to solve the underlying problems."[52] In short, those problems cannot be solved until it is recognized that 500,000 Catholics have a right to participate in community affairs, a right which, to date, has been denied them.

The London Viewpoint

Since the passage of the 1920 Act, Britain has endeavored to allow the people of Northern Ireland to govern themselves and to ensure that, at the very least, the human rights of all persons in Ulster are protected. Although Britain has been subjected to periodic attack for its actions in pursuing these objectives, it has nevertheless attained them. In doing

51 Cardinal Conway, quoted in Rose, GOVERNING WITHOUT CONSENSUS 250 (1971).

52 Lynch, *Presidential Address to the Fianna Fail Ard Fheis, 20th February, 1971*, in Lynch, SPEECHES 41, 42.

223

so, Britain has also fulfilled all of its international obligations.

By far the most controversial measure that Britain permitted to be placed on the Northern Ireland Statute Book was the Special Powers Act. Unquestionably, it was a harsh act. It must be remembered, however, that the Special Powers Act was promulgated at a time when "violence and sudden death were frequent happenings on the streets of northern towns"[53] and that it was "designed to facilitate extraordinary and swift action by the executive to counter this menace, even at the price of abandonment of many of the traditional safeguards of British justice."[54] It must also be recognized that while the Special Powers Act created the opportunity for violations of civil liberties, that opportunity was minuscule when juxtaposed with the potential deprivation of civil liberties resulting from the imposition of violence and death. Accordingly, even though the Special Powers Act may have been viewed either as a necessary or an outright evil, it was certainly the lesser of two obvious evils.

Despite countless justifications for legislation even stronger than the Special Powers Act, Britain sought to meet the recurring terrorist crises with that act. Moreover, before the introduction of internment in 1971, it carefully reviewed the request of the Prime Minister of Northern Ireland to determine that internment was in fact strictly required by the exigencies of the situation and that, as such, it came within the meaning of Article 15 (1) of the European Convention.

In particular, Britain decided that the increase in terrorist activity—explosions and murders of civilians, police officers, and soldiers—clearly demanded the introduction of internment. Even then, though, Britain determined that whenever possible the normal processes of the criminal law should be followed, that internment should be ordered only

[53] Calvert, CONSTITUTIONAL LAW 380.
[54] Ibid., 380–81.

in those cases where, after careful examination by a senior police official, the Minister of Home Affairs was satisfied that the person to be interned was either an active IRA member or had been actively implicated in IRA activities, that an advisory committee should be created pursuant to Regulation 12 (1) to give due consideration to any representations made by the person subject to the internment order, that internment should be phased out as quickly as possible, and that alternatives to internment should be developed if at all possible.[55]

By 1972 an alternative to Regulation 12 had been promulgated. Although Regulation 12 itself met Britain's international obligations, since it had more built-in safeguards than existed in Ireland at the time of the *Lawless Case*—and the European Court had determined in the *Lawless Case* that sufficient safeguards existed—it was replaced by the 1972 Order. Under the terms of the 1972 Order, the safeguards afforded to accused persons are in accord not only with the requirements of the European Convention but also with *any* reasonable standards, since the commissioner or Detention Appeal Tribunal must be satisfied that the detainee has been personally concerned with the use or attempted use of violence for political ends.

Still, Britain continued to try to improve its procedures. For that reason, it formed the Diplock Commission. As it stated in its report[56]—a report that confirmed many of the findings of the Bowen Report[57]—the main obstacle to trying terrorists in the regular courts of justice is witness intimidation. While this obstacle might be partially overcome by oral evidence of police officers or soldiers, physical evidence such as fingerprints, or confessions, and while it might be further

---

55 See generally EUROPEAN COMMISSION 56–61.

56 Diplock, REPORT OF THE COMMISSION TO CONSIDER LEGAL PROCEDURES TO DEAL WITH TERRORIST ACTIVITIES IN NORTHERN IRELAND (Cmnd. 5185) (1972) (hereinafter cited as DIPLOCK REPORT).

57 See Bowen, REPORT BY MR. RODERIC BOWEN, Q.C., ON PROCEDURES FOR THE ARREST, INTERROGATION AND DETENTION OF SUSPECTED TERRORISTS IN ADEN: 14 November 1966. (Cmnd. 3165) (1971 reprint) 12.

overcome by in camera hearings in which the witness is screened from sight, his name and address are withheld, the press and public are excluded, and the physical presence of the accused is prohibited,[58] the fact remains that, on the one hand, the evidence derived without witnesses is often insufficient and, on the other hand, witnesses would still be subject to possible intimidation by both Catholic and Protestant terrorists. The Diplock Commission therefore concluded that there was a definite need for an even-handed policy of detention.[59]

The Diplock Commission also concluded, however, that not all crimes require detention. With a few changes in criminal procedure, crimes which could only be dealt with by detention could be disposed of by a public trial in a court of law. Chief among those changes were trial by a single judge rather than trial by jury for certain scheduled offenses. Given the nature of the crimes and the lack of adequate safeguards against the danger of perverse jury acquittals, a change was indeed needed. "The jury system . . . may not yet have broken down, but . . . the time [was] already ripe to forestall its doing so."[60]

In addition, the Diplock Commission recommended—and its recommendations were enacted in the 1973 Emergency Powers Act—that members of the armed services be granted the power to arrest without a warrant and to detain

[58] See DIPLOCK REPORT 9–11.

[59] *Ibid.*, 10–14. "The only hope of restoring the efficiency of criminal courts of law in Northern Ireland to deal with terrorist crimes is by using an extra-judicial process to deprive of their ability to operate in Northern Ireland, those terrorists whose activities result in the intimidation of witnesses. With an easily penetrable border to the south and west the only way of doing this is to put them in detention by an executive act and to keep them confined, until they can be released without danger to the public safety and to the administration of criminal justice" (14). The reference throughout the report is to "detention" and not "internment," which is distinguished as an arbitrary executive directive.

[60] *Ibid.*, 18.

any arrested person for a period of not more than four hours for the purpose of establishing his identity.[61] It suggested, furthermore, that bail be granted only by a judge of the High Court and that bail be refused unless the judge was satisfied that hardship existed and that there was no risk that the person would commit an offense, interfere with witnesses, or fail to surrender.[62] Finally, it recommended "that upon proof by the prosecution of particular facts capable of implicating the accused in the offense with which he [was] charged the onus [would] lie upon him to furnish an explanation of them which [was] consistent with his innocence,"[63] that a confession be admissible "unless it [was] proved on a balance of probabilities that it was obtained by subjecting the accused to torture or to inhuman or degrading treatment,"[64] and that signed statements by witnesses who were dead, unfit to attend the trial, or missing or who had left the province be admissible.[65]

Individually, the Special Powers Act, 1972 Order, Diplock Report, and 1973 Emergency Powers Act reflect British efforts to balance state needs with human rights; collectively, they are evidence of the fact that Britain is constantly trying to improve, and is succeeding in improving, upon those efforts. Until both state needs and human rights are fully secured, Britain will continue to search for new approaches to deal with the modern terrorists' exacerbation of the age-old Irish problem, approaches which, as was the case with past plans and is the case with present ones, will be well within the parameters of international law.

The Belfast Viewpoint

The controversy over the Special Powers Act is the classic case of "much ado about nothing." Born in the difficult days

---

61 *Ibid.*, 21. 62 *Ibid.*, 24.

63 *Ibid.*, 25 and, generally, 25–28.

64 *Ibid.*, 32, and, generally, 28–33.

65 *Ibid.*, 33–34.

227

of the 1920s, when Ulster was fighting for its very existence, the Special Powers Act was "in a respectable line of succession to many similar acts which the troubled state of Ireland has rendered necessary in times past."[66] It was, moreover, required by—and not a violation of—the Rule of Law, for "the Rule of Law presupposes a tolerably orderly community where the authorities are not impeded in their task of government by deliberate violence."[67]

Even though the Special Powers Act was a reasoned response to the indiscriminate violence to which Ulster has been subjected through the years, it was employed infrequently—and then only when no viable alternative existed and adequate safeguards had been established to prevent potential abuses. For instance, from 1926 to 1934, no one was interned; in 1935, two persons were held; from 1936 to 1938, no one was imprisoned; in the war years of 1939 to 1945—when the IRA was consorting with the Axis powers—82, 302, 73, 243, 112, 12, and 3 persons, respectively, were interned; and, from 1946 to 1956, no one was deprived of his liberty.[68] By any means of measurement, therefore, the use of internment was restricted as fully as possible and constituted an appropriate, if little used, weapon against IRA violence. And, by way of comparison, it should be realized that the Republic has, despite far less justification and pressure, employed internment without trial far more often than has Ulster.

When the IRA launched its insane campaign of violence in 1970, it became obvious to the Government of Northern Ireland that internment would have to be introduced. Without internment it would be possible to capture only some of the murderous IRA gunmen; without internment it

[66] Newark, *The Constitution of Northern Ireland: The First Twenty-Five Years*, 8 N. IR. L. Q. 52, 57 (1948). For the view that the Special Powers Act was similar to British statutes, see Shearman, NORTHERN IRELAND: 1921–1971, at 24 (1971).

[67] *Ibid.*

[68] See Carson, ULSTER AND THE IRISH REPUBLIC 25 (1957).

would be impossible to incarcerate any of the men who planned the violence, since they would be far from the scene of the death and destruction. Yet Britain dragged its feet for months, and it was not until August 1971 that Britain gave its consent to the reintroduction of internment.

Once again, however, internment orders were issued only with regard to those men who constituted a serious and continuing threat to public order and safety and "only after a careful scrutiny of information furnished to [Prime Minister Faulkner] in respect of each such person, sufficient to convince [him] that the individual in question [was] a threat to the preservation of peace and the maintenance of order."[69] Even then, the internment orders were subject to review by an advisory committee that would hear any individual's representations and make recommendations to Faulkner concerning that individual's case. Invariably, the Prime Minister would accept the advice of the advisory committee.[70]

While the controversy over internment is misguided, the accusations concerning discrimination in Northern Ireland are nothing short of lies. From the very beginning, the Unionist Government attempted to bring Catholics and Protestants together. At the suggestion, for instance, of Lord Londonderry, Northern Ireland's first Minister of Education, integrated education was to be attained by transferring all schools to state control. Catholics, however, refused to participate, and only Protestant schools were shifted to public control by the Education Act (Northern Ireland) 1923.[71] Instead, therefore, of a uniform education system, a "three-

69 British Information Service, Statement by Mr. Brian Faulkner, Prime Minister of Northern Ireland in Belfast on August 9, 1971, 2.

70 See generally British Information Service, Northern Ireland: Advisory Committee on Internment, October 19, 1971.

71 For a more detailed discussion of the 1923 Act and for a discussion of the 1930 and 1947 Acts, which dealt with the amount of state assistance, see Barritt & Booth, ORANGE AND GREEN 30–31; Edwards, SINS OF OUR FATHERS 226–28; Stetler, BATTLE OF BOGSIDE 34–35.

school" system of education was created: "wholly maintained" schools, run by the Government for all students (the Protestant schools transferred in 1923 form the nucleus of this group); "voluntary maintained" schools, run by a six-member board (most Catholic schools fit into this category); and "nonmaintained" schools, completely controlled by the church (the remaining Catholic schools come under this heading).[72] Still, in spite of Catholic opposition to a unified education system and contrary to Catholic complaints of discrimination, the Government has long provided assistance for all schools, for, aside from the aid granted to "wholly maintained" schools, "voluntary maintained" schools receive 80 percent of all building costs and 100 percent of maintenance costs and teachers' salaries, and "nonmaintained" schools are awarded grants equal to 65 percent of their expenses.[73]

From the beginning, too, the Unionist Government attempted to establish employment opportunities that were free of discrimination. Consequently, when the RUC was created in 1922, the Government reserved one-third of the positions for members of the Catholic community. In this instance, as in the case of its efforts in the education arena, the Unionist Government was rebuffed, since Catholics never occupied more than one-seventh of the positions in the RUC.[74] Nevertheless, those Catholics who did join the RUC were treated fairly, as the recent appointment of a Catholic, Jamie Flanagan, to the position of Chief Constable clearly demonstrates.[75]

[72] See generally Menendez, *Ulster's Educational Apartheid*, 26 CHURCH & STATE 13 (June 1973).

[73] *Ibid.*, 14. For additional views on the "three-school" system, see Hastings, BARRICADES IN BELFAST 36; O'Neill, ULSTER AT THE CROSSROADS 113.

[74] See Barritt & Booth, ORANGE AND GREEN 29.

[75] See generally "Flanagan Named R.U.C. Chief Constable," *Irish Times*, September 12, 1973, 1, col. 1. It should also be noted that the first Lord Chief Justice of Northern Ireland was a Catholic. See Shearman, NORTHERN IRELAND 30.

Another appointment in the public sector that undermines the claim of discrimination was the naming of Gerard Newe as Minister of State in Faulkner's cabinet. Although Newe was in fact the first Catholic cabinet member in Northern Ireland's 55-year history, his appointment cannot be taken as evidence of discrimination—unless it is Catholic discrimination against the Unionist Party and the concomitant refusal of Catholics to become members of that party.

Efforts are also being made to dispel any claims of discrimination in the private sector. Through the Working Party on Discrimination in the Private Sector of Industry, the Unionist Government is promoting full equality in all aspects of employment within that area. While the Working Party "has not attempted to assess the present extent of discrimination on religious grounds,"[76] it has proposed, in its interim report, that a declaration of principle and intent be signed jointly by employers and trade union organizations, a guide to manpower policy and practice—based on manifestly fair principles and sound management procedures—be prepared and issued, and an agency be established to investigate individual discrimination complaints and to initiate inquiries into patterns of employment.[77]

In passing, it might be well to note that, as the 1971 White Paper pointed out, the Unionist Government has been quick both to take action whenever there is reason to believe that discrimination exists and to ensure that justice is seen to be done.[78] Accordingly, the Northern Ireland Government es-

[76] *Full Equality in All Aspects of Job Opportunity*, ULSTER COMMENTARY 5 (May 1973).

[77] See generally *ibid.*; *Fair Employment Agency*, ULSTER COMMENTARY 15 (September 1973). Recent statistics show that employment is on the rise in areas where, formerly, unemployment ran rampant. In Londonderry, for example, "employment figures for men are the best since records were started 24 years ago," See *Londonderry "Go-go" Instead of "No-go,"* ULSTER COMMENTARY 12 (July 1973).

[78] For the view that the Government must work "not so much at ensuring that justice was done, for it was pretty amply done in the past, as at ensuring that justice is seen to be done," see Shearman, 27 MYTHS ABOUT ULSTER 11 (1972).

tablished a Commissioner for Complaints to deal with citizens' grievances against local councils and public bodies, adopted universal adult suffrage—one man, one vote—for local council elections where the franchise had previously been restricted to ratepayers, provided for antidiscrimination clauses in government contracts, set up a Ministry of Community Relations, established a model points scheme for housing allocation, and created the Northern Ireland Housing Executive to be responsible for all public authority house building and allocation.[79]

Finally, it would be well to recognize that to the extent discrimination does exist in Northern Ireland, it is the Catholics who have, by direct and indirect actions, initiated it. They have "deliberately refused to accept the responsibility of U.K. citizenship while demanding all its benefits."[80] They have, until 1971, prohibited members of the Gaelic Athletic Association from taking part in or watching "foreign" games.[81] They have continued to support a church that stated in the recent past that it was a mortal sin for any "Catholic to enter the Protestant University of Trinity College without the previous permission of the Ordinary of the Diocese."[82] And they have unhesitantly paid homage to a church that forced the resignation of Dr. Noel Browne,

[79] See generally THE FUTURE DEVELOPMENT OF THE PARLIAMENT AND GOVERNMENT OF NORTHERN IRELAND: A CONSULTATIVE DOCUMENT (Cmd. 560) (1971). See also Barritt & Booth, ORANGE AND GREEN 26 for the observation that, in Londonderry, housing allocations have reflected population proportions and that the housing program has made satisfactory strides; and McIvor, transcript of *The Advocates* 15 (April 25, 1972) for the view that the points system favors Catholics, who tend to have larger families, as evidenced by the fact that they rent 58 percent of the public housing authority houses but constitute only 22 percent of the family units in Ulster.

[80] Ulster Group, RECENT EVENTS IN NORTHERN IRELAND IN PERSPECTIVE 2 (1972).

[81] *Ibid.*, 4.

[82] Statement by Most Rev. Dr. McQuaid, Archbishop of Dublin and Primate of Ireland, in Carson, ULSTER AND THE IRISH REPUBLIC 41. See also Hone, IRELAND SINCE 1922 21 (1932) for a similar expression.

Minister of Health for the Republic of Ireland, for setting up a mother-and-child health plan that the church felt interfered with the sacred right of parents to provide for the health of their children.[83]

CONCLUSIONS

It is indeed difficult to comprehend how, despite the wartime conditions that exist in parts of Ulster, "the nation that gave Magna Carta, habeas corpus, due process and the common law to the world [could have] imprisoned hundreds of citizens in Northern Ireland without warrant, charge or trial, often on evidence of the rankest hearsay and deception."[84] Although provocation in the form of murder and vast destruction has been great, it cannot—it can never—justify the practices set forth, seriatum, by the Special Powers Act, 1972 Order, Diplock Report, and 1973 Emergency Powers Act. To come to any other conclusion would be suspiciously similar to embracing the universally rejected principle that the end justifies the means.

Yet, paradoxically, one of the most enlightened international instruments, the European Convention, would probably require a different conclusion. While its precursors, the United Nations Charter and the Universal Declaration, would appear to condemn the aforementioned British statutes as human rights impediments, the European Convention would seem to provide Britain with a legal justification for its manifestly inhumane acts and actions. Indeed, it would be surprising, in light of the *Lawless Case*, if Article 15 were not interpreted by the European Commission or European Court to permit derogation from the prescriptions

[83] See Carson, ULSTER AND THE IRISH REPUBLIC 40; Gray, THE IRISH ANSWER: AN ANATOMY OF MODERN IRELAND 276–78 (1966); Stone, *Ireland: "The Killing Sickness,"* 214 NATION 390 (1972). The Browne Affair, a head-on confrontation with the church in 1951, confirmed the feelings of Ulsterites that partition was still the only answer.

[84] Kennedy, *Ulster is an International Issue,* 11 FOREIGN POL. 57, 60–61 (September 1973).

of Articles 5 and 6 of the European Convention. Nonetheless, under the circumstances existing in Ulster today, Article 15 should not be available to Britain to circumvent the problem of witness intimidation, for the article should be restricted to those instances in which "there is an interruption of the administration of justice or a breakdown in the court system due to war or other similar emergencies."[85] Until such an interruption or breakdown occurs, Britain should not have recourse to Article 15; until such time, it should be required to rely on ordinary criminal courts, special criminal courts, or military courts and on some of the methods that the Diplock Report so frivolously discarded—*even if some terrorists are able to remain at large.*

Of course, the human rights issue does not end with a determination as to the legality of the procedures employed to combat terrorism. International law and human decency both demand that all human beings be treated fairly and equally. In this regard, the Government of Northern Ireland—and, accordingly, Britain—appears to have been derelict in fulfilling its duty, although the deprivations of human rights, past and present, do not seem to be as serious or as widespread as many Catholic spokesmen would have one believe.

Job discrimination, housing differentials, gerrymandering, voting barriers, and disparities in education assistance did and, to some extent, do exist. But the degree of prejudice to which Catholics were subjected has been somewhat exaggerated and largely eliminated.[86] Employment, a serious problem in the past, is today adequately protected in the public sector and reasonable suggestions are being proposed

[85] Rauch, *Compatability of the Detention Order* 27.

[86] In addition, it has been argued that Catholics "brought a good deal of [discrimination] on themselves by pretty much refusing, right up to the time of the first civil-rights marches, to do anything to help themselves." Buckley, *Double Troubles of Northern Ireland–A Visit with the Protestant Militants*, NEW YORK TIMES MAG. 36, 130 (December 10, 1972).

for the private sector; housing, another valid complaint in the past, is now assigned on an equitable basis; gerrymandering, which applied only to local elections and did not exist province-wide, has been eliminated; and discrepancies in support for education, though they still exist, are hardly a form of discrimination, since the aid given to schools over which the state has no control—the Catholic schools—is extremely generous.

Significantly, however, it must be recognized that discrimination never existed in all areas of the North.[87] As conversations with both Catholics and Protestants will confirm and as evidenced in detailed studies,[88] the members of the two communities thought of themselves as equals. When separation of the groups occurred, it was not a rigid segregation resulting from an official or unofficial discrimination. Instead, it was a form of self-exclusion from various activities and organizations.[89]

Where it did and does exist, discrimination might best be described as "relative deprivation." Usually defined in terms of three inequalities—economic, political, and social—relative deprivation occurs "when a comparison is made between [a group's] situation and that of another identifiable group and [the group] is shown to be at a disadvantage."[90] If the deprivation—which in Northern Ireland exists both

[87] In 1969, 76 percent of the Catholic community felt that discrimination existed, and 77 percent of the Protestant community that it did not. See Rose, GOVERNING WITHOUT CONSENSUS 272.

[88] By far the best study is that of "Ballybeg," a town in the West of Ulster whose name was, for obvious reasons, changed by the author. The town was studied in 1952–1953, and the contacts maintained by the author until 1965. See Harris, PREJUDICE AND TOLERANCE.

[89] The activities—church and sports (the Catholics play Gaelic football and hurling, and the Protestants take part in hockey, rugby, and soccer); the organizations (the Ancient Order of Hibernians and the Orange Lodges); see *ibid.*, 132–48.

[90] Birrell, *Relative Deprivation as a Factor in Conflict in Northern Ireland*, 20 SOCIOLOGICAL REV. 317 (1972). See also Rose, GOVERNING WITHOUT CONSENSUS 291–92.

within the Catholic community and within the Protestant working class which begins "to feel relatively deprived if working-class Catholics begin to catch up"[91]—is not assuaged, it leads to frustration. Later, if the frustration of rising expectations is not relieved, it leads to aggression.

That is what happened in Ulster. Human wrongs, perpetrated over the years in contravention of the principles of human decency and of the obligations in the United Nations Charter and Universal Declaration to which Britain had assented, produced frustrations terminating in the justifiable demonstrations and marches of 1968. Like the civil rights movement in the United States in the early 1960s, which led to strong laws outlawing discrimination and to greater opportunities for the Black community, the Northern civil rights efforts were quickly successful; unlike the American movement which, with a few glaring exceptions, remained peaceful, the Ulster movement erupted into unjustifiable violence almost as quickly as the civil rights demands were granted.[92] With the outbreak of violence the human rights gains evaporated, and human wrongs—incurred and inflicted by Northern Irish citizens (Catholics and Protestants) and British soldiers—again appeared. Northern Ireland had come full circle.

[91] Birrell, *Relative Deprivation* 331 and, generally, 333–38.

[92] "Yes, the grievance is justified, but no, it does not justify the means being used to seek its redress, and the moral course is to endure the grievance until redress can be won some more civilized way." "A Spirit of Fanaticism," *Wall Street Journal*, November 7, 1972, at 28, col. 1.

CHAPTER VII

The Internationalization of Civil Strife: A Possible Role for the United Nations in Northern Ireland

HAVING concluded that human rights are being violated in Northern Ireland, what must be asked is who has the responsibility to remedy the wrongs. More specifically, it must be determined whether the deprivations are a matter of domestic or international concern, and, concomitantly, whether they constitute a threat to the peace that necessarily triggers the full mechanisms of the United Nations Charter.

Humanitarian Intervention before 1945

Under customary or traditional international law, it was well established both that a state possessed a wide discretion with which to deal with persons in its territorial jurisdiction and that other states were justified at times in exercising forcible self-help or in undertaking humanitarian intervention. Whenever, for instance, a state endangered the lives or property of the nationals of another state residing within its borders, it opened the door to the use of forcible self-help by the state of those nationals. In addition, whenever "the treatment meted out by a State to its own population, particularly to minorities, was so arbitrary, persistently abusive, and cruel that it shocked the conscience of mankind, other States, usually the great powers of the period, took it upon themselves to threaten, or even to use, force in order to come to the rescue of the oppressed minority."[1] In point of fact,

---

[1] Schwelb, HUMAN RIGHTS AND THE INTERNATIONAL COMMUNITY 14 (1964). For a list of authorities supporting this position, see Brownlie, INTERNATIONAL LAW AND THE USE OF FORCE BY STATES 338 (1963); Lillich,

the right of humanitarian intervention was so accepted that the greatest criticism that can be leveled against it was that it was not exercised often enough. Indeed, unless the state against whom the intervention was contemplated was militarily weak, the action was not taken, as the inaction with regard to Germany's treatment of its Jewish population made patently clear.

While customary international law's sanctioning of humanitarian intervention is beyond dispute, the doctrine itself has often been attacked as belonging "to an era of unequal relations"[2] and creating "a musty aura of racial-religious superiority mixed with self-interest."[3] More recently, it has been challenged by the proponents of the nonintervention theory, who assert that one state must not interfere in the affairs of another state. Both assaults are at best unjustified: the former one because the need for humanitarian intervention overshadows the fact that the doc-

---

Forcible Self-Help by States to Protect Human Rights, 53 IOWA L. REV. 325, 325–34 (1967). See also Greenspan, THE MODERN LAW OF LAND WARFARE 623 (1959) for the observation that a right of humanitarian intervention by states exists "in a civil war where cruelties not permitted by the laws of international warfare are practised in a systematic manner." But see Ganji, INTERNATIONAL PROTECTION OF HUMAN RIGHTS 43 (1962) for the view that humanitarian intervention does not have the authority of a customary rule of international law.

The terms "forcible self-help" and "humanitarian intervention" appear to be clearly distinguishable, since the former label would seem to cover situations involving one's own nationals and the latter one would appear to apply to the nationals of another state. Yet the two terms are sufficiently similar to justify a single label. For purposes of the analysis which follows, therefore, the term "humanitarian intervention" will describe both situations.

[2] Brownlie, INTERNATIONAL LAW 341. Brownlie furthermore asserts (340) that "no genuine case of humanitarian intervention has occurred, with the possible exception of Syria in 1860 and 1861" (when the French entered the country following the killing of nearly 4,000 Christians).

[3] Franck & Rodley, *After Bangladesh: The Law of Humanitarian Intervention by Military Force*, 67 AM. J. INT'L. L. 275, 285 (1973).

trine has been abused in the past; and the latter one because the "use of force *primarily* to protect the lives and property of nationals of the intervening state, depending upon one's conceptualistic preference, either was not an intervention at all or, if it was, then [it was] a legally justifiable one."[4]

Humanitarian Intervention after 1945

A more valid dispute arises, however, concerning the status of humanitarian intervention in the post-1945 period. To some scholars "it is extremely doubtful if this form of intervention has survived the express condemnations of intervention which have occurred in recent times or the general prohibition of resort to force to be found in the United Nations Charter."[5] Conversely, other writers reject the contention that humanitarian intervention contravenes the United Nations' limitation on the use of force. They argue, instead, that the cumulative effect of the United Nations Charter is both to prevent international warfare and "to create a coordinate responsibility for the active protection of human rights: members may act jointly with the Organization in what might be termed a new organized, explicitly conventional, humanitarian intervention or singly or collectively in the customary or international common law humanitarian intervention."[6]

To deal intelligently with these contentions the Charter of the United Nations itself must be examined in some detail. In particular, the prescriptions of Articles 2 (4) and 51 and Articles 2 (7) and 39 must be analyzed. At the same time, the interplay of Articles 55 and 56 with these articles must be established.

[4] Lillich, *Forcible Self-Help* 330–31.

[5] Brownlie, INTERNATIONAL LAW 342. See also Franck & Rodley, *After Bangladesh* 299–300.

[6] McDougal & Reisman, *Response by Professors McDougal and Reisman*, 3 INT'L LAWYER 438, 444 (1969). See also Reisman, *Humanitarian Intervention to Protect the Ibos*, in R. Lillich, ed., HUMANITARIAN INTERVENTION AND THE UNITED NATIONS 167, 178 (1973).

239

Taking the last articles first, it will be remembered that Article 55 states that "the United Nations shall promote . . . universal respect for, and observance of, human rights and fundamental freedoms for all without distinction as to race, sex, language, or religion." It will also be recalled that Article 56 provides that "all Members pledge themselves to take joint and separate action in cooperation with the Organization for the achievement of the purposes set forth in Article 55." Quite obviously, therefore, both the individual member states of the United Nations and the United Nations itself are committed to the protection of human rights and fundamental freedoms. Quite obviously, too, the right of humanitarian intervention *appears* to be preserved by Article 56, whether the intervention is by individual states or the United Nations.

Appearances, however, can be deceptive—and in this instance they are. Since Article 2 (4) categorically and clearly asserts that "all Members shall refrain in their international relations from the threat or use of force against the territorial integrity or political independence of any state, or in any other manner inconsistent with the Purposes of the United Nations," the conclusion that Article 56 preserves the right of humanitarian intervention is hardly "obvious." There are, in fact, writers who flatly reject the conclusion and believe instead that Article 2 (4) prohibits the use of all force by states across state lines.[7]

It has nevertheless been suggested that "Article 2 (4) does not forbid the threat or use of force simpliciter,"[8] but only that force which is directed against the territorial integrity or political independence of a state; that good faith humani-

[7] See Kelsen, THE LAW OF THE UNITED NATIONS 27–32 (1951); Franck & Rodley, *After Bangladesh* 299–300; Moore, *The Control of Foreign Intervention in Internal Conflict,* 9 VA. J. INT'L L. 205, 261–64 (1969). The complexity of the legality of individual and United Nations intervention is vividly demonstrated in Lillich, ed., HUMANITARIAN INTERVENTION.

[8] Stone, AGGRESSION AND WORLD ORDER 95 (1958).

240

tarian intervention does not, by reason of the nonpermanent nature of the forages made in its name, violate either the territorial integrity or the political independence of any state; that the protection of human rights should not be made subordinate to the proposition that force should not be used across state lines; and that a broad reading of Article 2 (4) is inappropriate, since the machinery for implementation envisaged by the Charter has not been established.[9] Moreover, it has been argued that Article 51—which provides that nothing in the Charter "shall impair the inherent right of individual or collective self-defense if an armed attack occurs against a Member of the United Nations, until the Security Council has taken measures necessary to maintain international peace and security"—sanctions the use of force in instances where a state, extending the "self" of "self-defense," is protecting either its nationals in a foreign state or persons with a religious affiliation in that state if they are the subject of an "attack" in violation of the provisions of Article 55.[10]

As for humanitarian intervention by the United Nations (and "humanitarian intervention" is here used in a general, loose sense to cover collective actions by the United Nations for the advancement of humanitarian objectives), the objections focus on Article 2 (7) of the Charter. Article 2 (7) provides that "nothing contained in the present Charter shall

[9] See generally Lillich, *Statement on the Record*, in Lillich, ed., HUMANITARIAN INTERVENTION 58–62.

[10] This point is made by Higgins in *The Legal Limits to the Use of Force by Sovereign States: United Nations Practice*, 37 BRIT. Y.B. INT'L L. 269, 316–18 (1961). For the observation, however, that there is no exception and should be no codified exception to the prohibition concerning the unilateral use of force, see Franck & Rodley, *After Bangladesh* 304–305. Their reasons are that it is difficult to define humanitarian intervention, past military intervention is not the type of intervention that should be encouraged (and the type that would be desirable would not, for reasons of self-interest, occur), and virtually no penalties are presently inflicted if the intervention is disinterested, effective, and neutral.

authorize the United Nations to intervene in matters which are essentially within the domestic jurisdiction of any state or shall require the Members to submit such matters to settlement under the present Charter; but this principle shall not prejudice the application of enforcement measures under Chapter VII."

According to adherents of the "Article 2 (7) position," the words of the article override all other provisions of the Charter. In their view, the prescriptions of Articles 55 and 56 are mere recommendations and, when juxtaposed with Article 2 (7), they have no force or effect. In their view, "intervene" is to be construed broadly to bar any measures short of the enforcement sanctions of Chapter VII, since a more restrictive interpretation of intervention—an interpretation that would permit debates, fact-finding missions, and recommendations—"would render otiose . . . the entire provision, for the limitation which it implies would exist even if all reference to matters of domestic jurisdiction were expunged from the Charter."[11] In their view, the words "essentially within the domestic jurisdiction" mean that a matter, so long as it is primarily in the national arena, remains a domestic concern, even if it has international effects. And in their view, each state is itself the judge of when and to what extent a matter falls within the parameters of Article 2 (7).

However, their collective views are subject to heavy scholarly attack. First of all, the assertion that the "nothing con-

---

[11] Preuss, *Article 2, Paragraph 7 of the Charter of the United Nations and Matters of Domestic Jurisdiction*, 74 RECUEIL DES COURS (Hague Academy of International Law) 553, 608 (1949). For a detailed discussion of "intervention" and Article 2 (7), see *ibid.*, 605–14; and for the observation that "the creation of a commission of inquiry, the making of a recommendation of a procedural or substantial nature, or the taking of a binding decision constitutes intervention under the terms of this paragraph," see Goodrich & Hambro, CHARTER OF THE UNITED NATIONS: COMMENTARY AND DOCUMENTS 120 (1949). See also Kelsen, *Limitations on the Functions of the United Nations*, 55 YALE L. J. 997, 999 (1946).

tained" language of Article 2 (7) takes primacy over the rest of the United Nations Charter is highly debatable. In practice, it is argued, the United Nations must adhere (and has adhered) to the belief that the Charter—like any treaty—is to be taken as a whole and understood in light of the United Nations' purposes.[12]

Secondly, "intervene" is held by some scholars to refer to dictatorial interference in the affairs of a state, not to measures such as placing a matter on the agenda of the General Assembly or Security Council or discussing it in either body. If "intervention" were defined in any way other than a " 'peremptory demand,' involving physical enforcement or threat of enforcement in the event of non-compliance"[13] with the provisions of the Charter, it would exclude the very measures that are provided in the Charter for the resolution of problems and, in the process, do violence to the obligations assumed by states in drafting or adhering to the Charter. A case in point is Article 62 (2) (which provides that the Economic and Social Council "may make recommendations for the purpose of promoting respect for, and observance of, human rights and fundamental freedoms for all"), for, if recommendations were barred as falling within the confines of Article 2 (7), Article 62 (2) would make no sense whatsoever.[14]

12 See Higgins, THE DEVELOPMENT OF INTERNATIONAL LAW THROUGH THE POLITICAL ORGANS OF THE UNITED NATIONS 65 (1963); Fawcett, *Human Rights and Domestic Jurisdiction*, in E. Luard, ed., THE INTERNATIONAL PROTECTION OF HUMAN RIGHTS 286, 290 (1967).

13 Korey, *The Key to Human Rights Implementation*, 570 INT. CONCILIATION 1, 10 (1968). See also H. Lauterpacht, INTERNATIONAL LAW AND HUMAN RIGHTS 167–73 (1950); Ermacora, *Human Rights and Domestic Jurisdiction (Article 2, §7 of the Charter)*, 124 RECUEIL DES COURS (Hague Academy of International Law) 371, 439 (1968); Fawcett, *Human Rights and Domestic Jurisdiction* 291; Wright, *Is Discussion Intervention?*, 50 AM. J. INT'L L. 102, 105–10 (1956).

14 See H. Lauterpacht, INTERNATIONAL LAW 181, where the author states that "there is no reason why the process of interpretation should transform the imperfections of the Charter into manifest absurdities." But see Higgins, *Development of International Law* 82 for a rejection

Thirdly, and of cardinal significance, "essentially within the domestic jurisdiction" is defined by some writers and by practice in a narrow, restrictive way. Although the replacement of "solely" in Article 15 (8) of the League of Nations Covenant with "essentially" in Article 2 (7) was intended by the framers of the Charter to place limitations on the United Nations' powers, "the very elasticity of the terminology which they employed has permitted a degree of interference by the United Nations in internal matters which would not have been possible under such a provision as Article 15 (8) of the Covenant."[15] By broadening the exception, these scholars assert, the framers paradoxically narrowed the jurisdiction of individual states.

The jurisdiction that remains appears indeed to be limited. While human rights are initially matters of domestic jurisdiction, it is now apparent to many jurists that the systematic denial of human rights to individuals has become a matter of international concern that justifies United Nations action.[16] In the years since the Charter was drafted,

---

of the view that recommendations are acceptable so long as they are not directed against one state: "The organs of the United Nations have no more authority to intervene in the affairs of its members at large than they have to intervene in the domestic affairs of any one member. If a recommendation is permissible *vis-à-vis* the many, it is permissible *vis-à-vis* the one."

15 Preuss, *Article 2, Paragraph 7* 649. See also Q. Wright, INTERNATIONAL LAW AND THE UNITED NATIONS 50–76 (1960). Article 15 (8) provided that "if the dispute between the parties is claimed by one of them, and is found by the Council [of the League], to arise out of a matter which by international law is solely within the domestic jurisdiction of that party, the Council shall so report, and shall make no recommendation as to its settlement."

16 See Ganji, INTERNATIONAL PROTECTION 133–36; Fawcett, *Human Rights and Domestic Jurisdiction* 293; Fawcett, *The Role of the United Nations in the Protection of Human Rights—Is it Misconceived?*, in A. Eide & A. Schou, eds., INTERNATIONAL PROTECTION OF HUMAN RIGHTS 95, 98–100 (1968); Markovic, *Implementation of Human Rights and the Domestic Jurisdiction of States, ibid.*, 56–58; Rudzinski, *Domestic Jurisdiction in United Nations Practice*, 9 INDIA Q. 313, 344–49 (1953).

the respect for and observance of human rights have become international obligations; in the years since that date, human rights have been "internationalized." As has been forcefully stated, in this intensely interdependent world, "the people in one territorial community may realistically regard themselves as being affected by activities in another territorial community, though no goods or people cross any boundaries."[17] Consequently, "domestic jurisdiction means little more than a general community concession of primary, but not exclusive, competence over matters arising and intimately concerned with aspects of the internal public order of states."[18]

When, however, either the nature of a situation or its repercussions are such as to constitute a direct or potential threat to international peace and security, the "concession of primacy," in the view of these writers, gives way to international jurisdiction and the activities cease to be, if they ever were, "matters essentially within the domestic jurisdiction" of a state.[19] If, indeed, the domestic jurisdiction clause were permitted to shield human rights violations despite the threat which those violations pose to international peace and security, "the principal purpose for which the whole constitutive structure [was] established and [is] maintained could be easily defeated."[20]

The mere threat to the peace occasioned by violations of

[17] McDougal & Reisman, *Rhodesia and the United Nations: The Lawfulness of International Concern*, 62 AM. J. INT'L L. 1, 12 (1968). See also H. Lauterpacht, INTERNATIONAL LAW 174–76.

[18] McDougal & Reisman, *Rhodesia and the United Nations* 15. The authors add (18) that "the impact of the flagrant deprivation of the most basic human rights of the great mass of the people of a community cannot possibly stop short within the territorial boundaries in which the physical manifestations of such deprivations first occur."

[19] See generally H. Lauterpacht, INTERNATIONAL LAW 176; Oppenheim, INTERNATIONAL LAW 115–16 (8th ed., 1955); Markovic, *Implementation of Human Rights* 55–58; McDougal & Reisman, *Rhodesia and the United Nations* 14–15.

[20] McDougal & Reisman, *Rhodesia and the United Nations* 14. See also Lillich, *Forcible Self-Help* 338–40.

245

human rights is enough, it is claimed, to justify United Nations action; an actual breach of the peace is not required to remove an activity from the protection of Article 2 (7). Under Article 39, the Security Council is empowered to "determine the existence of *any threat to the peace*, breach of the peace, or act of aggression and shall make recommendations, or decide what measures shall be taken in accordance with Articles 41 and 42, to maintain or restore international peace and security."[21] Furthermore, in order to accord the Security Council additional flexibility and freedom "to make *ad hoc* determinations after a full, contextual examination of the peculiar features of each specific situation of threat or coercion,"[22] the drafters left the words "threat," "breach," and "act of aggression" undefined.

Nonetheless, jurists argue that the Security Council, given the polarizations of the superpowers, has not fully exercised its powers under Article 39. With the notable exception of the Rhodesian conflict, where it voted selective mandatory sanctions against the rebel government, the Security Council has shied away from its powers under Article 39 in human-rights situations.[23] Yet concomitant with the failure of the Security Council to take the requisite action, the General Assembly, under Articles 10 and 11, has moved into this area. Picking up the Security Council slack, the General Assembly has examined many ostensibly domestic conflicts and issued numerous resolutions.[24]

A fourth and final attack is made by scholars on the

---

[21] Emphasis added. Article 41 provides for enforcement measures "not involving the use of armed force"; Article 42 provides for the use of armed force if the "measures provided for in Article 41 would be inadequate or have proved to be inadequate."

[22] McDougal & Reisman, *Rhodesia and the United Nations* 7.

[23] The best analysis of the Rhodesian situation is *ibid.* The Security Council's 1966 condemnation of Rhodesia may be found in SC Res. 232 (1966); 61 AM. J. INT'L L. 654 (1967).

[24] Article 10 states that the General Assembly may discuss any questions or matters within the scope of the Charter and may make recommendations to United Nations members, to the Security Council, or to both; Article 11 provides specifically for General Assembly con-

conclusion that each state may determine for itself when Article 2 (7) applies. Rejecting the assertion out of hand, they assert that the organs of the United Nations, not the individual state, must decide (despite the omission of a specific reference to an organ authorized to do so) the applicability of Article 2 (7), if the Charter is to have any meaning and the members of the United Nations are to have any obligations.[25] Indeed, were Article 2 (7) "construed—in an interdependent world in which matters of international concern and domestic concern, in a factual sense, are wholly and irrevocably commingled—to authorize each particular state by its own exclusive decision to determine the matters within its domestic concern, [it] could, of course, mean the complete negation of obligation."[26] Accordingly, the organs of the United Nations, not the individual state, must decide what falls within the domestic jurisdiction of a state.

Summary

In the post-Charter period, humanitarian intervention remains an acceptable, if not widely accepted, concept, for the most reasonable view is that humanitarian intervention —by either individual states or the United Nations—is legally permissible when the United Nations Charter is read as

---

sideration of and recommendations with regard to any matter dealing with international peace and security. For discussions of these resolutions, see Cohen, *Human Rights under the United Nations Charter*, 14 LAW & CONTEMP. PROB. 430, 434–35 (1949); Korey, *Key to Human Rights* 31–32. For a detailed examination of twenty-three instances of United Nations action where the Article 2 (7) defense was raised, see United Nations, 1 REPERTORY OF PRACTICE OF UNITED NATIONS ORGANS (Art. 1–22) 61–156 (1955).

25 See generally Higgins, DEVELOPMENT OF INTERNATIONAL LAW 61–67; H. Lauterpacht, INTERNATIONAL LAW 181–82; Ross, CONSTITUTION OF THE UNITED NATIONS 130–31 (1950); Stone, LEGAL CONTROLS OF INTERNATIONAL CONFLICT 254 (1954); Markovic, *Implementation of Human Rights* 55; Preuss, *Article 2, Paragraph 7* 596–97; Rudzinski, *Domestic Jurisdiction* 318–20.

26 McDougal & Feliciano, LAW AND MINIMUM WORLD PUBLIC ORDER 360 (1961).

a whole. If, indeed, humanitarian intervention is exercised when and how it should be, the provisions of Articles 2 (4) and 2 (7) will not be violated, while those of Articles 55 and 56 will be given their full meaning.

Still, it is not enough to assert that humanitarian intervention is legal. It must be recognized, instead, that such action might well give rise to a threat to the peace under Article 39. For that reason, humanitarian intervention must be carefully weighed to determine that human rights and international peace are not in conflict; for that reason, too, humanitarian intervention "would thus appear to belong to that category of acts which may be generally legal, but which may be deemed impermissible in a given case."[27]

In that connection, recent General Assembly resolutions directed at certain African regimes are most discouraging. Contrary to the laudable aspirations of the Declaration on Principles of International Law concerning Friendly Relations and Cooperation among States in accordance with the Charter of the United Nations,[28] the resolutions dealing with, among others, South Africa[29] and Namibia[30] called for material, moral, and political assistance to liberation movements in each area. In doing so, the General Assembly may well have been advancing international human rights. Yet, in doing so, it was simultaneously creating a serious threat to the peace that threatened and continues to threaten destruction of values at least as great as the human rights at stake.[31]

In brief, therefore, humanitarian intervention would ap-

[27] Higgins, *Legal Limits* 317. See also Fenwick, *When is There a Threat to the Peace?—Rhodesia*, 61 AM. J. INT'L L. 753, 755 (1967).

[28] G.A. Res. 265 (XXV), 25 U.N. GAOR Supp. 28, at 121, U.N. Doc. A/8028 (1970).

[29] G.A. Res. 2396 (XXIII), 23 U.N. GAOR Supp. 18, at 19, U.N. Doc. A/7348 (1968).

[30] G.A. Res. 2871 (XXVI), 26 U.N. GAOR Supp. 29, at 105–06, U.N. Doc. A/8429 (1971).

[31] See generally Bilder, *Rethinking International Human Rights: Some Basic Questions*, 1969 WISC. L. REV. 171, 188–89.

pear legally permissible by either individual states or the United Nations. It should, however, be employed by states only in situations of extreme deprivation to avoid what one scholar has called "a general license to vigilantes and opportunists to resort to hegemonial intervention";[32] and it should be exercised by the United Nations only at a level which, unless a threat to or breach of the peace exists, falls short of "dictatorial interference" or "peremptory demands." Until effective international machinery to protect human rights is developed, individual states must and will retain the right to "intervene humanely," since "to require a state to sit back and watch the slaughter of innocent people in order to avoid violating blanket prohibitions against the use of force is to stress blackletter at the expense of far more fundamental values."[33] Until, too, international bodies such as the General Assembly exercise greater restraint when dealing with colonial-oriented interventions than has been evidenced in the recent past, such machinery will remain an unrealized and vain hope.

THE DUBLIN VIEWPOINT

To right the human wrongs in the North of Ireland, humanitarian intervention—be it by states or the United Nations—is necessary and proper. Either the Republic or the United Nations, therefore, may take the requisite action.

Leaving aside the fact that the North is part of the Republic and assuming for the sake of argument that it is legally separate from the South, humanitarian intervention by the Republic would be justifiable, given the long period of discrimination, the policy of internment, the barbaric tortures practiced on innocent civilians, and the loss of life that has occurred and undoubtedly will continue to occur in

[32] Brownlie, *Thoughts on Kind-Hearted Gunmen*, in Lillich, ed., HUMANITARIAN INTERVENTION 139, 147–48.

[33] Lillich, *Forcible Self-Help* 344. See also Moore, *Statement on the Record*, in Lillich, ed., HUMANITARIAN INTERVENTION 49.

the lawless North. Such an intervention would be in accord with the stringent proscriptions of Article 2 (4) of the United Nations Charter, since it would not be directed against either the territorial integrity or political independence of the North. Such an intervention would fall within the parameters of Article 51, because the action might well be deemed self-defense, with the Catholics of the North representing an extension of the Southern "self." And such an intervention would be nothing more than the fulfillment of Ireland's obligations under Article 56.

Intervention by the United Nations is justifiable on three grounds: first, the deprivations endured by the Catholic minority are in clear violation of the provisions of Article 55; second, the situation in the North of Ireland constitutes a definite threat to international peace and security under Article 39; and, third, the Ulster Defense Association's gangster-like forays into the South, are, by any definition, acts of aggression under Article 2 (4), which set in motion the machinery of Article 39.[34] Unfortunately, however, neither the Security Council nor the General Assembly has seen fit to take any action.

After being rebuffed by Britain in its attempt to get Britain to ask for United Nations assistance or to form a joint British-Irish force to patrol the troubled North,[35] Ireland took its case to the Security Council. Pursuant to Article 35,[36] Ireland asked for an urgent meeting of that body. The

34 See generally *UN Forces for N. Ireland?*, 1 CIVIL RIGHTS (October 28, 1972).

35 By proposing these alternatives, the Republic would appear to have fulfilled its obligations under Article 33 (which requires members to resolve disputes by "peaceful means of their own choice" before bringing an action to the Security Council). See Boyd, FIFTEEN MEN ON A POWDER KEG: A HISTORY OF THE U.N. SECURITY COUNCIL 325 (1971).

36 Article 35 provides, in part, that "any Member of the United Nations may bring any dispute, or any situation of the nature referred to in Article 34, to the attention of the Security Council or of the General Assembly"; Article 34 states that the "Security Council may investigate any dispute, or any situation which might lead to inter-

request was granted, and, in August 1969, the Security Council met. However, the meeting proved to be a farce, for Britain immediately raised the black shield of Article 2 (7), asserted that United Nations intervention against British wishes would be a violation of Article 2 (7), and claimed that United Nations action was in fact unnecessary because Britain was taking the requisite measures to deal with the problem. Then, after Ireland exposed the hypocrisy of arguing that a United Nations discussion of the Northern "troubles" was barred by Article 2 (7) (hypocrisy because the question of apartheid in South Africa had for years been discussed despite South African objections), after it revealed the true facts about the inequality that existed in the North, and after it pleaded for a United Nations peacekeeping force to replace the British Army (which constituted a basic, age-old factor in the perpetuation of the Ulster struggle), the meeting was "adjourned"—never to be reconvened.[37]

Following this abortive exercise, Ireland turned in September 1969 to the General Assembly. This action also proved to be an exercise in futility. In the end, Ireland, realizing that it did not have the required votes and relying on the British assurance that the long-overdue reforms would be placed into effect, withdrew its request that the matter be placed on the General Assembly's agenda.[38]

Since, therefore, the United Nations has failed to exercise its powers, Ireland has again been forced to rely on its own resources to remedy the wrongs perpetrated in the North. Although the United Nations has the power to intervene

---

national friction or give rise to a dispute, in order to determine whether the continuance of the dispute or situation is likely to endanger the maintenance of international peace and security."

[37] See Schwelb, *Northern Ireland and the United Nations*, 19 INT'L & COMP. L. Q. 483, 483–86 (1970); 24 U.N. SCOR. 1503rd meeting 2–5 (1969).

[38] See Schwelb, *Northern Ireland* 488–90; 24 U.N. GAOR, Annexes, at 5, U.N. Doc. A/7651 (1969); Hillery, 24 U.N. GAOR, Gen'l Comm. 4–6 (1969).

under Article 39 or, at the very least, to place the conflict on the agenda of the Security Council or General Assembly for purposes of discussion, establish a fact-finding mission, adopt resolutions, and make recommendations, it has to date chosen instead to follow a "hands-off" policy. Until that policy is reversed and the United Nations uses its powers, Ireland will retain the legal and moral right to intervene in the North of Ireland whenever conditions require such humanitarian action.

The London and Belfast Viewpoints

If ever there was an instance that clearly fit within the limits of Article 2 (7), that instance is the sporadic terrorism in Northern Ireland today. If, instead of isolated acts of terrorism, there were a province-wide, all-out conflict in which people were being massacred daily or in which the threat of the outbreak of hostilities with the Republic of Ireland loomed large, an argument *might* be made that the enforcement language of Article 2 (7) should apply and that the United Nations should assume jurisdiction under Article 39. But the fact remains that the isolated acts of terrorism are precisely that—isolated acts of terrorism. As such, they do not constitute a conflict; as such, they do not justify the application of any provision of the Charter other than Article 2 (7); and, as such, they do not warrant United Nations—or any other individual or organizational—interference in the affairs of the United Kingdom.

The correctness of these statements was borne out by the actions of the Security Council and General Assembly during the August-September 1969 efforts of Ireland to place the Northern Ireland problem on the respective bodies' agendas. In each instance, the United Nations organ acted immediately and wisely. Aware that the Irish presentation was weak, that no member state could long remain immune to the consequences of the breach of Article 2 (7) of the Charter and the concomitant introduction of internal disputes into the United Nations, that a political discussion in the United Nations might inflame controversy, that "a peace-keeping force introduced against the wishes of the country concerned [was] a contradiction in terms,"[39] and that Britain "was already doing, and doing effectively, what the [Security Council and the] General Assembly at best could have recommended to it to do,"[40] the two United Nations bodies, without taking further action, adjourned after listening to the Irish arguments. In doing so, they did precisely what they should do in the case of matters that are "essentially within the domestic jurisdiction of any state." Any other action by either body would have caused and would cause great consternation—first to Britain, then to other sovereign states, and, eventually, to the United Nations itself.

CONCLUSIONS

Despite the undeniable existence and permissibility of humanitarian intervention in the post-Charter world, the Ulster conflict hardly seems a proper setting for the applicability of the doctrine by individual states. Although human rights are daily being violated, the deprivations endured are not of the requisite magnitude, harsh and cold-blooded as that may sound, to justify humanitarian intervention by Ireland. If, indeed, intervention were deemed justifiable in the Northern Ireland struggle, notwithstanding the great strides that have been taken by Britain in recent years to eliminate discrimination, the cry of vigilantism would fill the air, and both international law and the people of the North would suffer serious setbacks. More progress—much more progress—is needed before full equality will be fact and not British fiction in Ulster. That progress, however, cannot result from an Irish intervention in Northern Ireland.

[39] Lord Caradon, 24 U.N. GAOR, Gen'l Comm. 6 (1969).
[40] Schwelb, *Northern Ireland* 491.

253

Humanitarian intervention by the United Nations (and here again it must be reiterated that "humanitarian intervention" is being loosely used to embrace collective actions by the United Nations in situations destructive of human values) is another matter. To be sure, there is no valid threat to the peace under Article 39, for neither the possibility of a British-Irish war nor the belief that Catholics in Europe and throughout the world feel "threatened" by the tragic events in the North is very realistic. Still, there is a role for the United Nations, a role which that body has to date unfortunately refused to play.[41]

Even though the conflict in Northern Ireland is in fact the responsibility of Britain, the United Nations is not estopped by Article 2 (7) or by British actions to ameliorate the situation from exercising its competence short of dictatorial interference. Certainly, the primary jurisdiction for remedying the Ulster wrongs belongs to Britain. Just as certain, however, is the assertion that those wrongs are, both traditionally and under the United Nations Charter, a matter of international concern. For that reason, and for

[41] However, one observer, it should be noted, feels that the United Nations action in August 1969 was beneficial. That action, he asserts, "admirably illustrates the way in which an apparently empty exchange of words in the [Security] Council, leading to no formally identifiable agreement or action, can sometimes help to stabilise a dangerous situation—if the trick is worked neatly, by people who understand how to operate the United Nations mechanism without letting it get out of hand." Boyd, FIFTEEN MEN 329.

In passing it should perhaps also be noted that the Republic's action before the United Nations was "predictably ineffective" because the Catholic church did not want communist support (the Soviet Union spoke on the Republic's behalf before the General Committee of the General Assembly), Britain was seriously annoyed, and the United States was even more troubled (in view of the conflict's impact on its citizens of Irish descent). See O'Brien, *The Embers of Easter 1916–1966*, 37 NEW LEFT REV. 3, 6 (1966). Although the article expressed the reasons why Ireland would not go to the United Nations, the arguments raised might explain why the Republic did not make more of an effort when it finally did go to that organization.

the benefit of all, it is to be hoped that rather than maintain their silence or partake in another charade along the lines of the August-September 1969 "hearings," the organs of the United Nations will act. For that reason, too, it is to be hoped that they will inscribe the Northern Ireland conflict on their respective agendas, discuss it, establish fact-finding missions to determine the validity of each claimant's contentions, and, after full and speedy deliberation, adopt resolutions and make recommendations—ranging conceivably from the determination that the Republic must take a firmer stand against the IRA terrorists' use of the Southern sanctuary to the decision to send a peacekeeping force to the North if Britain concurs—which might contribute to the termination of hostilities and the righting of wrongs in Ulster.

CHAPTER VIII

Vox Clamantis in Deserto: Proposed Solutions and Yesable Propositions

IN PIECING together the Ulster puzzle, it is apparent that each of the participants to the struggle must bear some of the blame for the conflict. What is perhaps less apparent at first blush is the fact that the struggle is capable of solution. Like any man-made problem the Northern Ireland tragedy is soluble by man. While an acceptable solution has yet to be found, a number of suggestions—which can be conveniently categorized once more under the Dublin-London-Belfast labels—have been advanced.

THE DUBLIN VIEWPOINT

Since "a divided Ireland will never be happy or at peace,"[1] the "only lasting settlement to the recurring cycles of bitterness, violence and reprisals is the re-unification"[2] of Ire-

[1] Lynch, Extracts from the Taoiseach's Presidential Address to the Fianna Fail Ard-Fheis 3, February 19, 1972.

[2] Lynch, *Address to Fianna Fail Ard Fheis (Convention), 17th January, 1970*, in Lynch, SPEECHES AND STATEMENTS ON IRISH UNITY, NORTHERN IRELAND AND ANGLO-IRISH RELATIONS 15, 16 (1972). In a more recent speech, Lynch stated that: "The division of Ireland has never been, and is not now, acceptable to the great majority of the Irish people who were not consulted in the matter when that division was made fifty years ago. No generation of Irishmen has ever willingly acquiesced in that division—nor can this problem remain for ever in its present situation." *Telegram Exchange with the British Prime Minister, Mr. Edward Heath, 19/20th August, 1971, ibid.*, 77, 81. See also Greaves, *Epilogue* to Jackson, IRELAND HER OWN: AN OUTLINE HISTORY OF THE IRISH STRUGGLE 484 (1970); Kramer, *Letter to the Editors*, 48 NEW YORKER 126 (April 15, 1972).

land. In reality, there is only one Ireland, and, until this fact is accepted and the two parts of the island are once again joined, the "troubles" in the North of Ireland are bound to continue.

The rationale for this conclusion is not mere nationalism. Rather the basis for the belief is the recognition that the Six Counties lack stability—and that stability can never be formed on the sectarian foundations of the North. More specifically, stability is impossible when the party in power —the Unionist Party—maintains its position by keeping all non-Unionists in a position of inequality and subservience. Just as it did fifty-odd years ago, when it emerged from the post-World War I difficulties at the head of an artificially created majority, the Unionist Party is today pursuing its dictatorial objectives by casually speaking in terms of democracy, equality, and the majority will, while simultaneously insuring—by discriminatory practices that force members of the Catholic community to emigrate—that the Six Counties remain an area of unequals.[3] In doing so, it has in fact insured temporarily that the Protestants, despite the recent effort at power-sharing, retain effective control over the North of Ireland. It has also insured itself a permanent place among the world's least enlightened governments. And it has insured a continuation of the turmoil that has embroiled the North since the Six Counties were sprung full blown as a political entity from the head of Britain's Conservative Party.

[3] The creation of the Six County Government and the recent plebiscite concerning the future of the North are, it has been argued, travesties. "If there is to be self-determination for Ulster, why not self-determination for Londonderry, or County Tyrone, or any other predominantly Catholic area in Ulster?" Kennedy, *Ulster is an International Issue*, 11 FOREIGN POL. 57, 67 (September 1973). Moreover, as John Hume stated, "when you create a deliberately created majority then you cannot talk of democracy." Public Broadcasting Service, transcript of *The Advocates* 35 (April 25, 1972). But see Wilson, ULSTER UNDER HOME RULE 204 (1955) for the assertion that "beyond a point the principle [of self-determination] cannot be applied at all, and some *modus vivendi* must be accepted by both sides."

257

To allow intransigent Protestants to exercise a permanent veto over peace and tranquility is, by any but the Protestant extremist point of view, clearly wrong. A way must be found to foster harmony, not friction, among the peoples of Ireland. That way is to recognize the fact that the people of Ireland are one and that the government of Ireland should therefore also be one.

A single, all-Ireland government does not and will not mean a takeover of the North by the South. Instead, it means a new Ireland, a new constitution, and a new beginning for the peoples of Ireland, which would result in greater prosperity since energies could be concentrated "on building better [lives] for [the] people—instead of dissipating them, as at present, in division and recrimination."[4] In addition, it means a federal form of government, with the North, though answerable to the new Irish government, retaining control over local problems such as agriculture, education, and health.[5]

By controlling the purse strings of the Six Counties, Britain can advance the cause of peace in Ireland simply by "informing" the leaders of the North that the experiment in Protestant hegemony is over and that they must now

[4] Lynch, *The Anglo-Irish Problem*, 50 FOR. AFF. 601, 615 (1972). A new Ireland, states Lynch, would "not involve any levelling down, on either side, of existing social or economic standards. There *are* discrepancies at present but they are not insurmountable and they are lessening. The real dividing line in Ireland so far as economic prosperity is concerned has always been an East-West and not a North-South one. At present the link with Britain provides substantial direct and indirect subsidies to Northern Ireland. In any settlement arrangements these subsidies would no doubt eventually have to be phased out; but this should be done over a period." See also Greaves, THE IRISH CRISIS 212–13 (1972) for the view that "loans for development, without political conditions, willingness to accept Irish produce on favourable terms for a transitional period, and possibly other forms of aid would be a small price for ending the era of hatred between two close neighbours."

[5] See Gray, THE IRISH ANSWER: AN ANATOMY OF MODERN IRELAND 381–88 (1966).

work towards the reunion of the two parts of Ireland which will provide the only real solution to the tragedy in the North. In this regard, Britain's insistence on a coalition of Catholics and Protestants to run the Six Counties and on the formation of a Council of Ireland was a sensible, if long-overdue, start. Unfortunately, however, that start came to a sputtering halt as British resolve dissipated in the spring of 1974 amid the work stoppage and threats of Protestant extremists.

To ask Britain to insist on reunification hardly seems to be asking too much. Since it was responsible for the creation of the Northern dictatorship in the first place and since it has chosen to tell the world that the conflict is a matter within its domestic jurisdiction, Britain must bear the sole responsibility for removing this poisonous, tyrannical growth from the face of Ireland. With its economic weapon and the knowledge of its dishonorable Irish past, Britain stands well armed to accomplish this objective.

The London Viewpoint

There is only one "solution"—a two-pronged solution—to the years of death and destruction in Northern Ireland: the restoration of the rule of law and the determination by the peoples of the province, through democratic processes, of the course that Ulster is to follow. This "solution" is, at once, flexible and highly rigid, for, although Britain will adhere to whatever decision the people of the province choose, it will neither permit terrorism to make that choice nor hesitate to employ whatever means are necessary to restore law and order.[6]

If there be any doubt about either of these assertions, it should quickly be laid to rest. Just as it has in years past,

[6] See generally NORTHERN IRELAND CONSTITUTIONAL PROPOSALS (Cmnd. 5259) 6–7 (1973) (hereinafter cited as 1973 WHITE PAPER); and THE NORTHERN IRELAND CONSTITUTION (Cmnd. 5675) (1974) (cited herein-after as 1974 WHITE PAPER).

259

Britain will continue to afford to its Northern Ireland citizens the fullest protection of the rule of law and to combat "the IRA terrorist campaign and, at the same time, the activities of Protestant extremists, both by the normal processes of the criminal law and by the provisions of [the Northern Ireland (Emergency Provisions) Act 1973]."[7] Indeed, "there has been, and remains, no more urgent or compelling task than to bring the present state of violence to an end,"[8] and, therefore, the "Army will remain for so long and in such strength as the situation requires."[9]

Concomitant with the restoration of law and order, Britain will strive to insure that the wishes of the majority determine the future of Northern Ireland. In that regard and "in accordance with the specific pledges given by successive United Kingdom Governments, Northern Ireland must and will remain part of the United Kingdom for as long as that is the wish of a majority of the people";[10] in that regard, too, Britain will respect and support the wishes of the majority for either independence or union with the Republic, although if Ulster were to choose independence, it could not expect its sovereignty to be combined with continued British economic, financial, and military guarantees.[11]

[7] 1973 WHITE PAPER 6.   [8] *Ibid.*
[9] *Ibid.*

[10] *Ibid.* 1. A statement by former Secretary of State William Whitelaw is instructive: "There can be no change in the constitutional position of Northern Ireland as part of the United Kingdom unless by the will of the majority. Equally, of course if the majority of the people in Northern Ireland were to opt for a United Ireland no British Government would stand in the way. But here I must simply say something to all those who want a United Ireland and who think they can get it by violence and by force who think they can somehow bomb the majority of the Protestant community into a United Ireland. I say to them that they cannot, that they will not and that there is no possible chance of their doing it. I say to them that the longer they go on with the violence, the further away will be the objective they seek to promote." Whitelaw, *Northern Ireland: Military and Political Action*, 39 VITAL SPEECHES, 93, 95 (November 15, 1972).

[11] See THE FUTURE OF NORTHERN IRELAND: A PAPER FOR DISCUSSION

With the exception of two possibilities, Britain will, indeed, accept without question the decision of the majority regarding the province's future. First of all, it will not permit the development of Northern Ireland as "a base for any external threat to the security of the United Kingdom."[12] Secondly, Britain will not allow the majority to dictate to the minority. For that reason, Britain insisted that the Northern Ireland Assembly be representative of the whole Ulster community; for that reason, Catholics and Protestants in 1974 shared executive power in a body that exercised the limited powers of self-government that Britain granted to Northern Ireland; and, for that reason, Britain promised in the 1974 White Paper to continue to press for a provision, in whatever formula is accepted by the 1975 consultative convention, that recognizes the special relationship between Ulster and the Republic of Ireland and that will enable Belfast and Dublin to carry out certain functions for the benefit of the people of the North and the South.[13]

THE BELFAST VIEWPOINT

First and foremost on the minds of all loyal Ulstermen is the continued separation of Northern Ireland from the Republic. Even though the solutions advanced by them may differ, these Ulstermen are in full agreement with respect to the need for the continued separation of Northern and Southern Ireland.

A recent solution is that proposed by the Vanguard Unionist Progressive Party. Flirting with the idea of a quasi-unilateral declaration of independence, the V.U.P.P. pro-

---

32 (1972). Ulster cannot expect independence that would guarantee such assistance "but would otherwise confer upon it virtually sovereign status. No United Kingdom Government could be a party to such a settlement."

12 *Ibid.*   13 1974 WHITE PAPER 16.

posal attacks the 1973 White Paper as a sell-out and advocates a negotiated independence along the lines of dominion status. In other words, the proposal espouses a federal Britain-Ulster relationship with Britain maintaining Northern Ireland social services at a level largely in accord with present contributions as "a type of alimony after the separation."[14]

A second proposal recommends reversion to the pre-1920 position of Northern Ireland, that is, full integration (or reintegration) with Britain. In brief, it "would do more to assert the prevailing opinion in Ulster than the maintenance of separate institutions, or the setting out on paper of declarations like that in the Ireland Act, 1949."[15] Moreover, it might be said to make the Ulsterman's position more secure by linking his fate to his fellow British citizens, although it might just as well be argued that Ulster would be more susceptible to British chicanery once the protections of the Ireland Act 1949 and the Northern Ireland Constitution Act 1973 have been removed.

By far the most widely accepted solution to the conflict in Northern Ireland is the proposal to provide Ulster with a worthwhile regional parliament and to continue to adhere to the idea of the United Kingdom under one flag and one monarch. As a result of this approach, Ulster's citizenry would benefit from the best of all political and economic worlds, since, on the one hand, it would have an effective local government, and, on the other hand, it would continue to obtain the half crown along with the British Crown.[16]

[14] Kingston, *Northern Ireland—If Reason Fails*, 44 POL. Q. 22, 30 (1973).

[15] Newark, *The Constitution of Northern Ireland*, in Institute of Public Administration, DEVOLUTION OF GOVERNMENT: THE EXPERIMENT IN NORTHERN IRELAND 7, 17 (1953).

[16] The question of finances is of cardinal significance in the struggle. It should be noted that in the Republic "the average welfare check is less than half as big as that paid in Northern Ireland." *Irish vs. Irish: Why They Keep Fighting*, 69 U.S. NEWS & WORLD REP. 80 (Oc-

In spite of their disagreement on specifics, the people of Northern Ireland—Catholics and Protestants alike—recognize that their interests require that they maintain a united front against the Republic and its agents in Britain and Ulster. That front is and will remain united until the present terrorist threat is terminated; and that front is and will remain united against the increasingly serious threat that Britain will perhaps try to absolve itself of its responsibilities and cede Ulster to Ireland.

Conclusions

At long last Britain seems to have recognized the century-old wisdom of a British historian concerning the corruptibility of absolute power[17] and, by suspending Stormont, introducing much-needed reforms, and working towards power-sharing, partnership, and provision for a special relationship with Dublin, to have taken the first important steps to bring the Northern Ireland treadmill to a screeching halt. Unfortunately, however, that recognition and those steps have been marred by a continued myopia in the related area of law and order, for Britain's insistence on making the defeat of terrorism and violence its principal focus seems misplaced.

In that regard, it might be well for Britain to turn to the experiences of its American progeny, not for the purpose of drawing parallels between American Blacks and Ulster

---

tober 26, 1970). Whereas in 1968–1969, £138 were spent for each person in Northern Ireland for social services, only £65 were spent per head in the Republic. And in 1972, estimates totaled £210 million in the Republic and £230 million in Northern Ireland—which had one half the population of Ireland. See Stone, *Ireland: "The Killing Sickness,"* 214 NATION 390, 391 (1972); see also Biggs-Davidson, CATHOLICS AND THE UNION 13 (1972).

[17] In the famous words of Lord Acton, "power tends to corrupt and absolute power corrupts absolutely." Acton, *Letter to Mandell Creighton, April 5, 1887*, in Acton, ESSAYS ON FREEDOM AND POWER 364 (1948).

Catholics or between Vietnam and Northern Ireland, but for the lessons that might be learned from United States efforts at law and order.[18] Whether during the civil rights marches of the mid-1960s, the Democratic Convention of 1968, the Jackson State and Kent State shootings, or the prison riots at Attica, the get-tough, law-and-order approach proved as ineffective and failed as miserably as it has in Northern Ireland. Yet, throughout those disturbing events, talk and action focused—and, to some extent, continue to focus—on the false gold glitter of law and order.

That is not to say that law and order is not an important and necessary factor in a truly free and just society. As Rousseau eloquently stated, "whoever shall refuse to obey the general will must be constrained by the whole body of his fellow citizens to do so: which is no more than to say that it may be necessary to compel a man to be free—freedom being that condition which, by giving each citizen to his country, guarantees him from all personal dependence and is the foundation upon which the whole political machine rests, and supplies the power which works it."[19]

However, law and order is not, as Britain ostensibly believes, the precursor to freedom and justice.[20] These societal

18 Ironically, one of the most astute British historians of the twentieth century has remarked (unfortunately incorrectly): "Our reasons for finding ourselves in possession of a large portion of the earth's surface may not always have been entirely reputable, but once in possession there can be no question as to the benefits of government which Britain conferred. . . . We benefited by that "Imperial lesson," which you in America had taught us, namely, to respect the rights of colonists to govern themselves in their own ways." Wheeler-Bennett, A WREATH TO CLIO 23 (1967).

19 Rousseau, *The Social Contract*, in E. Barker, ed., SOCIAL CONTRACT: ESSAYS BY LOCKE, HUME, AND ROUSSEAU 167, 184 (1962).

20 Aleksandr Solzhenitsyn has decried what might best be described as "law-and-order violence": "It is this form of established, permanent violence of the state, which has managed to assume all the 'juridical' forms through decades of rule, to codify thick compilations of violence-ridden 'laws' and to throw the mantle over the shoulders of its 'judges,' it is this violence that represents the most frightening danger

factors are instead interdependent: if there is to be a non-despotic reign of law and order, there must be freedom and justice; and if there is to be freedom and justice, there must be law and order. Accordingly, law and order must be pursued simultaneously with freedom and justice, not seriatum.

How best to bring about these conditions in Ulster has been "debated" by bullets and words for longer than anyone cares to remember. While the "debate" will undoubtedly and unfortunately continue for some time, one possible solution stands out. Although this proposed two-step solution will appear naive to some readers, it is workable; and although the solution will neither fully satisfy all of the participants nor bring true peace to the Six Counties for another generation, it offers—through its immediate and long-range stages—the best chances for the attainment of that peace.

To begin with, step one (the immediate stage) aims, as the various White Papers did, at ending terrorism. Unlike the White Papers, though, which spoke of force as the weapon to combat terrorism, this approach places added emphasis on extending full equality and justice to *all* citizens of Ulster. By substituting equitable and desired treatment for the discrimination of the past, it is hoped that the succor granted by the Northern citizenry to the Catholic and Protestant extremists, either through outright assistance or indifference, will be superseded by the citizen opposition required to defeat urban guerrillas.

Secondly, step one envisions a British request for a United Nations, North Atlantic Treaty Organization, or, more realistically, European Economic Community (whose members have an economic interest in seeing that the conflict is terminated, since the struggle is a drain on British resources) peacekeeping force to replace the British Army.

---

to the peace, although few realize it." Solzhenitsyn, "Peace and Violence," *New York Times*, September 15, 1973, at 31, col. 2.

Even though Britain has asserted that the Ulster conflict is a matter within its domestic jurisdiction, the fact remains that Britain's Irish heritage makes it difficult for the British Army to keep the peace; and even though an international peacekeeping force will not necessarily have more success than the British Army in maintaining order, it will most assuredly be better able to convey the feeling that it is treating all citizens of Northern Ireland fairly.[21] For these reasons, it is to be hoped that Britain will reverse its stand and consent to the formation of a Northern Ireland peacekeeping force.

Finally, step one recommends that the status of Northern Ireland remain unchanged unless and until the people of the Six Counties decide, by democratic means, to alter that status. While it is certainly true that many persons would prefer one of the aforementioned options, it is also certainly true, as evidenced by the recent plebiscite and supported by studies,[22] that the vast majority of the Ulster citizenry finds the quality of its life of far greater importance than whether it is governed by Dublin, London, or Belfast; it is furthermore true that if the problem of sectarianism cannot be solved in a six-county microcosm, it cannot be solved simply by taking the problem and putting it into a

[21] Such a force, of course, is dependent on host country consent. See generally Bloomfield, INTERNATIONAL MILITARY FORCES (1964); Russell, UNITED NATIONS EXPERIENCE WITH MILITARY FORCES: POLITICAL AND LEGAL ASPECTS (1964); Seyersted, UNITED NATIONS FORCES IN THE LAW OF PEACE AND WAR (1966); Garvey, *United Nations Peacekeeping and Host State Consent*, 64 AM. J. INT'L L. 241 (1970); Hillenbrand, *Department States Position on Irish Crisis*, 66 DEPART. STATE BULL. 448, 448–49 (March 20, 1972).

It has, however, been stated that the "Loyalists would never accept an international force and would have no reservations about attacking it." Interview with William Craig, in Belfast, August 17, 1972.

[22] As Rose states, Catholics want to abolish the border and Protestants want no change in the border—but few Catholics or Protestants in the Six Counties mention the abolition or maintenance of the border as a matter of "immediate importance." See Rose, GOVERNING WITHOUT CONSENSUS 213 (1971).

thirty-two county context;[23] and, it is true, despite the lamentations and protestations of those persons who assert that "half a century is not enough to stamp the Ulster state with any acceptable seal of legitimacy in the eyes of those who truly believe in self-determination,"[24] that Northern Ireland has attained, both legally and politically, a certain legitimacy over the years. Ulster's creation was admittedly an error and an injustice. Yet can it be seriously denied, in view of the German, Korean, and Vietnam bifurcations, that errors and injustices eventually are clothed in a mantle of legitimacy? And is it not laughable to contend that once reforms are granted, there can be no justification for two Irelands simply because the original purpose of the Ulster Government was the maintenance of the "apparatus of Protestant supremacy"?[25]

Simultaneously with the implementation of the first part of the two-pronged solution, the second step (the long-range stage) must be commenced. That step—the integration of the schools of Northern Ireland—is both rarely mentioned as part of the "solution" to the Ulster conflict and exceedingly difficult to accomplish given the "traditions" of the North. If, however, complete and lasting peace is to come

[23] "If we cannot solve in a microcosm the problem of sectarianism in Northern Ireland, how do you solve it by simply taking it out and putting it into a thirty-two county context?" Oliver Napier in Public Broadcasting Service, transcript of *The Advocates* 30 (April 25, 1972).

[24] Kennedy, *Ulster is an International Issue* 67–68. The natural extension of this argument is that there can be no legitimacy without self-determination, at least not within a fifty-year time span. If that argument is valid, international affairs would be in an interesting state. As an example, the September 1973 admission of East and West Germany to the United Nations would have to be nullified.

[25] In the view of this writer, the Ulster creation was partially to perpetuate the Protestant Ascendancy—and partially to give the British Conservative Party a vehicle to power. But it seems foolish to argue that the elimination of discrimination removes the need for a separate government. Under that theory, there would be few governments in the world today. See Edwards, THE SINS OF OUR FATHERS: ROOTS OF CONFLICT IN NORTHERN IRELAND 307 (1970).

to Ulster, the subtle discrimination of segregated education (subtle because it was voluntarily imposed by the Catholic and Protestant communities) must at long last be rejected, for, unless children learn to live together and understand each other, it seems both certain and logical that they will neither be able to live together in peace nor understand each other when they become adults.

Some persons may argue that there are many lands where education is conducted on a sectarian basis and where there is no hostility among or between the religions involved. Perhaps. Even if true, though, those countries have neither the heritage nor the prejudices of Northern Ireland. For those reasons, their examples serve no useful purpose. In any case, however, it stands to reason that sectarian bitterness can at any time explode "when children grow up in ignorance of each other's attitudes, and without the decent respect for contrary opinions which only the closeness of long-standing *comraderie* can bring."[26]

At first blush, it is indeed ironic that Ulster's funding of Catholic schools, the "most liberal aspect of Northern Ireland's treatment of its minority, ha[s] the unhappy effect of helping to reinforce the communal division, for nowhere below the university level d[o] the children of the two communities study and play together."[27] Upon reflection, though, that irony turns first to skepticism and then to anger when it is realized that the dual educational system was, in all likelihood, conceived as another tool to keep the Ulster citizenry divided. In fact, it is difficult to imagine a more effective tool, since "hostility . . . is an index of unfamliarity"[28] and since the system guarantees that each sect will remain ignorant of the beliefs and teachings of the other sect.[29]

[26] *Ibid.*, 229 and, generally, 219–32.

[27] Boyd, FIFTEEN MEN ON A POWDER KEG: A HISTORY OF THE U.N. SECURITY COUNCIL 321 (1971).

[28] Cole, *Introduction* to O'Neill, ULSTER AT THE CROSSROADS 14 (1969).

[29] Not only are children "rarely even [given] the chance to hear

Although integrated education is a delicate question—
whether in Northern Ireland or, as recent events have demonstrated, in the Northern United States—it must become
a reality, for the present "education system [does] perhaps
more than any other factor to make for a divided community in Northern Ireland"[30] and constitutes the major
obstacle in the path of communal understanding. To be
sure, the battle will be difficult, since, it is argued, the
control of education "is an essential part of the whole
fabric of Roman Catholicism"[31] and since many parents—
Catholic and Protestant alike—will object to integrated
education (and, unfortunately, undo at home what is done
in school). But the battle—and the war—can be won. It
can be won because approximately 65 percent of the adult
population, realizing that there is nothing Christian about
Catholic and Protestant children learning in school to "hate
each other in the name of Jesus Christ,"[32] favors integrated

the other side explained or discussed" (15), but when they are presented with facts concerning their religious counterparts, those facts
are often false or exaggerated. See Ayearst, THE REPUBLIC OF IRELAND:
ITS GOVERNMENT AND POLITICS 91 (1970).

[30] Edwards, SINS OF OUR FATHERS 219. Edwards adds that "in the
zeal to preserve a theoretical hold on Catholic youth, a greater evil
than the danger of insufficient religious instruction has been allowed
to grow, to wit the taking of lives, the open hatred of man against
man, and the blasphemy of bloody conflict in the name of Christ" (220).

[31] Plunkett, IRELAND IN THE NEW CENTURY 96 (1970). An influential
Catholic cardinal has stated that he does "not think that [children]
would grow up with a strong and virile faith if all they got at school
was an agreed syllabus Christianity, watered down to the lowest common denominator of different persuasions and taught by persons who
may not even be believing Christians themselves." Quoted in Rose,
GOVERNING WITHOUT CONSENSUS 250.

[32] Devlin, THE PRICE OF MY SOUL 53 (1969). In a stinging attack,
Devlin adds that: "Among the best traitors Ireland has ever had,
Mother Church ranks at the very top, a massive obstacle in the path
to equality and freedom. She has been a force for conservatism, not
on the basis of preserving Catholic doctrine or preventing the corrup-

269

education.[33] It can also be won because Britain can put economic pressure on the Catholic schools by cutting off or reducing state funding of sectarian education, thereby making it financially difficult for those schools to survive or, in the alternative, making those schools so expensive that parents will voluntarily send their children to state schools. Admittedly, this hard-line approach—which in no way interferes with the free exercise of religion that must be carefully guarded and protected—runs the risk of exacerbating an already horrendous situation. Yet if the next generation of Ulster's citizenry is to live in peace, it will take a momentous decision—as momentous as the 1954 decision of the United States Supreme Court regarding dual school systems—to shake Northern Ireland loose from its sectarian foundations and move it forward.

This two-step solution lacks the appeal of instant success or the drama of suggesting that the Archbishop of Canterbury and the Pope walk arm-in-arm down the streets of Belfast. Moreover, if it were effectuated, the result would hardly please the IRA extremists, who desire the union of North and South, or Protestant reactionaries, who want to maintain the twentieth-century version of the seventeenth-century Ascendency. It would, however, end the eye-for-an-eye brand of sectarianism now and in the future. It would provide Catholics and Protestants with rights that

---

tion of her children, but simply to ward off threats to her security and influence" (71).

The Catholic church is, however, in a difficult position. Although it should be leading efforts to bring Catholics and Protestants together, it is somewhat restricted "by the dead hand of the past." Indeed, it cannot "repudiate all disobedience to civil authority without repudiating its own history, when [during the era of the Penal Laws] the Catholic religion was kept alive in Ireland by priests who were technically outlaws." Rose, GOVERNING WITHOUT CONSENSUS 265.

[33] Sixty-four percent of all adults and 65 percent of all youths favor integrated education. Interestingly, 69 percent of all Catholics favor it. See Rose, GOVERNING WITHOUT CONSENSUS 336 and, generally, 335–75. See also Bleakley, PEACE IN ULSTER 61 (1972) and, generally, 61–65.

have in the past been withheld from them by devious businessmen, politicians, and religious leaders who, employing the age-old, divide-and-conquer principle for their own economic and political purposes, convinced them that they should forsake their own advancement and focus instead on the destruction of their Christian brothers.[34] It would provide Britain, at once, with the honorable out that every state always desires and with the opportunity to right its past dishonorable wrongs. And it would set the stage for cooperation that might lead eventually to the union of North and South and would lead immediately to the amelioration of living conditions for all the peoples of Ulster.

Of course, all these assertions might prove to be wrong, and the so-called solution might be a colossal failure. One thing, though, is certain: the assertions and the solution stand a better chance of bringing peace to Northern Ireland than the bombs and bullets and empty rhetoric that have become so much a part of Ulster's everyday life.

[34] "Civil Rights are not merely Catholic Rights . . . the Protestants also suffer from the undemocratic nature of the [Protestant] regime. They are constrained to suffer their own disabilities because those of the Catholics are worse." Greaves, THE IRISH CRISIS 216.

BIBLIOGRAPHY

British Documents

Bowen, Roderic. Report by Mr. Roderic Bowen, Q.C., on Procedures for the Arrest, Interrogation and Detention of Suspected Terrorists in Aden: 14 November 1966. CMND. No. 3165. 1971 (reprint).

Cameron, John. Disturbances in Northern Ireland: Report of the Commission Appointed by the Governor of Northern Ireland. CMD. No. 532. 1969.

A Commentary by the Government of Northern Ireland to Accompany the Cameron Report. CMD. No. 534. 1969.

Compton, Edmund. Report of the Enquiry into Allegations against the Security Forces of Physical Brutality in Northern Ireland Arising out of Events on the 9th August, 1971. CMND. No. 4823. 1971.

Diplock, Lord. Report of the Commission to Consider Legal Procedures to Deal with Terrorist Activities in Northern Ireland. CMND. No. 5185. 1972.

The Future Development of the Parliament and Government of Northern Ireland: A Consultative Document. CMD. No. 560. 1971.

The Future of Northern Ireland: A Paper for Discussion. London, H.M.S.O., 1972.

Hunt, John. Report of the Advisory Committee on Police in Northern Ireland. CMD. No. 535. 1969.

Judgment of the International Military Tribunal for the Trial of Major German War Criminals (Misc. No. 12). CMND. No. 6964. 1946.

The Northern Ireland Constitution. CMND. No. 5675. 1974.

Northern Ireland Constitutional Proposals. CMND. No. 5259. 1973.

Northern Ireland: Financial Arrangements and Legislation. CMND. No. 4998. 1972.

Parker, Lord. Report of the Committee of Privy Counsellors Appointed to Consider Authorized Procedures for the In-

TERROGATION OF PERSONS SUSPECTED OF TERRORISM. CMND. No. 4901. 1972.

POLITICAL SETTLEMENT: STATEMENTS ISSUED ON FRIDAY 24 MARCH 1972 BY THE PRIME MINISTER AND THE GOVERNMENT. CMD. No. 568. 1972.

A RECORD OF CONSTRUCTIVE CHANGE. CMD. No. 558. 1971.

Scarman, Leslie. VIOLENCE AND CIVIL DISTURBANCES IN NORTHERN IRELAND IN 1969: REPORT OF TRIBUNAL OF INQUIRY. CMD. No. 566. 2 vols. 1972.

Widgery, Lord. REPORT OF THE TRIBUNAL APPOINTED TO INQUIRE INTO THE EVENTS OF SUNDAY, 30TH JANUARY 1972, WHICH LED TO LOSS OF LIFE IN CONNECTION WITH THE PROCESSIONS IN LONDONDERRY ON THAT DAY. H.L. No. 101, H.C. No. 220. 1972.

CASES

Chung Chi Cheung v. The King, A.C. 160 (1939).
Forde v. McEldowney, N.IR.L.R. 11 (1972).
The State (O'Laighleis) vs. O'Sullivan & Min. for Justice, 2 YEARBOOK OF EUROPEAN CONVENTION 308, 474, and 608 (1958–1959); 3 YEARBOOK OF EUROPEAN CONVENTION 492 (1960); and 4 YEARBOOK OF EUROPEAN CONVENTION 430 (1961).
The Three Friends, 166 U.S. 1 (1896).

NEWSPAPERS

The Christian Science Monitor
Civil Rights
The Irish Times
The Times (London)
The New York Times
Nuacht Naisiunta (Official IRA newspaper)
The Protestant Telegraph
Unionist Review
The Wall Street Journal

BOOKS

Acton, John Emerich Edward Dahlberg. ESSAYS ON FREEDOM AND POWER. Glencoe, Ill.: Free Press, 1948.

274

THE AMERICAN COMMISSION ON CONDITIONS IN IRELAND: INTERIM REPORT. New York, 1921.

AMNESTY INTERNATIONAL REPORT OF AN ENQUIRY INTO ALLEGATIONS OF ILL-TREATMENT IN NORTHERN IRELAND. London: Amnesty International, 1972.

Ardell, John Roche. THE CLOSING OF THE IRISH PARLIAMENT. Dublin: Hodges, 1907.

Armour, W. S. FACING THE IRISH QUESTION. London: Duckworth, 1935.

————. ULSTER, IRELAND, BRITAIN: A FORGOTTEN TRUST. London: Duckworth, 1938.

Ayearst, Morley. THE REPUBLIC OF IRELAND: ITS GOVERNMENT AND POLITICS. New York: New York University Press, 1970.

Ballinger, W. A. THE MEN THAT GOD MADE MAD. New York: G. P. Putnam's, 1969.

Barker, Ernest, ed. SOCIAL CONTRACT: ESSAYS BY LOCKE, HUME, AND ROUSSEAU. New York: Oxford University Press, 1962.

Barnet, Richard J. INTERVENTION AND REVOLUTION: THE UNITED STATES IN THE THIRD WORLD. New York: World, 1968.

Barritt, Denis P. and Arthur Booth. ORANGE AND GREEN. Kendal, Ireland: Northern Friends Peace Board, 1972.

Barritt, Denis P. and Charles F. Carter. THE NORTHERN IRELAND PROBLEM: A STUDY IN GROUP RELATIONS. London: Oxford University Press, 1962.

Bassiouni, M. Cherif and Ved P. Nanda, eds. A TREATISE ON INTERNATIONAL CRIMINAL LAW. Springfield, Ill.: C. C. Thomas, 1973.

Battersby, T. S. Frank. A MODERN EYE-OPENER: 60 POINTS AGAINST HOME RULE. Dublin: Unionist Association, 1912.

Beckett, J. C. THE MAKING OF MODERN IRELAND 1603–1923. London: Faber & Faber, 1966.

————. A SHORT HISTORY OF IRELAND. London: Hutchinson's University Library, 1961.

Bell, J. Bowyer. THE SECRET ARMY: THE IRA, 1916–1970. New York: John Day, 1971.

Bennett, Richard. THE BLACK AND TANS. Boston: Houghton, Mifflin, 1960.

Bestic, Alan. THE IMPORTANCE OF BEING IRISH. New York: Morrow, 1969.

Betham, William. THE ORIGIN AND HISTORY OF THE CONSTITUTION

OF ENGLAND AND OF THE EARLY PARLIAMENTS OF IRELAND. Dublin: W. Curry, 1934.

Biggs-Davidson, John. CATHOLICS AND THE UNION. Belfast: Unionist, 1972.

Birch, A. H. THE BRITISH SYSTEM OF GOVERNMENT. New York: Praeger, 1967.

Bishop, William W., ed. INTERNATIONAL LAW: CASES AND MATERIALS. Boston: Little, Brown, 1971.

Black, Cyril Edwin. THE DYNAMICS OF MODERNIZATION. New York: Harper & Row, 1966.

Bleakley, David. PEACE IN ULSTER. London: Mowbrays, 1972.

Blenerhasset, Thomas. THE PLANTATION IN ULSTER. Amsterdam: Theatrum Orbis Terrarom Ltd., 1972 (reprint of London: Ed. Allde, 1610).

Bloomfield, Lincoln P. INTERNATIONAL MILITARY FORCES. Boston: Little, Brown, 1964.

Bluntschli, Johannes Kaspar. LE DROIT INTERNATIONAL CODIFIÉ. Paris: Guillaumin, 1874.

Bolton, G. C. THE PASSING OF THE IRISH ACT OF UNION: A STUDY IN PARLIAMENTARY POLITICS. London: Oxford University Press, 1966.

Bond, James E. INTERNAL CONFLICT AND THE LAW OF WAR. Princeton: Princeton University Press, 1974.

Bothe, Michael. DAS VOLKERRECHTLICHE VERBOT DES EINSATZES CHEMISCHER UND BAKTERIOLOGISCHER WAFFEN. Cologne: Heymannas, 1973.

Boyd, Andrew. BRIAN FAULKNER AND THE CRISIS OF ULSTER UNIONISM. Tralee, Ireland: Anvil, 1972.

———. FIFTEEN MEN ON A POWDER KEG: A HISTORY OF THE U.N. SECURITY COUNCIL. New York: Methuen, 1971.

———. HOLY WAR IN BELFAST. New York: Grove, 1969.

Boyle, C. Kevin. WIDGERY—A CRITIQUE. Belfast: Civil Rights Association, 1972.

Brayden, W. H. THE IRISH FREE STATE. Chicago: Chicago Daily News, 1925.

Brierly, James L. THE LAW OF NATIONS. Oxford: Clarendon Press, 1963.

Briggs, Herbert W. THE LAW OF NATIONS. New York: Appleton-Century-Crofts, 1952.

British Information Service. NORTHERN IRELAND. New York: British Information Service, 1973.

BRITISH VS. GERMAN IMPERIALISM: A CONTRAST. New York: Neutral Publishing Co., 1915.

Bromage, Mary C. CHURCHILL AND IRELAND. South Bend, Ind.: University of Notre Dame Press, 1964.

————. DEVALERA AND THE MARCH OF A NATION. New York: Noonday, 1956.

Brown, Irene K. CONSISTENT OR INCONSISTENT. Newtownards, Ireland: UDUA, 1972.

Brownlie, Ian. INTERNATIONAL LAW AND THE USE OF FORCE BY STATES. Oxford: Clarendon Press, 1963.

Bryan, Walter. THE IMPROBABLE IRISH. New York: Taplinger, 1969.

Burke, Edmund. LETTERS, SPEECHES AND TRACTS ON IRISH AFFAIRS. London: Macmillan & Co., 1881.

Burtt, Edwin A., ed. THE ENGLISH PHILOSOPHERS FROM BACON TO MILL. New York: Random House, 1939.

Calvert, Harry. CONSTITUTIONAL LAW IN NORTHERN IRELAND. London: Stevens, 1968.

Campaign for Social Justice in Northern Ireland. NORTHERN IRELAND—THE MAILED FIST: A RECORD OF ARMY & POLICE BRUTALITY FROM AUGUST 9–NOVEMBER 9, 1971. Portglenoe, Ireland: Bethlehem Abbey Press, 1972.

Campbell, T. J. FIFTY YEARS OF ULSTER: 1890–1940. Belfast: Irish News, 1941.

Carey, John. INTERNATIONAL PROTECTION OF HUMAN RIGHTS. Dobbs Ferry, N. Y.: Oceana, 1968.

Carnegie Endowment. THE LAW OF ARMED CONFLICTS. New York: Carnegie Endowment, 1971.

Carson, William A. ULSTER AND THE IRISH REPUBLIC. Belfast: W. W. Cleland, 1957.

Carter, Gwendolen M. THE BRITISH COMMONWEALTH AND INTERNATIONAL SECURITY. Toronto: Ryerson, 1947.

Casement, Roger. THE CRIME AGAINST IRELAND AND HOW THE WAR MAY RIGHT IT. New York, 1914.

Casserley, D. HISTORY OF IRELAND. Dublin: Talbot Press, 1943.

Castren, Erik. THE PRESENT LAW OF WAR AND NEUTRALITY. Helsinki: Suomalaisen Kirjallisuuden Seuran Kirjapainon, 1954.

277

Central Office of Information. NORTHERN IRELAND. London: British Information Services, 1970.

Chakravarti, Reghubir. HUMAN RIGHTS AND THE UNITED NATIONS. Calcutta: Progressive Publishers, 1958.

Chauvire, Roger. A SHORT HISTORY OF IRELAND. New York: Devin-Adair, 1956.

Chen, Ti-Chiang and L. C. Green. THE INTERNATIONAL LAW OF RECOGNITION. London: Stevens, 1951.

Chubb, Basil. THE GOVERNMENT AND POLITICS OF IRELAND. Stanford, Cal.: Stanford University Press, 1970.

Churchill, Winston S. THE AFTERMATH. New York: Scribner's, 1929.

———. LORD RANDOLPH CHURCHILL. New York: Macmillan Co., 1906.

Clausewitz, Carl von. PRINCIPLES OF WAR. Harrisburg, Pa.: Military Service Publishers, 1942.

Collins, Michael. THE PATH TO FREEDOM. Dublin: Talbot, 1922.

COMMENTARY UPON THE WHITE PAPER (COMMAND PAPER 558) ENTITLED "A RECORD OF CONSTRUCTIVE CHANGE" PUBLISHED BY THE GOVERNMENT OF NORTHERN IRELAND ON 20 AUGUST, 1971. Belfast, 1971.

Coogan, Timothy Patrick. THE I.R.A. New York: Praeger, 1970.

———. IRELAND SINCE THE RISING. New York: Praeger, 1966.

Corish, Brendan. THE NEW REPUBLIC. Dublin: Abbey Printing Service, 1969.

Cranston, Maurice. WHAT ARE HUMAN RIGHTS? London: Ampersand, 1962.

Crozier, Brian. THE REBELS. Boston: Beacon Press, 1960.

Curtis, Edmund and R. B. McDowell. IRISH HISTORICAL DOCUMENTS: 1172–1922. New York: Barnes & Noble, 1943.

Dash, Samuel. JUSTICE DENIED: A CHALLENGE TO LORD WIDGERY'S REPORT ON "BLOODY SUNDAY." New York: International League for Rights of Man, 1972.

De Paor, Liam. DIVIDED ULSTER. Baltimore: Penquin, 1970.

DeValera, Eamon. IRELAND'S STAND. Dublin: M. H. Gill & Son, 1946.

Devlin, Bernadette. THE PRICE OF MY SOUL. New York: Knopf, 1969.

Dicey, A. V. INTRODUCTION TO THE STUDY OF THE LAW OF THE CONSTITUTION. New York: St. Martin's, 1959.

————. A Leap in the Dark. London: John Murray, 1911.

Donaldson, Alfred Gaston. Some Comparative Aspects of Irish Law. Durham, N. C.: Duke University Press, 1957.

Douglas, A. B. Ireland and the War against Hitler. London: Richards, 1940.

Draper, G.I.A.D. The Red Cross Conventions. London: Stevens, 1958.

Drost, Pieter Nicolaas. Human Rights as Legal Rights: The Realization of Individual Human Rights in Positive International Law. Leiden: Sijthoff, 1951.

Durant, Will and Ariel Durant. The Lessons of History. New York: Simon and Schuster, 1968.

Eagleton, Clyde. The Responsibility of States in International Law. New York: New York University Press, 1928.

Eckstein, Harry I., ed. Internal War: Problems and Approaches. Glencoe, Ill.: Free Press, 1964.

Eden, Anthony. Full Circle. Boston: Houghton, 1960.

Edwards, Lyford. The Natural History of Revolution. Chicago: University of Chicago Press, 1927.

Edwards, Owen Dudley. The Sins of Our Fathers: Roots of Conflict in Northern Ireland. Dublin: Gill and Macmillan, 1970.

Eide, Asbjorn and August Schou, eds. International Protection of Human Rights. New York: Interscience, 1968.

Eire Nua: The Social and Economic Programme of Sinn Fein. Dublin: Sinn Fein, 1971.

Eliot, R.S.P. and John Hickie. Ulster: A Case Study in Conflict Theory. London: Longmans, Green, 1971.

Emden, Cecil S. Principles of British Constitutional Law. London: Methuen, 1925.

England, Germany and the Irish Question. London: Hodder, 1917.

Ervine, John G. Sir Edward Carson. New York: Dodd, Mead, 1916.

Evans, Richardson. Ireland in the Realm and Ulster in Ireland. London: Constable, 1917.

Ezejiofor, Gaius. Protection of Human Rights under the Law. London: Butterworths, 1964.

Falk, Richard A., ed. The International Law of Civil War. Baltimore: Johns Hopkins University Press, 1971.

Falk, Richard; Gabriel Kolko; and Robert J. Lyton, eds. CRIMES OF WAR. New York: Random House, 1971.

Fanon, Frantz. STUDIES IN A DYING COLONIALISM. New York: Monthly Review Press, 1965.

————. THE WRETCHED OF THE EARTH. New York: Grove Press, 1968.

Faul, Denis and Raymond Murray. BRITISH ARMY AND SPECIAL BRANCH RUC BRUTALITIES. Cavan: Abbey, 1972.

Fawcett, J.E.S. THE APPLICATION OF THE EUROPEAN CONVENTION ON HUMAN RIGHTS. Oxford: Clarendon Press, 1969.

Finerty, John F. IRELAND: THE PEOPLE'S HISTORY OF IRELAND. New York: Cooperative Publishing Society, 1904.

Fisher, Joseph R. THE END OF THE IRISH PARLIAMENT. London: E. Arnold, 1911.

Fisher, Roger. INTERNATIONAL CONFLICT FOR BEGINNERS. New York: Harper & Row, 1969.

Forester, Margery. MICHAEL COLLINS—THE LOST LEADER. London: Sidgwick & Jackson, 1971.

Friedmann, Wolfgang. THE CHANGING STRUCTURES OF INTERNATIONAL LAW. New York: Columbia University Press, 1964.

Gallagher, Frank. THE ANGLO-IRISH TREATY. London: Hutchinson, 1965.

————. THE INDIVISIBLE ISLAND: THE HISTORY OF THE PARTITION OF IRELAND. London: Gollancz, 1957.

Ganji, Manouchehr. INTERNATIONAL PROTECTION OF HUMAN RIGHTS. Geneva: E. Droz, 1962.

Garcia-Mora, Manuel R. INTERNATIONAL RESPONSIBILITY FOR HOSTILE ACTS OF PRIVATE PERSONS AGAINST FOREIGN STATES. The Hague: M. Nijhoff, 1962.

Giap, Vo Nguyen. PEOPLE'S WAR PEOPLE'S ARMY. New York: Praeger, 1962.

Gardner, Louis. RESURGENCE OF THE MAJORITY. N.p., 1971.

Gibbons, John. IRELAND—THE NEW ALLY. London: R. Hale, 1938.

Good, James Winder. ULSTER AND IRELAND. London: Maunsel, 1919.

Goodrich, Leland M. and Edvard Hambro. CHARTER OF THE UNITED NATIONS: COMMENTARY AND DOCUMENTS. Boston: World Peace Foundation, 1949.

Grattan, Henry. SPEECHES. Dublin: James Duffy, 1868.

280

Gray, Tony. THE IRISH ANSWER: AN ANATOMY OF MODERN IRE-LAND. London: Heineman, 1966.

Great Britain, Government of. MANUAL OF MILITARY LAW. London: Her Majesty's Stationery Office, 1968.

Greaves, Desmond. THE IRISH CASE AGAINST PARTITION. London: Connolly Association, 1956.

———. THE IRISH CRISIS. London: Lawrence & Wishand, 1972.

Greenspan, Morris. THE MODERN LAW OF LAND WARFARE. Berkeley and Los Angeles: University of California Press, 1959.

Grotius, Hugo. THE LAW OF WAR AND PEACE. New York: Black, 1949.

———. PROLEGOMENA TO THE LAW OF WAR AND PEACE. New York: Bobbs-Merrill, 1957.

Guevara, Ernesto (Che). GUERRILLA WARFARE. New York: Monthly Review, 1961.

Gwynn, Denis. THE HISTORY OF PARTITION (1912–1925). Dublin: Browne & Nolan, 1950.

Hackworth, Green Haywood. DIGEST OF INTERNATIONAL LAW. Washington, D.C.: U.S. Gov't Printing Office, 1940.

Hall, William Edward. INTERNATIONAL LAW. 1909.

———. THE RIGHTS AND DUTIES OF NEUTRALS. London: Longmans, Green, 1874.

HALSBURY'S STATUTES OF ENGLAND. London: Butterworths, 1970.

Hand, Geoffrey J. REPORT OF THE IRISH BOUNDARY COMMISSION 1925. Dublin: Irish University Press, 1969.

Harkness, D. W. THE RESTLESS DOMINION: THE IRISH FREE STATE AND THE BRITISH COMMONWEALTH OF NATIONS, 1921–31. New York: New York University Press, 1970.

Harmon, Maurice, ed. FENIANS AND FENIANISM. Dublin: Scepter, 1968.

Harris, Rosemary. PREJUDICE AND TOLERANCE IN ULSTER. Manchester: Manchester University Press, 1972.

Harrison, Henry. IRELAND AND THE BRITISH EMPIRE, 1937. London: Hale, 1937.

———. THE NEUTRALITY OF IRELAND: WHY IT WAS INEVITABLE. London: Hale, 1942.

———. ULSTER AND THE BRITISH EMPIRE 1939. London: Hale, 1939.

Harwood, Jeremy; Jonathan Guinness; and John Biggs-Davison. IRELAND—OUR CUBA? London: Monday Club (n.d.).

281

Hastings, Max. BARRICADES IN BELFAST: THE FIGHT FOR CIVIL RIGHTS IN NORTHERN IRELAND. New York: Taplinger, 1970.

Hawkins, John. THE IRISH QUESTION TODAY: THE PROBLEMS AND DANGERS OF PARTITION. London: Gollancz, 1941.

Healy, David. LIBERTY VS. LANDLORDISM. Rochester, N. Y.: Union, 1881.

Heatley, Robert W. DIRECT RULE. Belfast: Civil Rights Association, 1972.

Heilbrunn, Otto. PARTISAN WARFARE. New York: Praeger, 1962.

Hershey, Amos Shortle. ESSENTIALS OF INTERNATIONAL PUBLIC LAW. New York: Macmillan, 1912.

Heuston, R.F.V. ESSAYS IN CONSTITUTIONAL LAW. London: Stevens, 1964.

Higgins, Rosalyn. THE DEVELOPMENT OF INTERNATIONAL LAW THROUGH THE POLITICAL ORGANS OF THE UNITED NATIONS. London: Oxford University Press, 1963.

Hobson, Bulmar. IRELAND YESTERDAY AND TOMORROW. Tralee, Ireland: Anvil, 1968.

Hogan, Albert E. and Isabel G. Powell. THE GOVERNMENT OF GREAT BRITAIN. London: University Tutorial Press, 1939.

Hogan, Vincent Paul. THE NEUTRALITY OF IRELAND IN WORLD WAR II. Ann Arbor, Mich.: University Microfilms, 1953.

Holcombe, Arthur Norman. HUMAN RIGHTS IN THE MODERN WORLD. New York: New York University Press, 1948.

Hone, J. M. IRELAND SINCE 1922. London: Faber and Faber, 1932.

Hull, Roger H. and John Novogrod. LAW AND VIETNAM. Dobbs Ferry, N. Y.: Oceana, 1968.

IMPERIALISM AND THE IRISH NATION. Dublin: National Book Service, 1972.

Inglis, Brian. WEST BRITON. London: Faber and Faber, 1962.

Ingram, Thomas Dunbar. A CRITICAL EXAMINATION OF IRISH HISTORY. London: Longmans, Green, 1900.

————. A HISTORY OF THE LEGISLATIVE UNION OF GREAT BRITAIN AND IRELAND. Port Washington, N. Y.: Kennikat, 1970.

Institute for the Study of Conflict. THE ULSTER DEBATE. London: Bodley Head, 1972.

Institute of Public Administration. DEVOLUTION OF GOVERNMENT: THE EXPERIMENT IN NORTHERN IRELAND. London: Allen & Unwin, 1953.

International Association of Democratic Lawyers. LEGAL ASPECTS OF NEUTRALITY. Brussels: IADL, 1962.

International Committee of the Red Cross. CONFERENCE OF GOVERNMENT EXPERTS ON THE REAFFIRMATION AND DEVELOPMENT OF INTERNATIONAL HUMANITARIAN LAW APPLICABLE IN ARMED CONFLICTS: REPORT ON THE WORK OF THE CONFERENCE. Geneva: ICRA, 1972.

THE I.R.A. SPEAKS. Dublin: National Book Service, 1972.

IRELAND: THE FACTS. Dublin: Sinn Fein, 1971.

Irish Association. IRELAND AND THE WAR. Belfast and Dublin: Irish Association, 1940.

Jabhet al-Tahrir al-Quami. WHITE PAPER ON THE APPLICATION OF THE GENEVA CONVENTIONS OF 1949 TO THE FRENCH-ALGERIAN CONFLICT. New York: Algerian Office, 1960.

Jackson, T. A. IRELAND HER OWN: AN OUTLINE HISTORY OF THE IRISH STRUGGLE. New York: International Publishing, 1970.

Jennings, W. Ivor. THE BRITISH CONSTITUTION. Cambridge: Cambridge University Press, 1941.

———. THE LAW AND THE CONSTITUTION. London: University of London Press, 1943.

Jessup, Phillip C. A MODERN LAW OF NATIONS. New York: Macmillan Co., 1948.

Jones, Thomas. WHITEHALL DIARY: IRELAND 1918–1925. London: Oxford University Press, 1971.

Kee, Robert. THE GREEN FLAG. London: Weidenfeld, 1972.

Keenan, Joseph Barry and Brendon Francis Brown. CRIMES AGAINST INTERNATIONAL LAW. Washington, D. C.: Public Affairs Press, 1950.

Kelly, George A. and Linda B. Miller. INTERNAL WAR AND INTERNATIONAL SYSTEMS: PERSPECTIVES ON METHOD. Cambridge, Mass.: Center for International Affairs, 1969.

Kelly, John Maurice. FUNDAMENTAL RIGHTS IN THE IRISH LAW AND CONSTITUTION. New York: Oceana, 1968.

Kelsen, Hans. THE LAW OF THE UNITED NATIONS. New York: Praeger, 1951.

———. PRINCIPLES OF INTERNATIONAL LAW. New York: Rinehart, 1966.

———. RECENT TRENDS IN THE LAW OF THE UNITED NATIONS. London: Stevens, 1951.

Kennan, George F. AMERICAN DIPLOMACY 1900–1950. New York: Mentor, 1962.

Kennelly, Brian, ed. THE PENQUIN BOOK OF IRISH VERSE. Middlesex, England: Penquin, 1970.

Kinsella, Thomas. BUTCHER'S DOZEN: A LESSON FOR THE OCTAVE OF WIDGERY. Dublin: Dolmen, 1972.

Kiralfy, Albert Kenneth Roland. THE ENGLISH LEGAL SYSTEM. London: Sweet & Maxwell, 1967.

Kotzsch, Lothar. THE CONCEPT OF WAR: CONTEMPORARY HISTORY AND INTERNATIONAL LAW. Geneva: Droz, 1956.

Lauterpacht, Elihu. BRITISH PRACTICE IN INTERNATIONAL LAW. London: British Institute of International and Comparative Law, 1962.

Lauterpacht, Hersch. AN INTERNATIONAL BILL OF THE RIGHTS OF MAN. New York: Columbia University Press, 1945.

———. INTERNATIONAL LAW AND HUMAN RIGHTS. New York: Praeger, 1950.

———. RECOGNITION IN INTERNATIONAL LAW. Cambridge: Cambridge University Press, 1947.

Lawrence, R. J. THE GOVERNMENT OF NORTHERN IRELAND: PUBLIC FINANCE AND PUBLIC SERVICES 1921–1964. Oxford: Clarendon Press, 1965.

Lecky, William Edward Hartpole. A HISTORY OF IRELAND IN THE EIGHTEENTH CENTURY. London: Longmans, Green, 1913.

Lenin, V. I. LENIN ON IRELAND. Dublin: New Books, 1970.

Lieberson, Goddard. THE IRISH UPRISING. New York: Macmillan Co., 1966.

Lillich, Richard B., ed. HUMANITARIAN INTERVENTION AND THE UNITED NATIONS. Charlottesville: University of Virginia Press, 1973.

Longford, Frank Pakenham and Thomas P. O'Neill. EAMON DE-VALERA. Boston: Houghton, Mifflin, 1971.

———. PEACE BY ORDEAL. London: Sidgwick & Jackson, 1967.

Luard, Evan, ed. THE INTERNATIONAL REGULATION OF CIVIL WARS. New York: New York University Press, 1972.

———. THE INTERNATIONAL REGULATION OF FRONTIER DISPUTES. New York: Praeger, 1970.

Lynch, John. SPEECHES AND STATEMENTS ON IRISH UNITY, NORTHERN IRELAND AND ANGLO-IRISH RELATIONS AUGUST 1969–OCTOBER 1971. Dublin: Government Information Bureau, 1972.

MacColl, Rene. ROGER CASEMENT: A NEW JUDGMENT. New York: W. W. Norton, 1956.

MacGiolla, Tomas. WHERE WE STAND—THE REPUBLICAN POSITION. Dublin: National Book Service, 1972.

Machiavelli, Niccolo. THE PRINCE. New York: Mentor, 1960.

MacIntyre, Tom. THROUGH THE BRIDEWELL GATE. London: Faber, 1971.

Mackey, Herbert O. ROGER CASEMENT: THE TRUTH ABOUT THE FORGED DIARIES. Dublin: Fallon, 1966.

MacManus, Seumas. THE STORY OF THE IRISH RACE. New York: Devin-Adair, 1972.

MacNeill, T. G. Swift. THE CONSTITUTIONAL AND PARLIAMENTARY HISTORY OF IRELAND TILL THE UNION. Port Washington, N. Y.: Kennikat, 1970.

———. THE IRISH PARLIAMENT. London: Cassell, 1886.

MacSwiney, Terence J. PRINCIPLES OF FREEDOM. Dublin: Irish Book Bureau, 1964.

Mansergh, Nicholas. THE COMMONWEALTH AND THE NATIONS. London: Royal Institute of International Affairs, 1948.

———. THE COMMONWEALTH EXPERIENCE. New York: Praeger, 1969.

———. DOCUMENTS AND SPEECHES ON BRITISH COMMONWEALTH AFFAIRS 1931–1952. New York: Oxford University Press, 1953.

———. THE GOVERNMENT OF NORTHERN IRELAND. London: George Allen & Unwin, 1936.

———. THE IRISH FREE STATE: ITS GOVERNMENT AND POLITICS. New York: Unwin, 1934.

———. THE IRISH QUESTION: 1840–1921. Toronto: University of Toronto Press, 1965.

———. SURVEY OF BRITISH COMMONWEALTH AFFAIRS: PROBLEMS OF EXTERNAL POLICY 1931–1939. New York: Oxford University Press, 1952.

Mao Tse-Tung. ON GUERRILLA WARFARE. New York: Praeger, 1961.

Marx, Karl and Frederick Engels. IRELAND AND THE IRISH QUESTION. New York: International Publishers, 1972.

MASSACRE AT DERRY. Belfast: Civil Rights Association, 1972.

McCaffrey, Lawrence J. THE IRISH QUESTION, 1800–1922. Lexington: University of Kentucky Press, 1968.

McCardle, Dorothy. THE IRISH REPUBLIC: A DOCUMENTAL CHRONI-

CLE OF THE ANGLO-IRISH CONFLICT AND THE PARTITIONING OF IRELAND. Dublin: Irish Press, 1951.

McDonnell, Michael F. J. IRELAND AND THE HOME RULE MOVEMENT. Dublin: Maunsel, 1908.

McDougal, Myres and Florentino Feliciano. LAW AND MINIMUM WORLD PUBLIC ORDER. New Haven: Yale University Press, 1961.

McGuire, James K. WHAT COULD GERMANY DO FOR IRELAND? New York: Wolfe Tone, 1916.

McLachlan, John. HUMAN RIGHTS IN RETROSPECT AND REALITY. London: Lindsey, 1968.

McNair, Lord A. and A. D. Watts. THE LEGAL EFFECTS OF WAR. Cambridge: Cambridge University Press, 1966.

Mitchell, J.D.B. CONSTITUTIONAL LAW. Edinburgh: W. Green & Son, 1964.

Moore, John Bassett. A DIGEST OF INTERNATIONAL LAW. Washington, D. C.: Government Printing Office, 1906.

Moore, John Norton. LAW AND THE INDO-CHINA WAR. Princeton: Princeton University Press, 1972.

Morgenthau, Hans. POLITICS AMONG NATIONS: THE STRUGGLE FOR POWER AND PEACE. 3rd ed. New York: Knopf, 1961.

Morrisson, Clovis C. THE DEVELOPING EUROPEAN LAW OF HUMAN RIGHTS. Leyden: Sijthoff, 1967.

Moskowitz, Moses. HUMAN RIGHTS AND WORLD ORDER: THE STRUGGLE FOR HUMAN RIGHTS IN THE UNITED NATIONS. Dobbs Ferry, N. Y.: Oceana, 1958.

————. THE POLITICS AND DYNAMICS OF HUMAN RIGHTS. Dobbs Ferry, N. Y.: Oceana, 1968.

Neeson, Eoin. THE CIVIL WAR IN IRELAND. Cork, Ireland: Mercier, 1966.

Neligan, David. THE SPY IN THE CASTLE. London: MacGibbon & Kee, 1968.

Northern Ireland Civil Rights Association. DISCRIMINATION! THE FACTS. Belfast: Civil Rights Association, 1972.

————. INNOCENT EQUALS GUILTY UNDER THE SPECIAL POWERS ACT. Belfast: Civil Rights Association, 1972.

————. PROPOSALS FOR PEACE: DEMOCRACY AND COMMUNITY RECONCILIATION. Belfast: Civil Rights Association, 1973.

NORTHERN IRELAND: THE HIDDEN TRUTH. Belfast: Unionist Party, 1972.

Nowlan, Kevin B. IRELAND IN THE WAR YEARS AND AFTER, 1939–1951. South Bend, Ind.: University of Notre Dame Press, 1969.

O'Donnell, Charles James. OUTRAGED ULSTER. London: C. Palmer, 1932.

O'Donnell, Terence. THE CASE FOR AMERICAN-IRISH UNITY. Washington, D. C.: American Council on Public Affairs, 1941.

O'Faolain, Sean. THE STORY OF IRELAND. London: Collins, 1946.

O'Neill, Terence. ULSTER AT THE CROSSROADS. London: Faber, 1969.

Oppenheim, Lassa F. L. INTERNATIONAL LAW. 2 vols. 4th ed., edited by A. McNair. London: Longmans, Green, 1968.

———. INTERNATIONAL LAW. 2 vols. 7th ed., edited by H. Lauterpacht. London: Longmans, Green, 1952.

———. INTERNATIONAL LAW. 2 vols. 8th ed., edited by H. Lauterpacht. London: Longmans, Green, 1955.

Paisley, Ian R. K. THE DAGGER OF TREACHERY STRIKES AT THE HEART OF ULSTER. Belfast, n.p., 1972.

———. NORTHERN IRELAND: WHAT IS THE REAL SITUATION? Greenville, S. C.: Bob Jones University Press, 1970.

———. THE ULSTER PROBLEM: SPRING 1972. Greenville, S. C.: Bob Jones University Press, 1972.

Palmer, R. R. A HISTORY OF THE MODERN WORLD. New York: Knopf, 1960.

Peacey, Howard. ISLAND OF DESTINY. London: Sidgwick & Jackson, 1933.

Pennefather, Frederick W. IS ULSTER RIGHT? London: J. Murray, 1913.

Phillimore, Robert. COMMENTARIES UPON INTERNATIONAL LAW. London: Butterworths, 1879.

Pictet, Jean S. COMMENTARY ON THE GENEVA CONVENTION FOR THE AMELIORATION OF THE CONDITION OF THE WOUNDED AND SICK IN ARMED FORCES IN THE FIELD. Geneva: ICRC, 1952.

———. COMMENTARY ON THE GENEVA CONVENTION RELATIVE TO THE TREATMENT OF PRISONERS OF WAR. Geneva: ICRC, 1960.

Plunkett, Horace C. IRELAND IN THE NEW CENTURY. Port Washington, N. Y.: Kennikat, 1970.

Pompe, C. A. AGGRESSIVE WAR: AN INTERNATIONAL CRIME. The Hague: M. Nijhoff, 1953.

Quekett, Arthur S. THE CONSTITUTION OF NORTHERN IRELAND. 3 vols. Belfast, n.p., 1928–1946.

287

Radcliffe, Geoffrey Reynolds Yonge. THE ENGLISH LEGAL SYSTEM. London: Butterworths, 1954.

Ragg, Nicholas M. SURVEY OF INTERNEES' FAMILIES. Belfast: CRA, 1972.

Rajan, M. S. UNITED NATIONS AND DOMESTIC JURISDICTION. New York: Asia Publishing House, 1961.

Remarque, Erich Maria. ALL QUIET ON THE WESTERN FRONT. Boston: Little, Brown, 1948.

Robertson, Arthur Henry. HUMAN RIGHTS IN EUROPE. New York: Oceana, 1963.

————. HUMAN RIGHTS IN THE WORLD. Manchester: Manchester University Press, 1972.

Rose, Richard. GOVERNING WITHOUT CONSENSUS. Boston: Beacon Press, 1971.

Rosenau, James N., ed. INTERNATIONAL ASPECTS OF CIVIL STRIFE. Princeton: Princeton University Press, 1964.

Rosenbaum, S., ed. AGAINST HOME RULE: THE CASE FOR UNION. London: Frederick Warne & Co., 1912.

Ross, Alf. CONSTITUTION OF THE UNITED NATIONS. Copenhagen: Ejnar Munksgrard, 1950.

Rougier, Antoine. LES GUERRES CIVILES ET LE DROIT DES GENS. Paris: L. Larose, 1903.

Rudd, George Poyston. THE ENGLISH LEGAL SYSTEM. London: Butterworths, 1962.

Russell, Bertrand. UNPOPULAR ESSAYS. New York: Clarion, 1969.

Russell, Ruth B. UNITED NATIONS EXPERIENCE WITH MILITARY FORCES: POLITICAL AND LEGAL ASPECTS. Washington, D. C.: Brookings Institution, 1964.

Ryan, A. P. ISLANDS APART: THE STORY OF IRELAND FROM ST. PATRICK TO DEVALERA. New York: W. Morrow, 1954.

Schaeffer, Werner. ENGLAND'S OPPRESSION OF IRELAND. Berlin, 1940.

Schwarzenberger, Georg. INTERNATIONAL LAW AS APPLIED BY INTERNATIONAL COURTS AND TRIBUNALS. London: Stevens, 1968.

————. POWER POLITICS: A STUDY OF WORLD SOCIETY. London: Stevens, 1964.

Schwelb, Egon. HUMAN RIGHTS AND THE INTERNATIONAL COMMUNITY. Chicago: Quadrangle, 1964.

Seyersted, Finn. UNITED NATIONS FORCES IN THE LAW OF PEACE AND WAR. Leyden: Sijthoff, 1966.

288

Shearman, Hugh. NORTHERN IRELAND: 1921–1971. Belfast: Baird, 1971.

———. NOT AN INCH: A STUDY OF NORTHERN IRELAND AND LORD CRAIGAVON. London: Faber, 1942.

———. 27 MYTHS ABOUT ULSTER. Belfast: Unionist Party, 1972.

Sheehy, Michael. DIVIDED WE STAND: A STUDY OF PARTITION. London: Faber, 1955.

Siotis, Jean. LE DROIT DE LA GUERRE ET LES CONFLITS ARMÉES D'UN CARACTÈRE NON-INTERNATIONAL. Paris: Librairie Générale, 1958.

Smyth, Clifford. THE AXIS AGAINST ULSTER. Belfast: Puritan, 1972.

Sohn, Louis B. and Thomas Buergenthal. INTERNATIONAL PROTECTION OF HUMAN RIGHTS. New York: Bobbs-Merrill, 1973.

Stetler, Russell. THE BATTLE OF BOGSIDE. London: Sheed & Ward, 1970.

Stewart, Edwina. THE CIVIL RIGHTS CASE. Belfast: Civil Rights Association, 1972.

Stone, Julius. AGGRESSION AND WORLD ORDER. Berkeley and Los Angeles: University of California Press, 1958.

———. LEGAL CONTROLS OF INTERNATIONAL CONFLICT. New York: Rinehart, 1954.

Stowell, Ellery Cory. INTERNATIONAL LAW. New York: Holt, 1931.

Sullivan, T. D.; A. M. Sullivan; and D. B. Sullivan. SPEECHES FROM THE DOCK. Dublin: Gill and Macmillan, 1968.

Sunday Times Insight Team. ULSTER. Baltimore: Penquin, 1972.

Sutherland, Hugh. IRELAND YESTERDAY AND TODAY. Philadelphia: North American, 1909.

Synge, John M. THE COMPLETE PLAYS OF JOHN M. SYNGE. New York: Vintage, 1960.

Taylor, A.J.P. ENGLISH HISTORY 1914–1945. Oxford: Oxford University Press, 1965.

Taylor, Telford. NUREMBERG AND VIETNAM: AN AMERICAN TRAGEDY. New York: Bantam, 1972.

Thomas, Ann van Wynen and A. J. Thomas, Jr. LEGAL LIMITS ON THE USE OF CHEMICAL AND BIOLOGICAL WEAPONS. Dallas: Southern Methodist University Press, 1970.

———. NON-INTERVENTION: THE LAW AND ITS IMPORT IN THE AMERICAS. Dallas: Southern Methodist University Press, 1956.

Thompson, William Irvin. THE IMAGINATION OF AN INSURRECTION: DUBLIN, EASTER 1916. New York: Oxford University Press, 1967.

289

TORTURE: THE RECORD OF BRITISH BRUTALITY IN IRELAND. Dublin: Northern Aid, 1972.

Trinquier, Roger. MODERN WARFARE. New York: Praeger, 1964.

Ulster Group. RECENT EVENTS IN NORTHERN IRELAND IN PERSPECTIVE. London: Madley, 1972.

ULSTER YEAR BOOK (1968–1972). Belfast: Her Majesty's Stationery Office, 1972.

United Ireland Association (Britain). STORMONT: AN ASSESSMENT. London: Hibernian, 1972.

United Nations. 1. REPERTORY OF PRACTICE OF UNITED NATIONS ORGANS (ART. 1–22). New York: United Nations, 1955.

United Nations, Division of Human Rights. HUMAN RIGHTS: A COMPILATION OF INTERNATIONAL INSTRUMENTS OF THE UNITED NATIONS. New York: United Nations, 1973.

United States, Department of the Army. THE LAW OF LAND WARFARE (FIELD MANUAL FM 27–10). Washington, D. C.: Department of the Army, 1956.

Utley, T. E. ULSTER: A SHORT BACKGROUND ANALYSIS. Belfast: Northern Whig, 1972.

Vattel, Emmerich de. THE LAW OF NATIONS. Philadelphia: Johnson, 1876.

Walker, R. J. and M. G. Walker. THE ENGLISH LEGAL SYSTEM. London: Butterworths, 1970.

Wallace, Martin. NORTHERN IRELAND: 50 YEARS OF SELF-GOVERNMENT. New York: Barnes & Noble, 1971.

Weil, Gordon L. THE EUROPEAN CONVENTION ON HUMAN RIGHTS. Leyden: Sijthoff, 1963.

Westlake, John. INTERNATIONAL LAW. 2 vols. Cambridge: Cambridge University Press, 1910–13.

Wheare, K. C. THE STATUTE OF WESTMINSTER AND DOMINION STATUS. Oxford: Oxford University Press, 1947.

Wheaton, Henry. ELEMENTS OF INTERNATIONAL LAW. Boston: Little, Brown, 1866.

Wheeler-Bennett, John W. JOHN ANDERSON: VISCOUNT WAVERLY. London: Macmillan & Co., 1962.

———. A WREATH TO CLIO. London: Macmillan & Co., 1967.

WHERE SINN FEIN STANDS. Dublin: Sinn Fein, 1972.

White, Albert C. THE IRISH FREE STATE: ITS EVOLUTION AND POSSIBILITIES. London: Hutchinson, 1923.

Whiteman, Marjorie. DIGEST OF INTERNATIONAL LAW. 10 vols. Washington, D. C.: Department of State, 1968.

Whitten, J. R.; R. Davison; and H. Millar. P.R. AND ULSTER. Belfast: Unionist Party, 1972.

Wiesse, Carlos. LE DROIT INTERNATIONAL APPLIQUÉ AUX GUERRES CIVILES. Lausanne: B. Benda, 1898.

Williams, Basil. HOME RULE PROBLEMS. London: King, 1911.

Wilson, George Grafton. HANDBOOK OF INTERNATIONAL LAW. St. Paul, Minn., West Publishing Co., 1910.

Wilson, Thomas. ULSTER UNDER HOME RULE. London: Oxford University Press, 1955.

Wright, Quincy. INTERNATIONAL LAW AND THE UNITED NATIONS. London: Asia Publishing House, 1960.

Younger, Calton. IRELAND'S CIVIL WAR. New York: Frederick Muller, 1968.

ARTICLES

Acheson, Dean. The Arrogance of International Law. 2 INTERNATIONAL LAWYER 591 (1968).

———. Remarks. 57 AMERICAN SOCIETY OF INTERNATIONAL LAW PROCEEDINGS 13 (1963).

Against Everybody. 35 TIME MAGAZINE 36 (June 10, 1940).

Aiken, Frank. Eire and the War. 104 NEW REPUBLIC 860 (1941).

American-Eire Relations. 6 CURRENT HISTORY 427 (1944).

Barkun, Michael. The Social Scientist Looks at the International Law of Conflict Management. 65 AMERICAN JOURNAL OF INTERNATIONAL LAW 97 (1971).

Baty, Thomas. Abuse of Terms: "Recognition": "War." 30 AMERICAN JOURNAL OF INTERNATIONAL LAW 477 (1936).

Beale, Joseph J., Jr. The Recognition of Cuban Belligerency. 9 HARVARD LAW REVIEW 406 (1896).

Bilder, Richard B. Rethinking International Human Rights: Some Basic Questions. 2 REVUE DES DROITS DE L'HOMME 557 (1969); also 1969 WISCONSIN LAW REVIEW 171.

Bindschedler-Robert, Denise. Biological and Chemical Weapons, in A TREATISE ON INTERNATIONAL CRIMINAL LAW 351 (M. C. Bassiouni & V. P. Nanda, eds., 1973).

Birrell, Derek. Relative Deprivation as a Factor in Conflict in Northern Ireland. 20 SOCIOLOGICAL REVIEW 317 (August 1972).

Black, C. E. *Greece and the United Nations.* 63 POLITICAL SCIENCE QUARTERLY 551 (1948).

Black, Robert J. *A Change in Tactics?: The Urban Insurgent.* 23 AIR UNIVERSITY REVIEW 50 (January–February 1972).

Bond, James E. *Protection of Non-Combatants in Guerrilla Wars.* 12 WILLIAM AND MARY LAW REVIEW 787 (1971).

Bowen, Elizabeth. *Eire.* 21 NEW STATESMAN AND NATION 382 (1941).

Boyd, Andrew. *Orange Bullies & British Tories.* 212 NATION 521 (1971).

Boyd, Ernest. *Ireland between Two Stools.* 19 FOREIGN AFFAIRS 426 (1941).

Boyle, Kevin. *The McElduff Case and the Law of Arrest under the Special Powers Act.* 23 NORTHERN IRELAND LEGAL QUARTERLY 334 (1972).

———. *Northern Ireland—Dismantling the Protestant State.* 52 NEW BLACKFRIARS 12 (1971).

Brennan, Robert. *Case for Ireland's Neutrality.* NEW YORK TIMES MAGAZINE 15 (April 4, 1943).

Breslin, Jimmy. *The Breslins of the Bogside.* 214 NATION 392 (1972).

Brett, C.E.V. *The Lessons of Devolution in Northern Ireland.* 41 POLITICAL QUARTERLY 261 (1970).

Britain Indicted. 2 CIVIL RIGHTS 1 (November, 1973).

Bromage, Arthur W. and Mary C. Bromage. *Ireland—No Man's Land.* INTERNATIONAL CONCILIATION 692 (1941).

Brownlie, Ian. *International Law and the Activities of Armed Bands.* 7 INTERNATIONAL AND COMPARATIVE LAW QUARTERLY 712 (1958).

———. *Interrogation in Depth: The Compton and Parker Reports.* 35 MODERN LAW REVIEW 501 (1972).

Buckley, Tom. *Double Troubles of Northern Ireland—A Visit with the Protestant Militants.* NEW YORK TIMES MAGAZINE 36 (December 10, 1972).

Buckley, William F. *Suspension of the Stormont.* 24 NATIONAL REVIEW 425 (1972).

Buergenthal, Thomas. *Comparative Study of Certain Due Process Requirements of the European Human Rights Convention.* 16 BUFFALO LAW REVIEW 18 (1966).

292

————. *The Effect of the European Convention on Human Rights on the Internal Law of Member States.* INTERNATIONAL AND COMPARATIVE LAW QUARTERLY SUPPLEMENT NO. 11, 79 (1965).

————. *Proceedings against Greece under the European Convention of Human Rights.* 62 AMERICAN JOURNAL OF INTERNATIONAL LAW 441 (1968).

Bunn, George. *Banning Poison Gas and Germ Warfare: Should the United States Agree?* 1969 WISCONSIN LAW REVIEW 375.

Burnham, James. *The British Vietnam.* 23 NATIONAL REVIEW 919 (1971).

Cameron Report. 209 NATION 300 (1968).

Carroll, W. Don. *The Search for Justice in Northern Ireland.* 6 NEW YORK UNIVERSITY JOURNAL OF INTERNATIONAL LAW AND POLITICS 28 (1973).

Carter, Gwendolen M. *Eire—Its Neutrality and Post-War Prospects.* 20 FOREIGN POLICY REPORT 278 (1945).

Catholics, Protestants, B Men, Revolutionaries, Barbed Wire and Gas—The Ulster Story Goes On. 232 ECONOMIST 20 (September 13, 1969).

Chinh, Truong. *Revolutionary War* in CONTEMPORARY COMMUNISM: THEORY AND PRACTICE 298 (H. Swearer & R. Longaker, eds.) Belmont, Cal.: Wadsworth Pub. Co., 1963.

Clark, Ramsey. *On Violence, Peace and the Rule of Law.* 49 FOREIGN AFFAIRS 31 (1970).

Clokie, M. McD. *The British Dominions and Neutrality.* 34 AMERICAN POLICY SCIENCE REVIEW 737 (1940).

Cohen, Benjamin V. *Human Rights under the United Nations Charter.* 14 LAW AND CONTEMPORARY PROBLEMS 430 (1949).

Cole, John. *Introduction* to ULSTER AT THE CROSSROADS by Terence O'Neill (1969).

Commager, Henry S. *Challenge to Ireland's Neutrality.* NEW YORK TIMES MAGAZINE 7 (March 7, 1943).

Connor, Walker. *Nation-Building or Nation-Destroying?* 24 WORLD POLITICS 319 (1972).

————. *Self-Determination: The New Phase.* 20 WORLD POLITICS 30 (1967).

Corkey, Robert. *Northern Ireland and Neutrality.* 129 NINETEENTH CENTURY 493 (1941).

293

Curtis, Roy Emerson. *The Law of Hostile Military Expeditions as Applied by the United States.* 8 AMERICAN JOURNAL OF INTERNATIONAL LAW 1 (1914).

Darlington & Civil Rights. 1 CIVIL RIGHTS 1 (September 30, 1972).

Delany, V.T.H. *The Constitution of Ireland: Its Origins and Development.* 12 UNIVERSITY OF TORONTO LAW REVIEW 1 (1957–1958).

Did Widgery Write Widgery? 1 CIVIL RIGHTS 3 (April 28, 1972).

The Diplock Report. 2 CIVIL RIGHTS 3 (January 14, 1973).

Donaldson, A. G. *The Constitution of Northern Ireland: Its Origin and Development.* 11 UNIVERSITY OF TORONTO LAW REVIEW 1 (1955–1956).

———. *Fundamental Rights in the Constitution of Northern Ireland.* 37 CANADIAN BAR REVIEW 189 (1959).

Draper, G.I.A.D. *The Geneva Conventions of 1949.* 114 RECUEIL DES COURS (Hague Academy of International Law) 63 (1965).

———. *Human Rights and the Law of War.* 12 VIRGINIA JOURNAL OF INTERNATIONAL LAW 326 (1972).

Droits et devoirs en cas d'insurrection. 18 ANNUAIRE DE L'INSTITUTE DE DROITS INTERNATIONAL 217 (1900).

Dulanty, John. *Eire Neutral or Hostile?* 172 SPECTATOR 291 (1944).

Edwards, J.Ll.J. *Special Powers in Northern Ireland.* CRIMINAL LAW REVIEW 7 (1956).

Eire Plays with Fire. 152 NATION 88 (1941).

Eire's Case. 39 COMMONWEAL 556 (1944).

Emerson, Rupert. *Self-Determination.* 75 AMERICAN JOURNAL OF INTERNATIONAL LAW 459 (1971).

Ermacora, Felix. *Human Rights and Domestic Jurisdiction (Article 2, §7, of the Charter).* 124 RECUEIL DES COURS (Hague Academy of International Law) 371 (1968).

Ervine, St. John. *Ulster and Her People.* 198 SPECTATOR 577 (May 3, 1957).

Fair Employment Agency. ULSTER COMMENTARY 15 (September 1973).

Falk, Richard A. *International Law and the United States Role in the Viet Nam War.* 75 YALE LAW JOURNAL 1109 (1966).

———. *Law, Lawyers, and the Conduct of American Foreign Relations.* 78 YALE LAW JOURNAL 919 (1969).

———. *New Approaches to the Study of International Law.* 61 AMERICAN JOURNAL OF INTERNATIONAL LAW 477 (1967).

————. *The United States and the Doctrine of Non-Intervention in the Internal Affairs of Independent States*. 5 HOWARD LAW JOURNAL 163 (1959).

Farer, Tom. *Harnessing Rogue Elephants: A Short Discourse on Foreign Intervention in Civil Strife*. 82 HARVARD LAW REVIEW 511 (1969).

————. *Humanitarian Law and Armed Conflicts: Toward the Definition of "International Armed Conflict."* 71 COLUMBIA LAW REVIEW 37 (1971).

————. *Intervention in Civil Wars: A Modest Proposal*. 67 COLUMBIA LAW REVIEW 66 (1967).

Faulkner, Brian. *The White Paper: We Must be Constructive*. UNIONIST REVIEW 5 (May 1973).

Fawcett, J.E.S. *Human Rights and Domestic Jurisdiction*, in THE INTERNATIONAL PROTECTION OF HUMAN RIGHTS 286 (E. Luard, ed., 1967).

————. *Intervention in International Law*. 103 RECUEIL DES COURS (Hague Academy of International Law) 347 (1961).

————. *The Role of the United Nations in the Protection of Human Rights—Is it Misconceived?*, in INTERNATIONAL PROTECTION OF HUMAN RIGHTS 95 (A. Eide & A. Schou, eds., 1968).

Fawcett, Sanford. *A British View of the Covenant*. 14 LAW AND CONTEMPORARY PROBLEMS 438 (1949).

Fenwick, C. *When is There a Threat to the Peace?—Rhodesia*. 61 AMERICAN JOURNAL OF INTERNATIONAL LAW 753 (1967).

Fenwick, Dennis T. *A Proposed Resolution Providing for the Authorization of Intervention by the United Nations, a Regional Organization, or a Group of States in a State Committing Gross Violations of Human Rights*. 13 VIRGINIA JOURNAL OF INTERNATIONAL LAW 340 (1973).

Fraleigh, Arnold. *The Algerian Revolution as a Case Study in International Law*, in THE INTERNATIONAL LAW OF CIVIL WAR 1791 (R. Falk, ed., 1971).

Franck, Thomas M. *Who Killed Article 2 (4)?* 64 AMERICAN JOURNAL OF INTERNATIONAL LAW 809 (1970).

Franck, Thomas M. and Nigel S. Rodley. *After Bangladesh: The Law of Humanitarian Intervention by Military Force*. 67 AMERICAN JOURNAL OF INTERNATIONAL LAW 275 (1973).

Friedmann, Wolfgang. *Intervention, Civil War and the Role of International Law*. 59 AMERICAN SOCIETY OF INTERNATIONAL LAW PROCEEDINGS 67 (1965).

A Future for Ulster. 232 ECONOMIST 13 (August 23, 1969).

Garcia-Mora, Manuel R. *International Law and the Law of Hostile Military Expeditions.* 27 FORDHAM LAW REVIEW 309 (1958–1959).

Garner, James W. *Questions of International Law in the Spanish Civil War.* 31 AMERICAN JOURNAL OF INTERNATIONAL LAW 66 (1937).

————. *Recognition of Belligerency.* 32 AMERICAN JOURNAL OF INTERNATIONAL LAW 106 (1938).

Garvey, Jack Israel. *United Nations Peacekeeping and Host State Consent.* 64 AMERICAN JOURNAL OF INTERNATIONAL LAW 241 (1970).

The Geneva Convention and the Treatment of Prisoners of War in Vietnam. 80 HARVARD LAW REVIEW 851 (1967).

George, David. *These are the Provisionals.* 82 NEW STATESMAN 680 (1971).

Gilly, Adolfo. *Introduction* to STUDIES IN A DYING COLONIALISM by Frantz Fanon (1965).

Giraud, E. *L'Interdiction du recours à la force—la theorie et la pratique des Nations Unis.* 67 REVUE GÉNÉRALE DE DROIT INTERNATIONAL PUBLIC 501 (1963).

Glod, Stanley J. and Lawrence J. Smith. *Interrogation Under the 1949 Prisoners of War Convention.* 21 MILITARY LAW REVIEW 145 (1963).

Gluckstadt, Hans. *American Protection for Eire.* 105 NEW REPUBLIC 363 (1941).

Golsong, H. *The European Convention on Human Rights Before Domestic Courts.* 38 BRITISH YEARBOOK OF INTERNATIONAL LAW 445 (1962).

Gottlieb, Gidon A. G. *International Assistance to Civilian Populations in Armed Conflicts.* 4 NEW YORK UNIVERSITY JOURNAL OF INTERNATIONAL LAW AND POLITICS 403 (1971).

Graber, Doris A. *The Truman and Eisenhower Doctrines in the Light of the Doctrine of Non-Intervention.* 73 POLITICAL SCIENCE QUARTERLY 321 (1958).

Greaves, C. Desmond. *Epilogue* to IRELAND HER OWN: AN OUTLINE HISTORY OF THE IRISH STRUGGLE by T. A. Jackson (1970).

Greenberg, Jack and Anthony R. Shalit. *New Horizons for Human Rights: The European Convention, Court and Commission of Human Rights.* 63 COLUMBIA LAW REVIEW 1384 (1963).

Gutteridge, Joyce A. C. *The Geneva Conventions of 1949.* 26 BRITISH YEARBOOK OF INTERNATIONAL LAW 294 (1949).

Gwynn, Stephen. *Ireland and the War.* 18 FOREIGN AFFAIRS 305 (1940).

Harris, D. J. *The European Convention on Human Rights and English Criminal Law.* CRIMINAL LAW REVIEW 205 (1966).

Henkin, Louis. *The United Nations and Human Rights.* 19 INTERNATIONAL ORGANIZATION 504 (1965).

Higgins, Rosalyn. *International Law and Civil Conflict,* in THE INTERNATIONAL REGULATION OF CIVIL WARS 169 (E. Luard, ed., 1972).

———. *The Legal Limits to the Use of Force by Sovereign States: United Nations Practice.* 37 BRITISH YEARBOOK OF INTERNATIONAL LAW 269 (1961).

———. *The Place of International Law in the Settlement of Disputes by the Security Council.* 64 AMERICAN JOURNAL OF INTERNATIONAL LAW 1 (1970).

Hillenbrand, Martin J. *Department States Position on Irish Crisis.* 66 DEPARTMENT OF STATE BULLETIN 448 (March 20, 1972).

Hoffmann, Stanley. *Introduction* to INTERNATIONAL LAW AND POLITICAL CRISES (L. Scheinman & D. Wilkinson, eds., 1969).

Hooker, Wade S. and David H. Savaster. *The Geneva Convention of 1949: Application in the Vietnamese Conflict.* 5 VIRGINIA JOURNAL OF INTERNATIONAL LAW 243 (1965).

Hudson, Manley O. *Integrity of International Instruments.* 42 AMERICAN JOURNAL OF INTERNATIONAL LAW 105 (1948).

Human Rights, Commission of. *Government of Ireland Against the Government of the United Kingdom (Appl. Nos. 5310/71 & 5451/72).* 41 COLLECTION OF DECISIONS 1 (1973).

Humphrey, John P. *The UN Charter and the Universal Declaration of Human Rights,* in THE INTERNATIONAL PROTECTION OF HUMAN RIGHTS 39 (E. Luard, ed., 1967).

Ijalaye, David A. *Was Biafra at Any Time a State in International Law?* 65 AMERICAN JOURNAL OF INTERNATIONAL LAW 551 (1971).

International Human Rights, Symposium on. 14 LAW AND CONTEMPORARY PROBLEMS 411 (1949).

Ireland—the Implications of Neutrality. 32 ROUND TABLE 496 (1942).

The Irish Inheritance. 48 NEW YORKER 135 (October 21, 1972).

Irish Neutrality. 21 NEW STATESMAN AND NATION 459 (1971).

Irish Neutrality and U.S. Foreign Policy. 104 AMERICA 684 (1961).

Irish vs. Irish: Why They Keep Fighting. 69 U.S. NEWS AND WORLD REPORT 80 (October 26, 1970).

Jackson, Robert. *The Challenge of International Lawlessness.* INTERNATIONAL CONCILIATION 683 (1941).

Johnson, Paul. *Saving Ulster from Itself.* 77 NEW STATESMAN 608 (1969).

Joseph, Jeffery H. *Beyond Khartoum: Peacekeeping Forces, Imposed Treaties and Regional Conflict.* 6 INTERNATIONAL LAWYER 516 (1972).

Kalshoven, Frits. *Human Rights, the Law of Armed Conflicts, and Reprisals.* 121 INTERNATIONAL REVIEW OF THE RED CROSS 183 (1971).

Kane, John J. *Civil Rights in Northern Ireland.* 33 REVIEW OF POLITICS 54 (1971).

Kelleher, John N. *Eire and the Allies.* 110 NEW REPUBLIC 501 (1944).

Kelly, Joseph B. *Legal Aspects of Military Operations in Counterinsurgency.* 21 MILITARY LAW REVIEW 95 (1963).

Kelsen, Hans. *Limitations on the Functions of the United Nations.* 55 YALE LAW JOURNAL 997 (1946).

Kennedy, Edward M. *Remarks—Biafra, Bengal, and Beyond: International Responsibility and Genocidal Conflict.* 66 AMERICAN SOCIETY OF INTERNATIONAL LAW PROCEEDINGS 89 (1972).

———. *Ulster is an International Issue.* 11 FOREIGN POLICY 57 (September 1973).

Kingston, William. *Northern Ireland—If Reason Fails.* 44 POLITICAL QUARTERLY 22 (1973).

Korey, William. *The Key to Human Rights Implementation.* 570 INTERNATIONAL CONCILIATION (1968).

Kramer, James. *Letter from Ireland.* 48 NEW YORKER 46 (February 19, 1972).

———. *Letter to the Editors.* 48 NEW YORKER 126 (April 15, 1972).

Kunz, Josef L. *General International Law and the Law of International Organizations.* 47 AMERICAN JOURNAL OF INTERNATIONAL LAW 456 (1953).

———. *Revolutionary Creation of Norms of International Law.* 41 AMERICAN JOURNAL OF INTERNATIONAL LAW 119 (1947).

298

————. *The Universal Declaration of Human Rights.* 43 AMERICAN JOURNAL OF INTERNATIONAL LAW 316 (1949).

Lalor, Fintan. *The Neutrality of Eire.* 168 SPECTATOR 233 (1942).

Lasswell, Harold D. *Introduction: Universality versus Parochialism* in LAW AND MINIMUM WORLD PUBLIC ORDER by Myres S. McDougal and Florentino P. Feliciano (1961).

Lauterpacht, Elihu. *The Contemporary Practice of the United Kingdom in the Field of International Law: Survey and Consent.* 8 INTERNATIONAL AND COMPARATIVE LAW QUARTERLY 146 (1959).

Lauterpacht, Hersch. *Revolutionary Activities by Private Persons against Foreign States.* 22 AMERICAN JOURNAL OF INTERNATIONAL LAW 105 (1928).

————. *Revolutionary Propaganda by Governments.* 13 TRANSACTIONS OF THE GROTIUS SOCIETY 143 (1928).

————. *The Universal Declaration of Human Rights.* 25 BRITISH YEARBOOK OF INTERNATIONAL LAW 354 (1948).

Law is Force. 1 CIVIL RIGHTS 4 (December 2, 1972).

Lawrence, William H. *The Status under International Law of Recent Guerrilla Movements in Latin America.* 7 INTERNATIONAL LAWYER 405 (1973).

Leman, Beverly. *The Prisoners of Vietnam.* VIET REPORT 5 (August/September 1966).

Lillich, Richard B. *Forcible Self-Help by States to Protect Human Rights.* 53 IOWA LAW REVIEW 325 (1967).

Lynch, John M. *The Anglo-Irish Problem.* 50 FOREIGN AFFAIRS 601 (1972).

MacBride, Sean. *The European Court of Human Rights.* 3 NEW YORK UNIVERSITY JOURNAL OF INTERNATIONAL LAW AND POLITICS 1 (1970).

Madness: British Intervention. 209 NATION 163 (1969).

Maloney, William J.M.A. *DeValera's Neutrality.* 154 NATION 141 (1942).

Markovic, Milan. *Implementation of Human Rights and the Domestic Jurisdiction of States,* in INTERNATIONAL PROTECTION OF HUMAN RIGHTS 47 (A. Eide & A. Schou, eds., 1968).

Matthews, Peter. *Eire's Neutrality.* 169 SPECTATOR 125 (1942).

————. *Neutrality of Eire.* 162 CONTEMPORARY 148 (September 1942).

McDougal, Myres S. *International Law and Social Science: A Mild*

Plea in Avoidance. 66 AMERICAN JOURNAL OF INTERNATIONAL LAW 77 (1972).

———. *Law and Power*. 46 AMERICAN JOURNAL OF INTERNATIONAL LAW 102 (1952).

———. *Rhodesia and the United Nations: The Lawfulness of International Concern*. 62 AMERICAN JOURNAL OF INTERNATIONAL LAW 1 (1968).

———. *Some Basic Theoretical Concepts about International Law: A Policy-Oriented Framework of Inquiry*. 4 JOURNAL OF CONFLICT RESOLUTION 337 (1960).

McDougal, Myres S. and Gerhard Bebr. *Human Rights in the United Nations*. 58 AMERICAN JOURNAL OF INTERNATIONAL LAW 605 (1964).

McDougal, Myres S. and Harold Lasswell. *The Identification and Appraisal of Diverse Systems of Public Order*. 53 AMERICAN JOURNAL OF INTERNATIONAL LAW 1 (1959).

McDougal, Myres S. and Gertrude C. K. Leighton. *The Rights of Man in the World Community: Constitutional Illusions versus Rational Action*. 14 LAW AND CONTEMPORARY PROBLEMS 490 (1949).

McDougal, Myres S. and Michael Reisman. *Response by Professors McDougal and Reisman*. 3 INTERNATIONAL LAWYER 438 (1969).

McMahon, Francis E. *A Catholic Writes to DeValera*. 104 NEW REPUBLIC 66 (1941).

McNair, A. D. *The Law Relating to the Civil War in Spain*. 53 LAW QUARTERLY REVIEW 471 (1937).

Menendez, Albert J. *Ulster's Educational Apartheid*. 26 CHURCH AND STATE 13 (June 1973).

Mitchell, Donald W. *Ireland's Strategic Position*. 154 NATION 134 (1942).

Moore, John Norton. *The Control of Foreign Intervention in Internal Conflict*. 9 VIRGINIA JOURNAL OF INTERNATIONAL LAW 205 (1969).

———. *Ratification of the Geneva Protocol on Gas and Bacteriological Warfare: A Legal and Political Analysis*. 58 UNIVERSITY OF VIRGINIA LAW REVIEW 419 (1972).

Morgenthau, Hans. *To Intervene or Not to Intervene*. 45 FOREIGN AFFAIRS 425 (1967).

Mosler, Hermann. *The Protection of Human Rights by Interna-*

tional Legal Procedure. 52 Georgetown Law Journal 800 (1964).

Moss, Norman. *War in North Ireland.* 163 New Republic 13 (August 15, 1970).

Neutral Eire. 15 Newsweek 23 (May 20, 1940).

Neutrality of Eire. 27 New Statesman and Nation 183 (1944).

New Measures against Terrorism. Ulster Commentary 16 (May 1973).

Newark, F. H. *The Constitution of Northern Ireland: The First Twenty-Five Years.* 8 Northern Ireland Legal Quarterly 52 (1948).

Novogrod, John. *Indirect Aggression,* in A Treatise on International Criminal Law 198 (M.C. Bassiouni and V. P. Nanda, eds., 1973).

Nyerere, Julius. *Rhodesia in the Context of Southern Africa.* 44 Foreign Affairs 373 (1966).

O'Brien, Conor Cruise. *The Embers of Easter 1916–1966.* 37 New Left Review 3 (1966).

O'Callaghan, John. *Paisley Waits in the Wings.* 83 New Statesman 380 (1972).

O'Higgins, Paul. *English Law and the Irish Question.* 1 Irish Jurist 59 (Summer 1966).

———. *The Lawless Case.* 16 Cambridge Law Journal 234 (1962).

O'Leary, Cornelius. *The Northern Ireland Crisis and Its Observers.* 42 Political Quarterly 255 (1971).

———. *Northern Ireland: The Politics of Illusion.* 40 Political Quarterly 307 (1969).

O'Rourke, Vernon A. *Recognition of Belligerency and the Spanish War.* 31 American Journal of International Law 398 (1937).

Over the Wall. 1 Civil Rights 3 (April 15, 1972).

Padelford, Norman J. *International Law and the Spanish Civil War.* 31 American Journal of International Law 226 (1937).

Paisley, Ian R. K. *Action to Defeat Republican Conspiracy.* 84 Northern Ireland Parliament Debates (March 14, 1972, reprint).

———. *Banning of Parades.* 83 Northern Ireland Parliament Debates (January 25, 1972, reprint).

———. *No to a United Ireland.* 84 Northern Ireland Parliament Debates (February 8, 1972, reprint).

301

Paisley, Ian R. K. *Union with Great Britain*. 84 NORTHERN IRE-LAND PARLIAMENT DEBATES (March 22, 1972, reprint).

Palley, Claire. *The Evolution, Disintegration and Possible Recon-struction of the Northern Ireland Constitution*. 1 ANGLO-AMERI-CAN LAW JOURNAL 368 (1972).

Paust, Jordan J. *My Lai and Vietnam: Norms, Myths and Leader Responsibility*. 57 MILITARY LAW REVIEW 99 (1972).

Pence, R. W. *Ireland, Friend or Enemy?* 155 NATION 427 (1942).

Pick, F. W. *German Eyes on Ireland*. 160 CONTEMPORARY 175 (1941).

Pictet, Jean S. *The New Geneva Conventions for the Protection of War Victims*. 45 AMERICAN JOURNAL OF INTERNATIONAL LAW 462 (1951).

Pratt, William V. *Britain's Great Need: Irish Bases*. 16 NEWSWEEK 22 (December 23, 1940).

Preuss, Lawrence. *Article 2, Paragraph 7 of the Charter of the United Nations and Matters of Domestic Jurisdiction*. 74 RE-CUEIL DES COURS (Hague Academy of International Law) 553 (1949).

———. *International Responsibility for Hostile Propaganda against Foreign States*. 28 AMERICAN JOURNAL OF INTERNATIONAL LAW 649 (1934).

Public Broadcasting Service. Transcript of *The Advocates* (April 25, 1972).

Punke, Harold H. *Common Mind and Common Law, as Basic Commonwealth*. 6 INTERNATIONAL LAWYER 635 (1972).

Rauch, Elmar. *The Compatibility of the Detention of Terrorists Order (Northern Ireland) with the European Convention for the Protection of Human Rights*. 6 NEW YORK UNIVERSITY OF INTERNATIONAL LAW AND POLITICS 1 (1973).

The Reflections of Leading Unionist Politicians. UNIONIST RE-VIEW 4 (May 1973).

Reik, Miriam. *Ireland: Religious War—or Class Struggle?* 55 SATURDAY REVIEW 25 (March 18, 1972).

Robertson, A. H. *The European Convention on Human Rights* in THE INTERNATIONAL PROTECTION OF HUMAN RIGHTS 99 (E. Luard, ed., 1967).

Rose, Richard. *Ulster Politics: A Select Bibliography of Political Discord*. 20 POLITICAL STUDIES 206 (1972).

Rudzinski, Aleksander Witold. *Domestic Jurisdiction in United Nations Practice*. 9 INDIA QUARTERLY 313 (1953).

Sartre, Jean-Paul. *Preface* to THE WRETCHED OF THE EARTH by Frantz Fanon (1968).

Sastry, K.R.R. *Neutrality*. 12 NEW REVIEW 314 (1940).

Savory, Douglas L. *Irish Republic and Neutrality in 1941*. 196 CONTEMPORARY 164 (1959).

Sayle and Humphrey. *The Verdict They Could Not Print*. 2 CIVIL RIGHTS 3 (June 16, 1973).

Schwelb, Egon. *Civil and Political Rights: The International Measures of Implementation*. 62 AMERICAN JOURNAL OF INTERNATIONAL LAW 827 (1968).

———. *Human Rights and the Teaching of International Law*. 64 AMERICAN JOURNAL OF INTERNATIONAL LAW 355 (1970).

———. *The International Court of Justice and the Human Rights Clauses of the Charter*. 66 AMERICAN JOURNAL OF INTERNATIONAL LAW 337 (1972).

———. *Northern Ireland and the United Nations*. 19 INTERNATIONAL AND COMPARATIVE LAW QUARTERLY 483 (1970).

———. *On the Operation of the European Convention on Human Rights*. 57 AMERICAN JOURNAL OF INTERNATIONAL LAW 804 (1963).

———. *The United Kingdom Signs the Covenants on Human Rights*. 18 INTERNATIONAL AND COMPARATIVE LAW QUARTERLY 457 (1969).

Sheean, Vincent. *Ireland: Back Door to Invasion*. 151 NATION 146 (1940).

Shirer, William S. *Will Hitler Take Ireland?* 154 NATION 132 (1942).

Should Eire Join the War? 34 COMMONWEAL 3 (1941).

Smyllie, R. M. *Unneutral Neutral Eire*. 24 FOREIGN AFFAIRS 317 (1946).

Stewart, Maxwell S. *Ireland's Dilemma*. 154 NATION 137 (1942).

Stone, Judy. *Ireland: "The Killing Sickness."* 214 NATION 390 (1972).

Stormont and Saigon. 213 NATION 165 (1971).

Taubenfeld, Howard J. *International Armed Forces and the Rules of War*. 45 AMERICAN JOURNAL OF INTERNATIONAL LAW 671 (1951).

303

Trainin, I. P. *Questions of Guerrilla Warfare in the Law of War.* 40 AMERICAN JOURNAL OF INTERNATIONAL LAW 534 (1946).

Through Irish Eyes. 176 ECONOMIST 599 (1955).

Ulster: The Children of Violence. 77 NEWSWEEK 46 (April 19, 1971).

UN Forces for N. Ireland? 1 CIVIL RIGHTS 1 (October 28, 1972).

Van Boven, T. C. *Some Remarks on Special Problems Relating to Human Rights in Developing Countries.* 3 REVUE DES DROITS DE L'HOMME 383 (1970).

Veuthey, Michel. *The Red Cross and Non-International Conflicts.* 113 INTERNATIONAL REVIEW OF THE RED CROSS 411 (1970).

———. *Some Problems of Humanitarian Law in Noninternational Conflicts and Guerrilla Warfare,* in A TREATISE ON INTERNATIONAL CRIMINAL LAW 422 (M. C. Bassiouni & V. P. Nanda, eds., 1973).

Waldock, Humphrey. *Human Rights in Contemporary International Law and the Significance of the European Convention.* INTERNATIONAL AND COMPARATIVE LAW QUARTERLY SUPPLEMENT No. 11, 1 (1965).

———. *The Regulation of the Use of Force by Individual States in International Law.* 81 RECUEIL DES COURS (Hague Academy of International Law) 455 (1952).

Warren, Earl. *It's Time to Implement the Declaration of Human Rights.* 59 AMERICAN BAR ASSOCIATION JOURNAL 1257 (1973).

Wehberg, Hans. *La Guerre civile et le droit international.* 63 RECUEIL DES COURS (Hague Academy of International Law) 7 (1938).

Weil, Gordon L. *The Evolution of the European Convention on Human Rights.* 57 AMERICAN JOURNAL OF INTERNATIONAL LAW 804 (1963).

Whitelaw, William. *Northern Ireland: Military and Political Action.* 39 VITAL SPEECHES 93 (November 15, 1972).

Widgery Waives the Rules. 83 NEW STATESMAN 547 (April 28, 1972).

Wilson, Robert R. *Recognition of Insurgency and Belligerency.* 31 AMERICAN SOCIETY OF INTERNATIONAL LAW PROCEEDINGS 136 (1937).

———. *The United Nations as Symbol and as Instrument.* 64 AMERICAN SOCIETY OF INTERNATIONAL LAW PROCEEDINGS 139 (1970).

Wilson, Thomas. *The Ulster Crisis: Reformed Government with a New Border?* 245 ROUND TABLE 37 (1972).

Woetzel, Robert K. *War Crimes by Irregular and Nongovernmental Forces*, in A TREATISE ON INTERNATIONAL CRIMINAL LAW 413 (M. C. Bassiouni & V. P. Nanda, eds., 1973).

Woolsey, L. H. *International Law and Civil Strife.* 53 AMERICAN SOCIETY OF INTERNATIONAL LAW PROCEEDINGS 145 (1959).

Wright, Quincy. *International Law and Civil Strife.* 53 AMERICAN SOCIETY OF INTERNATIONAL LAW PROCEEDINGS 145 (1959).

―――. *International Law and Ideologies.* 48 AMERICAN JOURNAL OF INTERNATIONAL LAW 616 (1954).

―――. *Is Discussion Intervention?* 50 AMERICAN JOURNAL OF INTERNATIONAL LAW 102 (1956).

―――. *Some Thoughts about Recognition.* 44 AMERICAN JOURNAL OF INTERNATIONAL LAW 548 (1950).

―――. *Subversive Intervention.* 54 AMERICAN JOURNAL OF INTERNATIONAL LAW 521 (1960).

―――. *United States Intervention in the Lebanon.* 53 AMERICAN JOURNAL OF INTERNATIONAL LAW 112 (1959).

Wyatt, Joan. *Battle of the Boyne II.* 94 COMMONWEAL 162 (April 23, 1971).

Yingling, Raymund T. and Robert W. Ginnane. *The Geneva Conventions of 1949.* 46 AMERICAN JOURNAL OF INTERNATIONAL LAW 393 (1952).

Young, Oran R. *International Law and Social Science: The Contributions of Myres S. McDougal.* 66 AMERICAN JOURNAL OF INTERNATIONAL LAW 60 (1972).

Library of Congress Cataloging in Publication Data

Hull, Roger H
  The Irish triangle.

  Bibliography: p.
  Includes index.
  1. Northern Ireland—Politics and government.
I. Title.
DA990.U46H84   320.9'416'0824   75-17424
ISBN 0-691-07576-X